TROIKA

A Month in the Country
Rasputin's Brother
Summerfolk

Three Russian Adaptations by

Carol Rocamora

BOOKS BY CAROL ROCAMORA:

Translations

Chekhov: The Early Plays
Chekhov: Four Plays
Chekhov: "The Vaudevilles" and other short works
Platonov, Acting Edition
Ivanov, Acting Edition
The Wood Demon, Acting Edition
The Seagull, Acting Edition
Uncle Vanya, Acting Edition
The Three Sisters, Acting Edition
The Cherry Orchard, Acting Edition

Biographies

Acts of Courage: Vaclav Havel's Life in the Theater
Anton Chekhov: A Life in Four Acts
Chekhov in an Hour (Playwrights in an Hour series)

Plays

"I take your hand in mine . . ."

www.smithandkraus.com

TROIKA

A Month in the Country
Rasputin's Brother
Summerfolk

Three Russian Adaptations by

Carol Rocamora

Smith and Kraus Publishers ❐ 2016

Troika: Three Russian Adaptations © 2016 By Carol Rocamora is fully protected under the copyright laws of the United States of America and of all countries covered by the International Copyright Union (including the Dominion of Canada and the rest of the British Commonwealth), The Berne Convention, the Pan-American Copyright Convention and the Universal Copyright Convention as well as all countries with which the United States has reciprocal copyright relations. All rights, including professional/amateur stage rights, motion picture, recitation, lecturing, public reading, radio broadcasting, television, video or sound recording, all other forms of mechanical or electronic reproduction, such as CD-ROM, CD-I, DVD, information storage and retrieval systems and photocopying, and the rights of translation into foreign languages, are strictly reserved.

All rights reserved.

ISBN 9781575258911

Library of Congress Control Number: 2016930398

Typesetting, layout, and cover design by Elizabeth E. Monteleone
Cover Art by: Mary Iselin —
  "Troika, Dawn, Daylight, and Night" 6x20 Oil on Linen
  maryiselinfineart.com

A Smith and Kraus book
177 Lyme Road, Hanover, NH 03755
editorial 603.643.6431 To Order 1.877.668.8680
www.smithandkraus.com

Printed in the United States of America

*To all the theatre artists who have
helped to develop these plays,
to Marisa Smith and Eric Kraus
for their abiding support,
and above all, to Jim, always.*

Contents

Acknowledgments	9
Introduction	11
A Month in the Country	21
Rasputin's Brother	151
Summerfolk	271

Acknowledgments

For *A Month in the Country:*

This translation of Turgenev's play was commissioned in 2007 by the Graduate Acting Program of New York University's Tisch School of the Arts. My heartfelt thanks go to Zelda Fichandler, chair, and Laurence Maslon, associate chair, for their support and enthusiasm, as well as to Cigdem Onat for her sensitive direction of the production at Tisch.

For *Rasputin's Brother:*

My initial translation/adaptation of Sukhovo-Kobylin's trilogy was commissioned by the graduate Acting Program of New York University's Tisch School of the Arts in 2011. My sincere thanks go to Mark Wing-Davey, chair, and Laurence Maslon, associate chair, for the opportunity to work on the early drafts with their actors. Thanks also go to Peter Pryor (associate artistic director) and The People's Light and Theatre Company (Malvern, Pennsylvania), where a newly conceived play, *Rasputin's Brother,* inspired the trilogy, was read in their "Hatchling Program." The most recent draft of *Rasputin's Brother* was read by the graduating acting class at Columbia's MFA Theatre Program (April 2015). My thanks go to all the actors who participated in these readings.

For *Summerfolk:*

Summerfolk was developed as a staged reading in July 2015 by the Martha's Vineyard Playhouse. My heartfelt thanks go to the cast, and I gratefully acknowledge M. J. Bruder-Munafo, artistic director, for her continued support. As one of the Vineyard "summerfolk" myself, it has been a special pleasure and privilege—as well as an inspiration—to hear it read before a Vineyard audience.

Introduction

For those of us who love the plays of Anton Chekhov, we tend to overlook other works in Russian drama. After all (we ask ourselves), where could we possibly find plays find as beautiful and as meaningful as his masterful creations? Just as others focus on the plays of Shakespeare or Molière, it's possible to devote an artistic lifetime to translating, directing, performing, and writing about Chekhov's dramatic works. His impressionistic plays change color with every interpretation, and one always finds new meaning in them. (And there's an endless supply of his wonderful short stories to be adapted for the stage, as well).

And yet if one ventures beyond Chekhov, there are rewarding dramatic discoveries to be made, of course. In the past few years, I've managed to stray off the Chekhovian path, and have been fascinated by the journey. The findings are in this volume—three Russian plays (two nineteenth century, one twentieth century). The first is a translation/adaptation of a well-known work; the second is a new play inspired by a long-lost trilogy; the third is a "reimagining" of a less familiar classic. They're presented here in chronological order.

A Month in the Country

Turgenev's classic (written from 1845–50, published in 1855, banned, and finally premiered in 1872) is hardly a "discovery." Its author is one of the giants of nineteenth-century Russian literature (along with Tolstoy and Dostoevsky). A celebrated prose writer as well as a playwright, he is considered one of the fathers of Russian realism—with a lingering strain of romantic idealism. *A Sportsman's Sketches* (1852), his collection of stories about the cruelty of serfdom, was one of the catalysts for its abolition in 1861. The controversy over his novel *Fathers & Sons* (1862), about the generation clash between the conservatives and nihilists, effectively exiled him from his native land.

Born into land and privilege, university-educated, multilingual, cultured, and European, Turgenev was a romantic figure. (He lived for many years in France and Germany and died in Paris). History classifies him as a "Westernizer." With these qualities he was the opposite of Chekhov, the son of a shopkeeper and grandson of a serf, a modest country doctor and an invalid for much of his adult life. That may have been one of the reasons Chekhov admired Turgenev—for his elegance and fame, as well as his glamour. "Charming and clever, but Turgenev is better," laments the writer Trigorin over how the critics judge him, in Chekhov's *The Seagull.* That could have been Chekhov's prophesy of his own fate.

Among Turgenev's dramatic works, *A Month in the Country* fascinates me in particular. As a translator of Chekhov, I've come to appreciate what a strong influence this particular play has on Chekhov's dramatic writing. Though in 1896 *The Seagull* (the first of Chekhov's four great plays) was considered a new form, one detects its roots in Turgenev's earlier play, published in 1855. The setting (country estate), the *dramatis personae* (landed gentry), the languid summer season, the long conversations, the themes of boredom and unrequited love, the absence of Aristotelian action—all these elements that characterize Chekhov's plays are to be found in Turgenev's *A Month in the Country.*

As for the specific characters themselves, I am struck by how many of them in *A Month in the Country* can be seen as prototypes for Chekhov's later works. The proud and passionate lady of the estate, the doctor, the confidant, the fussy mother-in-law, the innocent young girl, the flighty maid, the clueless neighbor, the bungler—all resurface decades later in Chekhov's plays, in subtler, multilayered incarnations.

Clearly, Chekhov was an admirer of *A Month in the Country*. He encouraged Stanislavsky to produce the play at the Moscow Art Theatre but never lived to see it performed there. The Art Theatre ultimately produced it—but not until five years after Chekhov's death, when Stanislavsky directed it and played the part of Rakitin opposite Olga Knipper (Chekhov's wife), who played Natalya Petrovna. It was during their rehearsals that Stanislavsky started experimenting with his theory of the actor's inner emotional life. This would become the basis of the famous Stanislavsky "method" that, a century later, many directors apply to Chekhov's plays today.

So on the one hand *A Month in the Country* can be enjoyed as a precursor to Chekhov' plays. On the other hand it can be enjoyed on its own terms—as an evocation of "old-world Russia" in the 1840s, a view of a lovely landscape in full summer bloom, and a seductive study of the perils of love. Indeed, the play seems suspended in time. Its colorful characters are insulated from the outside world on a country estate, with no foreshadowing of the decline to come. Turgenev may be called "the father of Russian realism," but *A Month in the Country* has its distinctly romantic strains, more concerned with unconscious drives and psychological yearnings of its characters than the historical inevitability that provides the haunting context to Chekhov's great plays.

My translation of *A Month in the Country* is faithful to the original. At the same time I found that some of the original dialogue sounds somewhat ornate and stilted to today's ear. So I've freshened it up in a few places (without modernizing it) and have made some selective and judicious trimmings—enough so to call it a translation/adaptation. At the same time I've kept the setting, time period, and flavor of the original.

Rasputin's Brother

Ever since graduate school, when I studied Russian literature in depth, I've admired its strong tradition of satire and farce. The volumes of satirical prose works (from Saltykov-Shchedrin to Gogol to Zoshcenko) and plays (including Griboyedov's *Wit Works Woe* and Gogol's *The Inspector General*) are prodigious. And yet rereading them in the original today, they often come across as archaic and inaccessible. Moreover, they present practical problems when it comes to production.

So when I was asked to adapt a long-lost satirical trilogy by a long-forgotten nineteenth-century Russian writer, I steeled myself for the challenge. To begin with, he wasn't really a bona fide literary figure. On the contrary, Aleksandr Sukhovo-Kobylin (1817–1903) was a Russian playboy aristocrat who gained notoriety in 1850 when he was accused of murdering his French mistress. Over the next four years he would be arrested, imprisoned, released, rearrested, and released again—without his name being cleared. During this period he wrote his first play (about a Russian playboy/opportunist) called *Krechinsky's Wedding* (1856). Meanwhile, his case followed a tortuous path from one government office to another, while he lost his family's fortune on legal fees and lived under the stigma of shame and suspicion.

Frustrated by this endless cycle, Sukhovo-Kobylin began a second play based on his experiences called *The Case*—about corruption of the Russian justice system, greed, and the triumph of evil over good. ("All Russia is under arrest," was the play's message). Despite the Tsar's pardon in 1857, he finished *The Case* in 1861 and continued to expose the corrupt Russian bureaucracy in a third play, *The Death of Tarelkin* (1869), a grotesquerie in which the police and government officials turn into werewolves and vampires.

Krechinsky's Wedding premiered in 1856, but it took years for the other two plays to see the light of day. *The Case* finally premiered at the Maly in 1881, but *Tarelkin* was banned until 1900, when it finally premiered. It wasn't until 1901 that the entire trilogy was performed for the first time in St. Petersburg. Vsevolod Meyerhold, the famous director, directed the trilogy and championed it for years (1917–33), but since then it has been neglected and infrequently performed.

The major challenge for the adapter is the enormity and unevenness of the trilogy. In the original Russian the three plays, each three hours in length, represent a total of nine hours of playing time, including dozens of characters, only a few of whom connect the plays. In my early drafts I condensed this massive material into one three-act play that ran three hours in the first reading. In subsequent drafts I kept editing the material down—until, after numerous readings, I saw that *Krechinsky's Wedding* worked consistently, while the other two parts simply didn't hold together. (After all, there had been years between the writing of each part. The tone of the trilogy wasn't consistent, segueing from farce to tragedy to the grotesque.)

So I decided to discard parts II and III of the trilogy entirely and use an abbreviated *Krechinsky's Wedding* (the most entertaining) as a springboard of a new full-length work, set in the same time period as the original (1850s). The result is essentially a new play about the adventures of Krechinsky, using some of the original material as Act One, and creating a completely new plot line for Act Two that retains the seminal themes of corruption and injustice. In essence, *Rasputin's Brother*, as I call it, honors the spirit of the original while telling a new, extended story. Dozens of characters were cut in the process, and a few new ones have been added to create a satirical farce in the tradition of Gogol's *The Government Inspector*. (An ensemble of ten actors can play the thirteen speaking roles plus other "walk-ons.")

During the writing process I was fortunate to see the Royal National Theatre's marvelous new farce called *One Man, Two Guvnors* (based on *A Servant of Two Masters,* Goldoni's 1743 classic.) Inspired by Richard Bean's hilarious adaptation, I strove to highlight the farcical elements of Sukhovo-Kobylin's original (improbable plot, physical comedy, mistaken identity, elements of the absurd, etc.), while paring the length down to a fast-paced, action-packed two hours. At the same time, I chose not to update, as Bean did with Goldoni. Instead, I've kept it in the original nineteenth-century setting to preserve its colorful qualities.

To my knowledge the original material is rarely if ever performed in translation on the English speaking stage today. I hope *Rasputin's Brother*, inspired by the trilogy of Aleksandr Sukhovo-Kobylin, will bring the delight of discovery.

(Another historical footnote: The first part of the trilogy, *Krechinsky's Wedding,* was popular in Chekhov's day. In *The Seagull*, Shamrayev, the stage-struck estate manager, marvels at the performance of a contemporary actor, saying: "His Raspluyev was immortal." Raspluyev is the name of Krechinsky's sidekick in the original. Sukhovo-Kobylin may have been an fledgling playwright, but he had a sharp satirical eye, and the role of Raspluyev has become a classic in Russian satire, just as the role of the rogue Mosca [in Ben Jonson's *Volpone*] is immortal in the English satirical tradition. Note: In my version, I've changed the name of "Raspluyev" to "Popov" because "Raspluyev" sounded too much like "Rasputin.")

Summerfolk

Maksim Gorky (1868–1936) looms large in Russian literature—a charismatic and fiery figure as well as a forceful writer. He lived in Tsarist as well as Soviet times and left a bold imprint on each era.

As a short story writer, novelist, playwright, and memoirist he drew heavily from his life experience, and his output was prolific. Gorky's childhood was traumatic. He came from the "lower depths" of Russian society, as he called it in his later eponymous play. Born into poverty, his father died when he was three and his mother abandoned him. Beaten and starved by his extended family, he fled home at age twelve and roamed all over Russia for a decade, holding a myriad of jobs from boatman to baker to icon maker. At one point he attempted suicide. Though he never received a higher education, he was a passionate reader. He began writing (essays, poems, and short stories) in his teens and landed a job as a journalist.

What kept Gorky going and focused was his compassion for the Russian people—in particular the "workers," with whose sufferings he strongly identified. He sent his early work to Tolstoy (who never responded); but Chekhov did, and they soon became close friends. Impressed by Gorky's outpouring of writings and the urgency of his voice, Chekhov mentored the younger writer, encouraging him to write plays and introducing him to the Stanislavsky. *The Lower Depths* was produced by the Moscow Art Theatre in 1902, and established Gorky in the Russian theatre community.

While his literary star rose, Gorky became a passionate political activist, writing and speaking out against the Tsarist regime and its censorship of free expression. He was soon put under surveillance by the police, was arrested several times, and was expelled from the Academy of Arts and Letters to which he had been recently elected. (In protest, Chekhov resigned from that organization). Subsequently, Gorky was exiled from Russia for two long periods, once under the Tsar, and once under the Soviets.

Just as Chekhov's plays evoke elements of Turgenev's *A Month in the Country,* so does *Summerfolk,* Gorky's next play, evoke elements of Chekhov's *The Cherry Orchard.* Chekhov's final play premiered in January 1904 at the Moscow Art Theatre, and three months later, Gorky finished *Summerfolk.* Gorky set his play in a community of summer dachas in the Russian countryside—just like the one that Lopakhin, the capitalist in *The Cherry Orchard,* dreams of developing after he buys the estate from Lyubov and Gayev, Chekhov's impoverished landowners. Gorky's character Uncle Yuri, capitalist and land developer, might as well be Lopakhin himself two years later, with his dream come true.

Chekhov died three months after Gorky finished his play. So he never saw its premiere a year later at Vera Kommisarzhevskaya's theatre in St. Petersburg—another ironic footnote in theatre history, since Kommisarzhevakaya had originated the role of "Nina" in *The Seagull* a decade earlier.

So it was the "Chekhov connection" that originally drew me to *Summerfolk,* among all Gorky's numerous plays. Initially, I found Gorky's play to be a large, colorful, overstuffed work, crammed with almost two dozen characters. Gorky the activist tried to pack his political theories—as well as those of others—into the play, and as a result the dialogue is often didactic and long-winded. What's missing, I felt, is a central focus—a charismatic character like the author himself to give the play vitality and drive.

So I've done something bold—I've put the author into his own play. First, I've pared down Gorky's original cast to ten characters and added four of my own, including Maksim Gorky and Vera Kommisarzhevskaya, both historical figures. Second, I've made the play about the writing of *Summerfolk* itself. I've kept the original setting (1904 Russian countryside) and some of the names of the ten characters, but I've rewritten the plot, with Gorky as the play's central focus. (Some of Gorky's dialogue comes from his original writings that I've translated.) I've also streamlined the length to roughly two hours. In the process I've taken a few literary liberties (see footnotes to the play text.). For these liberties, mea culpa.

Finally, there is a personal element in my attraction to *Summerfolk.* All my life, my family and I have spent summers on Martha's Vineyard, an island off the coast of Massachusetts that has a community of writers, artists, and professionals very much like the summer community in Gorky's play. For me, the similarities between the Vineyard's summer houses and Gorky's dachas (where people, in both settings, sit around and read and talk) are unmistakable. I think I understand what it means to be one of Gorky's "summerfolk."

Note: Whether I call them "adaptations," "versions," "reimaginings," or "inspired by," my work on these plays has been done from the original Russian texts.

Additional note:

The title of this volume of three adaptations is *Troika*, an antiquated Russian term meaning a vehicle drawn by three horses. All footnotes to Russian and other foreign names and terms are to be found at the end of each adaptation.

A MONTH IN THE COUNTRY

A COMEDY IN FIVE SCENES

IVAN TURGENEV

Cast of Characters

Arkady Sergeyevich Islayev, a wealthy landowner
Natalya Petrovna, his wife
Kolya, their son, age ten
Verochka, their ward
Anna Semyonovna Islayeva, Islayev's mother
Lizaveta Bogdanovna, a companion
Schaaf, a German tutor
Mikhail Aleksandrovich Rakitin, a friend of the family
Aleksey Nikolayevich Belyayev, a student, Kolya's tutor
Afanasy Ivanovich Bolshintsov, a neighbor
Ignaty Ilyich Shpigelsky, a doctor
Matvey, a servant
Katya, a young servant

The action takes place on Islayev's estate in the Russian countryside, over three days in July. The time is the early 1840s. There is an interval of one day between Scenes I and II, Scenes II and III, and Scenes IV and V.

Scene One

The drawing room of Islayev's country estate. It's afternoon on a summer day. Stage right, there is a card table and a door to the study. Upstage center, there is a door leading into an outer room; stage left, there are two windows and a round table. In the corners, there are sofas. At the card table, Anna Semyonovna, Lizaveta Bogdanovna and Schaaf are playing Preference.[1] Natalya Petrovna and Rakitin sit at the round table; she is embroidering, he has a book in his hands.

SCHAAF: Hartz.[2]

ANNA SEMYONOVNA: Again? You're killing us, man.

SCHAAF: *(Feigning boredom.)* Eight of hartz.

ANNA SEMYONOVNA: *(To Lizaveta.)* See that! You just can't play with him.

NATALYA PETROVNA: *(To Rakitin):* Why did you stop reading? Go on.

RAKITIN: *(Reading.)* "Monte-Cristo se redressa haletant"[3]— Natalya Petrovna, tell me truly, does this interest you?

NATALYA PETROVNA: Not at all.

RAKITIN: Then why are we reading it?

NATALYA PETROVNA: Do you really want to know? The other day, a lady remarked: "Haven't you read *Monte-Cristo* yet? You must—it's charming!" I didn't

25

reply, but now I can tell her I read it and didn't find it charming in the least.

RAKITIN: Oh, well, if you've already made up your mind, then why should I bother?

NATALYA PETROVNA: You're just lazy!

RAKITIN: Have it your way. *(Resumes reading.)* "*Se redressa haletant—*"

NATALYA PETROVNA: *(Interrupting.)* Have you seen Arkady today?

RAKITIN: I saw your good husband down by the dam. He was standing knee-deep in the sand, explaining something to the workmen.

NATAYLA PETROVNA: Typical. He's so intense. It's a fault, don't you think?

RAKITIN: I agree.

NATAYLA PETROVNA: *(Playfully.)* How boring! You always agree with me. Go on, read.

RAKITIN: Oh, so now you want me to quarrel with you—

NATALYA PETROVNA: *(Subtly.)* What I really want is … never mind. Read.

RAKITIN: At your service. *(Picks up the book again.)*

SCHAAF: Hartz.

ANNA SEMYONOVNA: What? Again? Intolerable! Natasha—

NATALYA PETROVNA: What?

ANNA SEMYONOVNA: Can you believe it? Schaaf beat us again. First seven, then eight of hearts.

SCHAAF: Und[4] again seven.

ANNA SEMYONOVNA: Did you hear? *C'est insupportable.*

NATALYA PETROVNA: Yes, it is ...

ANNA SEMYONOVNA: How about a game of whist! *(To Natalya Petrovna.)* Where's Kolya?

NATALYA PETROVNA: He's taking a walk with the new tutor.

ANNA SEMYONOVNA: Come, Lizaveta Bogdanovna, let's play.

LIZAVETA BOGDANOVNA: As you wish.

RAKITIN: What new tutor?

NATALYA PETROVNA: Ah! I forgot to tell you a Russian one, this time.

RAKITIN: Who is he?

NATALYA PETROVNA: A young student. We've taken him on for the summer—till the princess sends us a French tutor from Moscow.

RAKITIN: Interesting ...

NATALYA PETROVNA: Tell you what, RAKITIN: you love observing people, analyzing them—

RAKITIN: Do I?

NATALYA PETROVNA: *(Teasing.)* You know you do. Go on, study him. I like him. Slender, spirited, strong, a sparkle in his eyes ...you'll see. Oh, and rather unsophisticated. You won't like that.

RAKITIN: You're giving me a hard time today, Natalya Petrovna.

NATALYA PETROVNA: No, really, he'll intrigue you. I think he'll make a fine man some day. Although you never know ...

RAKITIN: You've aroused my curiosity.

NATALYA PETROVNA: Have I? Go on. Read.

RAKITIN: *(Reading.)* "Se redressa haletant, et ..."

NATALYA PETROVNA: *(Suddenly.)* Where's Vera? I haven't seen her all day. *(To Rakitin.)* Put the book away. I can see we're not going to get any reading done today. Let's talk about something else.

RAKITIN: What can I tell you? Let's see ... I spent several days at the Krinitsyns. Imagine, the happy young couple is bored already.

NATALYA PETROVNA: How can you tell?

RAKITIN: You can't hide boredom, can you? Anything else, but not boredom.

NATALYA PETROVNA: *(Subtly.)* Anything else?

RAKITIN: As a matter of fact, I was bored there myself. Awful, isn't it? To be bored by your friends? You're fond of them, and yet when you're with them, there's a gnawing feeling, like a hunger in your heart.

NATALYA PETROVNA: You must often be bored with your friends.

RAKITIN: As if you didn't know what it's like to live with someone who loves you and who bores you to tears!

NATALYA PETROVNA: Someone who loves you … hmm … you're too subtle for me today.

RAKITIN: Subtle?

NATALYA PETROVNA: Do you know what, Rakitin? Sometimes we talk as though we were making lace. Have you ever seen lace-makers? They sit absolutely still in their stuffy little rooms; they never move an inch. Lace is lovely, but a sip of sparkling water on a hot day is lovelier still.

RAKITIN: Natalya Petrovna, you're annoyed with me.

NATALYA PETROVNA: No I'm not—

29

ANNA SEMYONOVNA: Ah! Finally! He's lost! *(To Natalya Petrovna.)* Our nemesis has lost, Natasha!

SCHAAF: *(Agitated.)* It's Lizaveta Bogdanovna's fault.

LIZAVETA BOGDANOVNA: *(Also agitated.)* Well, excuse me, but how did I know that Anna Semyonovna didn't have any hearts?

SCHAAF: In ze future, I don't play mit Lisafeta Bogdanovna.

LIZAVETA BOGDANOVNA: So what! Who cares!

RAKITIN: The more I look at you today, Natalya Petrovna, the less I recognize you.

NATALYA PETROVNA: Really?

RAKITIN: Yes, really. Something's changed in you.

NATALYA PETROVNA: Since you know me so well, then tell me—what?

RAKITIN: Well—*(Kolya suddenly bursts into the room with a clamor and rushes over to Anna Semyonovna.)*

KOLYA: Babushka![5] Babushka! Look what I have! *(He shows her a bow and arrow.)* Look!

ANNA SEMYONOVNA: Show me, darling … oh, what a lovely bow! Who made it for you?

KOLYA: He did—my tutor! *(Points to Belyayev, who appears at the door to the hall.)*

ANNA SEMYONOVNA: And how beautifully he has made it.

KOLYA: I shot a tree with it, Babushka, and hit it—twice! *(Jumps up and down.)*

NATALYA PETROVNA: Show me, Kolya. (*Kolya runs to her and shows her the bow.*)

KOLYA: *Maman!*[6] You should see how Aleksey Nikolayevich climbs trees! He wants to teach me to climb to the top, and to swim too. He's going to teach me everything!

NATALYA PETROVNA: *(To Belyayev.)* I'm grateful for your attentiveness to Kolya.

BELYAYEV: It's my duty, Madame …

ANNA SEMYONOVNA: Speaking of duty, young man, I hope that includes giving my grandson his lessons.

SCHAAF: *Natürlich!*[7]

NATALYA PETROVNA: Never mind, *Maman*, I'm sure Belyayev will instruct Kolya well. Won't you?

BELYAYEV: I'll do my best—

KOLYA: *(Excited.)* I like him so much, *Maman,* so, so much!

NATALYA PETROVNA: Belyayev will make a young man out of him, won't you? (*Belyayev bows.*)

KOLYA: Aleksey Nikolayevich, let's go down to the stables and bring the horses some bread.

ANNA SEMYONOVNA: *(To Kolya.)* Come here and give me a kiss first.

KOLYA: Later, Babushka, later! *(Runs into the hall; Belyayev runs after him.)*

ANNA SEMYONOVNA: *(Looking after Kolya.)* Such a dear child, isn't he?

LIZAVETA BOGDANOVNA: Indeed he is. And what a lively young tutor—

SCHAAF: *(Playing cards.)* Und I pass.

NATALYA PETROVNA: *(To Rakitin.)* So? How does he strike you?

RAKITIN: Who?

NATALYA PETROVNA: You know who I mean. The tutor …

RAKITIN: There's something about him that I can't quite—

NATALYA PETROVNA: What if you and I were to take him on? Finish his education. An excellent opportunity for sensible people like you and me.

RAKITIN: This young man interests you, doesn't he? If he knew, he'd be flattered.

NATALYA PETROVNA: Don't judge him by our standards.

He's not at all like us. That's our problem, my dear; we spend all this time analyzing ourselves and then assume we understand everyone else.

RAKITIN: "Another man's soul is a dark, dark forest,"[8] as they say. But what are you hinting at? Are you teasing me again?

NATALYA PETROVNA: Whom can one tease if not one's own friends? You are my friend, you know ... *(Squeezes his hand.)* My old friend.

RAKITIN: I'm only afraid that ... you're bored with this old friend.

NATALYA PETROVNA: Come now ... *(Lowering her voice.)* As if you don't know *ce que vous êtes pour moi.*[9]

RAKITIN: Natalya Petrovna, you're playing "cat and mouse" with me. Never mind; the mouse doesn't mind.

ANNA SEMYONOVNA: Twenty from you, Adam Ivanovich ... Ah-ha!

SCHAAF: In ze future I don't play viz Anna Semyonovna, either.

LIZAVETA BOGDANOVNA: Insulting man!

MATVEY: *(Entering from the hall, announcing.)* Ignaty Ilyich has arrived.

SHPIGELSKY: *(Entering after.)* Don't bother, man—doctors are never announced. *(Matvey exits.)* My humblest respects to the entire family. *(Kisses Anna Semyo-*

novna's hand.) Good day, dear lady. I take it you're winning?

ANNA SEMYONOVNA: What do you mean, winning? I've barely won back what I lost! He's to blame. *(Points to Schaaf.)*

SHPIGELSKY: Tsk-tsk, Herr Schaaf, you're playing with ladies. For shame!

SCHAAF: *(Muttering.)* Ladies, vat ladies?

LIZAVETA BOGDANOVNA: You see what we have to put up with?

SHPIGELSKY: Yes, Lizaveta Bogdanovna, and I'll bet you're beating him, anyway! Hello, Natalya Petrovna! Hello, Mikhail Aleksandrovich!

NATALYA PETROVNA: Greetings, Doctor. How are you?

SHPIGELSKY: Perfect, as usual! A good doctor never gets ill—he just goes off and dies somewhere. Ha-ha!

NATALYA PETROVNA: Sit down, please. I am well, thank you. But I'm not in a good mood. That's a kind of illness too, I suppose.

SHPIGELSKY: *(Sits next to Natalya Petrovna.)* Allow me to take your pulse. *(Feels her pulse.)* Ah yes, nerves, nerves. Maybe I'll prescribe some drops. You don't walk enough, Natalya Petrovna. You don't laugh enough.

NATALYA PETROVNA: I'm not adverse to laughter. So why don't *you* amuse us, Doctor? You're a clever fellow.

SHPIGELSKY: At your service. But wait, you've caught me off guard. Allow me, first, a pinch of snuff. *(Takes it.)*

NATALYA PETROVNA: *(Teasing.)* Doctor's orders?

SHPIGELSKY: So. As you very well know, my dear Natalya Petrovna, there is humor and there is humor. It depends on your audience. Hm. Oh well, here goes. Do you know my friend, Verenitsyn? I just came from a visit.

NATALYA PETROVNA: Slightly, yes, I've heard of him.

SHPIGELSKY: He has a daughter, a greenish little thing, you know the type—pale eyes, pink nose, yellow teeth, a charming creature—plays the piano, lisps, everything a young lady should be. Owns two hundred souls, plus her aunt's one hundred and fifty on top of that. The aunt's still alive and plans to be so for a while—the mad always live longest—but never mind, every misfortune has its advantages. Anyway, the mad aunt writes a will leaving everything to her greenish-colored niece (the day before I doused the old lady's head with cold water—a complete waste of time, since she's beyond curing). So now Verenitsyn's daughter, the greenish-colored one, is somewhat of a catch. And suitors are appearing, including one Perekuzov, an anemic-looking young man, but impeccably mannered. Well, the father really goes for Perekuzov, and so does the greenish-colored daughter. No problem, then, get them to the altar and get it over with! So everything is going swimmingly, Verenitsyn is already patting the young fellow on the back and so on, when all of a sudden out of the blue an officer appears named Protobekasov! He sees Verenitsyn's daughter at the noblemen's ball, dances three polkas with her, rolls his eyes at her—and right on the spot she loses her mind. Tears, sighs, oohs, aahs. ... She ignores Perekuzov, won't even look at Perekuzov; the word "wedding" causes spasms. All right, thinks Verenitsyn, if it's meant to be Protobekasov, then it's going to be Protobekasov. So Protobekasov is invited to call—he arrives, flirts, falls in love, and proposes. Now you're thinking that Verenitsyn's daughter accepts with joy? Not so fast! In fact, on the contrary! Tears again, sighs, hysterics. The father's at his wit's end. Now what? "But father, I don't know which one I love, this one or the other one!" "What?!" "I swear, I don't know, so it's better not to marry either of them, although I'm still in love, I truly am." Verenitsyn is stricken with cholera on the spot, of course, and neither suitor knows which end is up. But the greenish-colored one sticks to her guns. And these are some of the wonders of our part of the world. *(General laughter.)*

NATALYA PETROVNA: I don't see anything especially wondrous in that. Why can't you love two people at once?

RAKITIN: You think it's possible, do you?

NATALYA PETROVNA: Perhaps it proves one might not love either.

SHPIGELSKY: Ah-ha ... *(Takes snuff.)*

NATALYA PETROVNA: It's a good story, but you didn't make me laugh.

SHPIGELSKY: Then that's not what you need at the moment, my dear lady.

NATALYA PETROVNA: What *do* I need?

SHPIGELSKY: God only knows.

NATALYA PETROVNA: You're as boring as Rakitin!

SHPIGELSKY: You give me too much credit.

ANNA SEMYONOVNA: *(Rising from her seat.)* At last ... *(Sighs.)* My leg's fallen asleep. *(Lizaveta Bogdanovna and Schaaf also rise.)* Ahhhh ...

LIZAVETA BOGDANOVNA: No wonder, if you're going to sit for that long.

ANNA SEMYONOVNA: *(To Schaaf.)* My dear man, you owe me seventy kopeks. *(Schaaf bows curtly.)* You can't win every time, you know. *(To Natalya Petrovna.)* You look pale today, Natasha. Are you well? Doctor, is she all right?

SHPIGELSKY: Absolutely!

ANNA SEMYONOVNA: Good. I'll have a little rest before dinner ... I'm dead tired. Liza, let's go.... Ach, my legs, my legs ...

SHPIGELSKY: Good-bye, ladies. Perhaps I'll have a moment with you later, Lizaveta Bogdanovna?

LIZAVETA BODGANOVA: *(Cryptically.)* Perhaps ... *(Exits with Anna Semyonovna.)*

SHPIGELSKY: *(Offers the snuffbox to Schaaf.)* So, Schaaf, wie gehts?[10]

SCHAAF: *(Taking the snuff ceremoniously.)* How am I? *Gut. Und* how are you?

SHPIGELSKY: Not bad, thank you kindly. *(To Rakitin, in a lowered voice.)* So you don't know what's bothering Natalya Petrovna today?

RAKITIN: That's right. I don't.

SHPIGELSKY: Well, if you don't know ... *(To Natalya Petrovna.)* I have small matter to discuss with you, Natalya Petrovna.

Rakitin sits, leafing through the book, while Schaaf plays a hand of solitaire.

NATALYA PETROVNA: What is it?

SHPIGELSKY: I need to speak with you in private.

NATALYA PETROVNA: Really? You're frightening me.

SHPIGELSKY: *(Taking Natalya Petrovna aside.)* The matter doesn't concern you alone.

NATALYA PETROVNA: What do you mean?

SHPIGELSKY: Here's the situation. One of my good friends has asked me to find out, shall we say, your intentions regarding your ward.

NATALYA PETROVNA: Vera Aleksandrovna?

SHPIGELSKY: Frankly speaking—

NATALYA PETROVNA: Does he wish to propose to her?

SHPIGELSKY: As a matter of fact, yes.

NATALYA PETROVNA: You're joking, aren't you?

SHPIGELSKY: As a matter of fact, no.

NATALYA PETROVNA: Good heavens, she's still a child—what a strange request!

SHPIGELSKY: What's so strange about it, Natalya Petrovna?

NATALYA PETROVNA: You're a smooth operator, Doctor. And who is this friend of yours?

SHPIGELSKY: Er ... my neighbor ...

NATALYA PETROVNA: *(Incredulous.)* You don't mean Bolshintsov?

SHPIGELSKY: Actually, I do.

NATALYA PETROVNA: *(Laughing.)* Bolshintsov? Why, he's old enough to be—

SHPIGELSKY: Even so, would you entertain the notion?

NATALYA PETROVNA: Enough. As I said, Vera is still a child. You know that full well, dear doctor. *(Laughs again.)* What a fantastic idea! Oh, by the way, here she is. *(Vera and Kolya rush in from the hall.)*

KOLYA: *(Runs to Rakitin, breathless.)* Mikhail Aleksandrovich, tell them to give us some glue, please, glue, right away—

NATALYA PETROVNA: *(To Vera.)* Where have you been? How flushed you are.

VERA: We've been out in the garden. *(Shpigelsky bows.)* Hello, Ignaty Ilyich.

RAKITIN: *(To Kolya.)* What do you want glue for?

KOLYA: We need it—Aleksei Nikolayevich is making us a kite! Tell them to find some, please!

SCHAAF: Von minute. Master Kolya hass not finished his lesson today. *(Takes Kolya by the hand.) Kommen Sie, Mein Herr!*[11]

KOLYA: *(Begging.) Morgen, Herr Schaaf, morgen!*[12]

SCHAAF: *(Scolding.)* "*Morgen, morgen, nur nicht heute/ sagen alle faule Leute ...*[13] "Do tomorrow, not today/ Zat's vat lazy people say!" *(Shpigelsky laughs.)*

NATALYA PETROVNA: Behave yourself, Kolya, you've been running around enough today.... It's time for your lesson. Go with Herr Schaaf.

SCHAAF: *(To Natalya.) Natürlich, Gnadige Frau.* (*To Kolya, scolding.) Es ist unerhört!*[14]

KOLYA: *(Whispering to Rakitin.)* Don't forget to ask for the glue …

RAKITIN: *(Conspiratorially.)* Will do!

Schaaf exits, pulling Kolya with him. Rakitin exits after them.

VERA: I'll go help them.

NATALYA PETROVNA: *(To Vera.)* Sit down, dear—you must be tired.

VERA: Not at all.

NATALYA PETROVNA: Look at her, Doctor. Doesn't she look tired?

SHPIGELSKY: It suits her, though!

NATALYA PETROVNA: *(To Vera.)* So tell me, what have you been doing in the garden?

VERA: *(Animated.)* Oh, playing, running around. First we watched them digging up the dam, then Aleksey Nikolayevich chased a squirrel up a tree! He climbed higher and higher, and then he started shaking the treetop. We were quite frightened!

NATALYA PETROVNA: And then?

VERA: Then Aleksey Nikolayevich made Kolya a bow and arrow, and then he crept up to our cow in the meadow and jumped on her back. The cow was scared to death and started kicking his hind legs—and Aleksey Nikolayevich was laughing so hard! Then he wanted to make us a kite, so we came in.

NATALYA PETROVNA: *(Patting her on the cheek.)* A child, a child, you're just a child—isn't she, Doctor? What do you think?

SHPIGELSKY: I agree.

NATALYA PETROVNA: You see?

SHPIGELSKY: But that's no obstacle. On the contrary—

NATALYA PETROVNA: *(To Vera.)* So you've been having fun?

VERA: Of course! Aleksey Nikolayevich is so amusing.

SHPIGELSKY: Oh, I forgot. Your coachman is ill—I haven't taken a look at him—

NATALYA PETROVNA: What's the matter?

SHPIGELSKY: Just a fever, nothing serious.

NATALYA PETROVNA: Will you dine with us tonight, Doctor?

SHPIGELSKY: With your permission. *(He exits into the hall.)*

NATALYA PETROVNA: *Mon enfant, vous feriez bien de mettre une autre robe pour le diner!*[15] *(Kisses her on the forehead.)* A child, a child. *(Vera kisses her hand.)*

Enter Rakitin.

RAKITIN: *(Softly, to Vera.)* I've arranged that Aleksey Nikolayevich be given the glue and everything he needs.

VERA: *(Softly.)* Thank you, Mikhail Aleksandrovich. *(Exits.)*

RAKITIN: At last, we're alone. Natalya Petrovna, tell me please, what's the matter?

NATALYA PETROVNA: Nothing, Michel,[16] nothing. Come, sit. *(Rakitin sits next to her.)* Why do you look at me that way?

RAKITIN: I look at you … and I'm happy.

NATALYA PETROVNA: Open the window, Michel. How lovely it is in the garden! *(Goes to the window.)* What a warm, fresh breeze! *(Laughs.)* It's as if it were waiting to whirl right in …

RAKITIN: You're as soft and as sweet as the evening air.

NATALYA PETROVNA: Do you know, Michel, I can't imagine a dearer, kinder man than you.

RAKITIN: Now you're being condescending—

NATALYA PETROVNA: No, really. Our relationship is so pure. We can look everyone in the eye—including my husband—in good conscience, can't we? And yet sometimes I feel so guilty it makes me angry, and then I take it out on everyone, especially you. Don't you mind?

RAKITIN: On the contrary.

NATALYA PETROVNA: Sometimes you take pleasure in tormenting the one you love—

RAKITIN: *(Startled.)* What are you saying?

NATALYA PETROVNA: *(Interrupting him.)* Of course, I love you, Michel. It's a clear and calm feeling, and yet I'm not moved by it. You've never made me cry. I mean, if it were truly love, well then.... Do you know what I mean?

RAKITIN: Not really—

NATALYA PETROVNA: We've known each other for such a long time.

RAKITIN: Four years.

NATALYA PETROVNA: Good old friends, that's what we are—

RAKITIN: Don't play with me, Natalya Petrovna. My happiness might vanish with a wave of your hand.

NATALYA PETROVNA: We won't let it.

RAKITIN: I'm under your spell. Do with me what you will.

ISLAYEV: *(Offstage.)* Where's the new tutor?

NATALYA PETROVNA: It's Arkady! I can't see him right now. *(She exits.)*

Enter Islayev, preoccupied. He removes his hat.

ISLAYEV: Hello, Misha. How are you today?

RAKITIN: You already asked me this morning!

ISLAYEV: Sorry … got a lot on my mind. *(Paces.)* Funny—isn't it? —about the Russian peasant … you explain things to him till you're blue in the face and still he doesn't get it. "Yes sir," he says, and meanwhile, he hasn't understood a word. Still, I respect him. Where's Natasha?

RAKITIN: She was here just a moment ago.

ISLAYEV: It's time for tea, I hope. Been on my feet since morning—so much to do— haven't even been down to the building site. How time flies! Can't get a damn thing done. Go ahead, laugh—I can't help it. I'm a practical man, born to manage my land— and that's it. Why isn't Belyayev here?

RAKITIN: Who?

ISLAYEV: The new Russian tutor. A shy sort of fellow, but he'll get used to us. He's nobody's fool. I asked him to take a look at the building site today. *(Enter Belyayev.)* Ah, here he is! So how are things down there? No progress, I suppose?

BELYAYEV: They're working on it, sir.

ISLAYEV: Have they finished the frame for the second barn?

BELYAYEV: They're already on the third.

ISLAYEV: Well, thank you, then! *(Natalya Petrovna enters.)* Ah! Natasha! Hello, darling!

RAKITIN: You've been greeting each of us twenty times today.

ISLAYEV: I already told you—got too much on my mind. Oh, by the way—did I show you my new sheafing machine? Come see it—it's marvelous, really. Works like a hurricane. Come on—we still have time before dinner—

RAKITIN: Why not?

ISLAYEV: What about you, Natasha, want to come with us?

NATALYA PETROVNA: What do I know about sheafing machines! You go—but mind you're not late!

ISLAYEV: *(Exiting with Rakitin.)* Back in a minute ... *(Belyayev starts to follow them.)*

NATALYA PETROVNA: Where are you going, Aleksey Nikolayevich?

BELYAYEV: Who, me? I—

NATALYA PETROVNA: Well, if you feel like taking a walk, then of course—

BELYAYEV: Actually, I've been outdoors all morning.

NATALYA PETROVNA: In that case, please sit down. I haven't had a proper conversation with you yet. And I would like to get to know you.

BELYAYEV: *(Bows and sits.)* I ... I'm very flattered, Madame.

NATALYA PETROVNA: *(Smiling.)* You're afraid of me, I see it. But wait a while, and you won't be, once you get to know me. Tell me—how old are you?

BELYAYEV: Twenty-two.

NATALYA PETROVNA: Are your parents living?

BELYAYEV: Just my father. My mother died a long time ago.

NATALYA PETROVNA: Do you remember her?

BELYAYEV: Yes of course I remember her, Madame.

NATALYA PETROVNA: Any siblings?

BELYAYEV: One sister.

NATALYA PETROVNA: And are you fond of her?

BELYAYEV: Very. She's much younger than I am.

NATALYA PETROVNA: And what's her name?

BELYAYEV: Natalya.

NATALYA PETROVNA: *(Animated.)* Strange. That's my name too.... Tell me, what do you think of my Kolya?

BELYAYEV: He's a very good boy.

NATALYA PETROVNA: Isn't he? And so affectionate! He's grown attached to you.

BELYAYEV: I'm glad. And I'll do my best.

NATALYA PETROVNA: I'd like him to grow up to be a worthwhile young man. And I want him to look back fondly on his childhood. You see, my upbringing was oppressive, Aleksey Nikolayevich. But here I am, talking about myself, instead of Kolya. I only wanted to say that I know from experience how important it is for a child to grow up free. I don't imagine you were stifled as a child, were you?

BELYAYEV: Not really—actually, no one paid attention to me.

NATALYA PETROVNA: And no one saw to your education?

BELYAYEV: No one, to tell you the truth. I'm well aware of my deficiencies.

NATALYA PETROVNA: By the way, was that you I heard singing in the garden yesterday?

BELYAYEV: When?

NATALYA PETROVNA: Last evening, down by the pond—

BELYAYEV: *(Embarrassed.)* I didn't dream you could hear it from here.

NATALYA PETROVNA: You have a lovely voice. Have you studied music?

BELYAYEV: Not at all. I sing by ear.

NATALYA PETROVNA: And how well you do it. I'll ask you to sing for me later, when we know each other better, when we are friends. We are going to be friends, aren't we, Aleksey Nikolayevich? *(She extends her hand. Belyayev takes it uncertainly, and after a moment kisses it. Natalya Petrovna, disarmed, withdraws her hand. Shpigelsky enters.)*

NATALYA PETROVNA: Ah, it's you, Doctor. I'm here with Aleksey Nikolayevich.

SHPIGELSKY: The things that go on in your house, Natalya Petrovna! I go to the servants' quarters to pay a call on your sick coachman, and what do I see? The patient at the table, gobbling down blini and onion. And I make a living by healing the sick!

NATALYA PETROVNA: Indeed. Oh, Aleksey Nikolayevich, I forgot to tell you—

VERA: *(Bursts into the room.)* Aleksey Nikolayevich! *(Sees everyone.)* Oh—

NATALYA PETROVNA: What's going on?

VERA: Kolya wants his tutor—

NATALYA PETROVNA: What for?

VERA: It's about the kite—

NATALYA PETROVNA: *(To Vera.)* On n'entre pas comme cela dans une chamber. ... Cela ne convient pas.[17] What time is it, Doctor?

SHPIGELSKY: *(Consults his pocket watch.)* Exactly 5:20.

NATALYA PETROVNA: You see. Almost time for dinner!

Vera whispers something to Belyayev.

BELYAYEV: *(Laughing, and lowering his voice.)* No, really?

VERA: *(Laughing.)* Absolutely—she fell down flat!

NATALYA PETROVNA: What happened? Who fell?

VERA: *(Embarrassed.)* Oh, it's nothing! Aleksey Nikolayevich built a swing, and Nanny thought she'd try it ... *(Vera and Belyayev dissolve in laughter.)*

MATVEY: *(Entering.)* Ladies and gentlemen, dinner is served.

NATALYA PETROVNA: Where's Arkady Sergeyevich? He'll be late again! And Rakitin?

MATVEY: They're already in the dining room. Anna Semyonovna too. *(Bows, exits.)*

NATALYA PETROVNA: *(Indicates Belyayev.)* Vera, allez en avant avec monsieur.[18] *(Belyayev and Vera exit.)* *(To Shpigelsky.)* We'll have another talk about your proposal.

SHPIGELSKY: Regarding Vera Aleksandrovna?

NATALYA PETROVNA: Yes. I'll think about it.

SHPIGELSKY: Really!

NATALYA PETROVNA: I'll think about it.

Both exit.

Scene Two

The afternoon of the next day, in the garden. To the left and the right are benches placed under the trees. Upstage, there is a patch of raspberry bushes. Katya and Matvey enter, stage right. Katya carries a basket in her hand.

MATVEY: So, what's it to be, Katerina Vasilyevna? Put me out of my misery please, and answer me—

KATYA: Matvey Yegorich, you're very kind to ask again, but I—

MATVEY: You know what my feelings are for you. I know, I'm older than you are—in years, that is. But I'm in my prime. Can't you tell? What's more, I'm a respectable fellow—and agreeable too. So agreeable. What more could you want?

KATYA: Matvey Yegorich, as I've told you before, again and again, I'm very touched, really and truly. But I think it's best to wait a bit.

MATVEY: Wait for what? You've never given that excuse before. Trust me, Katerina Vasilyevna, you'll never find another man more attentive than I am. Just let me carry your basket—I'll show you. *(He clumsily tries to take the raspberry basket Katya is carrying.)*

KATYA: *(Resisting.)* Really, I'm fine— *(The basket falls, and raspberries tumble out on the grass.)*

MATVEY: *(Dismayed, fumbling to pick them up.)* Oh no, I've done it again—

KATYA: Don't worry, I've got it—

MATVEY: *(Anxiously.)* But I do worry, Katerina Vasilyevna. I worry a lot. I'm trying to impress you, to show you what a fine fellow I am. And I can't seem to pull it off. I'm loyal, I assure you. I don't drink. And you've never heard my masters complain about me, have you?

KATYA: I don't know what to say, truly. *(She continues to refill the basket with the fallen raspberries.)*

MATVEY: Katerina Vasilyevna, permit me to make an observation—

KATYA: If you must—

MATVEY: *(Blurting.)* Something has changed in you lately—

KATYA: *(Blushing.)* What do you mean?

MATVEY: I don't know. It's just that before … you didn't used to act like this.

KATYA: Like what?

MATVEY: Like ... you're so excited all the time, it's as if you—

KATYA: *(Sees Schaaf entering, with a fishing rod on his shoulder.)* Look out! Here comes the German! That old stork!

MATVEY: Please, Katerina Vasilyevna, we must speak again. *(Exits.)*

SCHAAF: Vat are you doing, Katerin?

KATYA: We've been told to pick raspberries, Herr Schaaf.

SCHAAF: Razberries? A very nize fruit. You lof razberries?

KATYA: I do.

SCHAAF: Hee hee! ... Zo do I, zo do I. I lof everyzing vat you lof.

Katerin attempts to leave.

SCHAAF: Vait a vile, Katerin.

KATYA: I can't. The housekeeper will scold me.

SCHAAF: Look—I'm going *(points to the rod)* —how do you say?—feeshing, yes? Feeshing ... to catch feesh. You like feesh?

KATYA: Well, yes.

SCHAAF: Heh-heh. And I like you. And do you know vat, Katerin? There's a little song in Churman: *(sings)* "Katrinchin, Katrinchin, wie lieb'ich dich so sehr!"—und zat means, in Russian: "O Katrinushka, o Katrinushka, you are so pretty und I like you very, very much!" *(He tries to put his arm around her.)*

KATYA: Stop! Shame on you, Herr Schaaf. Uh oh—here comes the mistress. *(She escapes into the raspberry patch.)*

Enter Natalya Petrovna stage right, arm in arm with Rakitin.

NATALYA PETROVNA: *(To Schaaf.)* Ah! Adam Ivanovich! Are you going fishing?

SCHAAF: Ja wohl, meine Frau. Good afternoon, Mein Herr.

NATALYA PETROVNA: Where's Kolya?

SCHAAF: Lizaveta Bogdanovna is giving him a piano lesson.

NATALYA PETROVNA: Good! *(Looks about.)* Are you alone?

SCHAAF: All alone. Hee-hee.

NATALYA PETROVNA: Have you seen Aleksey Nikolayevich, by any chance?

SCHAAF: No, I haf not.

NATALYA PETROVNA: Would you mind if we come along with you, Herr Schaaf? To watch you catch fish?

SCHAAF: It vud be my pleashure.

RAKITIN: *(Softly, to Natalya Petrovna.)* Must we?

Natalya Petrovna laughs. All three exit stage right.

KATYA: *(Cautiously raising her head above the raspberry bushes.)* They've gone ... *(She emerges and stops, deep in thought.)* Lord, that German! *(Sighs and resumes her raspberry picking, singing in an undertone.)*

> "It's not the fire burning, burning ...
> It's not the pitch that's churning, churning,
> It's my poor heart that's yearning, yearning,
> And not for papa ... and not for mama ..."

Mmmm ... what a juicy raspberry ... *(Continues her singing.)*

> Not for papa, not for mama,
> It burns for—"[19]

Belyayev and Vera enter from stage left; Belyayev carries a kite. Katya hides in the bushes.

BELYAYEV: *(Continuing the song.)* "It burns for a lovely maiden/It burns for a lovely maiden—"

KATYA: *(Emerging, embarrassed.)* It doesn't go like that.

BELYAYEV: What are you doing? Picking raspberries? Let's have a taste. *(Katya offers Belyayev and Vera the basket—they select a few.)*

KATYA: Go on, take them—take them all!

BELYAYEV: No, thank you, Katya, really. *(Katya resumes her raspberry picking and wanders off.)*

BELYAYEV: Let's sit here on the bench, Vera Aleksandrovna. You can help me build the kite. *(They both sit. Belyayev places the kite in her hands.)* Here, hold it straight, like this. *(He starts to attach the tail.)*

VERA: *(Eagerly.)* I want to see how you do it. *(They sit close together.)*

(Offstage, Katya begins to sing softly. Her song will be heard intermittently throughout the following scene.)

VERA: Tell me, Aleksey Nikolayevich, do you ever flight kites in Moscow?

BELYAYEV: There's no time! Wait—hold the string for a moment—like that …

VERA: What do you actually do in Moscow?

BELYAYEV: Let's see … we study, we attend lectures, we—

VERA: Do you have any friends in Moscow?

BELYAYEV: Of course.

VERA: I envy you. I don't have any friends.

BELYAYEV: What about me?

VERA: Well, you ... that's a different story.

BELYAYEV: Did you go to school in Moscow, too?

VERA: Yes, at Madame Beauluce's. Natalya Petrovna wanted me to have a proper European education. She took me out last year.

BELYAYEV: Are you fond of Natalya Petrovna?

VERA: Very fond of her. She's so kind.

BELYAYEV: And a little afraid of her too I'll bet.

VERA: Yes, a little. I grew up in her house. I'm an orphan.

BELYAYEV: My parents are gone too. So we're both orphans.

VERA: They say that orphans seek one another out.

BELYAYEV: Really? Do you think so?

VERA: I do. I'm glad you're here.

BELYAYEV: *(Laughing, and continuing his work on the kite.)* How long have I been here, anyway?

VERA: Twenty-eight days today.

BELYAYEV: A month in the country ...

VERA: Yes ...

BELYAYEV: Here, the kite's finished. Why do you sigh?

VERA: I don't know. Look how clear the sky is!

BELYAYEV: Is that why you're sighing? Are you bored?

VERA: Bored? Not at all! On the contrary. Yesterday I was going upstairs to get a book—and suddenly I sat down on the stairs and burst into tears—God knows why. And yet I feel happy, so happy …

BELYAYEV: You're growing up. It happens. Is that why your eyes looked so red last night?

VERA: You noticed?

BELYAYEV: Of course.

VERA: You notice everything …

They listen for a moment to Katya's distant singing. Belyayev fixes the kite.

VERA: Aleksey Nikolayevich?

BELYAYEV: What?

VERA: What was I going to ask you? Oh, yes! You said you were fond of Natalya Petrovna.

BELYAYEV: I admire her.

VERA: Tell me—am I like her?

BELYAYEV: You're much lovelier.

VERA: *(Embarrassed.)* You mustn't say that! I'll never be

as grand as she is.

BELYAYEV: You will be—when you're mistress of your own house ...

VERA: Do you really think so?

BELYAYEV: You'll see. We'd better go get Kolya now, don't you think, Vera Aleksandrovna?

VERA: Why don't you call me Verochka?

BELYAYEV: If you'd call me Aleksey—

VERA: Why not? *(With sudden start.)* Oh!

BELYAYEV: What's the matter?

VERA: Natalya Petrovna's coming.

BELYAYEV: Where?

VERA: There—down the path, with Mikhail Aleksandrovich.

BELYAYEV: Let's go get Kolya. He must have finished his lesson by now.

VERA: Yes, let's. I'm afraid she'll scold me. *(They exit quickly.)*

Enter Natalya Petrovna and Rakitin. She carries a parasol.

NATALYA PETROVNA: Isn't that Belyayev walking with Vera?

RAKITIN: Indeed it is.

NATALYA PETROVNA: It looks as though they're running away from us.

RAKITIN: Perhaps they are.

NATALYA PETROVNA: I don't think that Verochka should be alone with a young man in the garden. She's only a child, of course; but still, it's not appropriate. I'll talk to her.

RAKITIN: How old is she?

NATALYA PETROVNA: Eighteen. Can you imagine?... It's hot today, isn't it? I'm tired. Let's sit. *(They sit on the bench.)*

NATALYA: Has the doctor gone already?

RAKITIN: He has.

NATALYA PETROVNA: What a shame. There's something I have to talk about with him.

RAKITIN: Concerning what, may I ask?

NATALYA PETROVNA: No, you may not. Must you know my every thought, Michel? It's tiresome. You watch me from morning till night—

RAKITIN: Then allow me to offer just one comment—

NATALYA PETROVNA: If you must.

RAKITIN: You won't get angry with me?

NATALYA PETROVNA: We'll see.

RAKITIN: All right, here goes. For some time now, you've been restless—

NATALYA PETROVNA: Really?

RAKITIN: It's as if there's a struggle going on inside you. You'll sigh so deeply, like one who is tired and can't find rest.

NATALYA PETROVNA: And what do you deduce from this, Monsieur L'Inspecteur?

RAKITIN: It worries me.

NATALYA PETROVNA: Let's change the subject—

RAKITIN: Forgive me—I've made you uncomfortable.

NATALYA PETROVNA: Never mind. You know Bolshintsov, don't you?

RAKITIN: Our neighbor, Afanasy Ivanich?

NATALYA PETROVNA: Yes.

RAKITIN: Whatever makes you ask about that foolish, tiresome man? Although I suppose that's the worst you can say about him.

NATALYA PETROVNA: He's not as foolish or tiresome as you think.

RAKITIN: Perhaps. And what has piqued your interest in him?

NATALYA PETROVNA: Oh, nothing ... *(Sighs.)*

RAKITIN: There's that sigh again ... there must be more on your mind than Bolshintsov, Natalya Petrovna.

NATALYA PETROVNA: I don't know. Perhaps.

RAKITIN: *(After a moment.)* Look at that dark green oak against the deep blue sky. It's bathed in sunlight, luxuriant in color. What astonishing strength it exudes, next to that willowy young birch. See her shimmering leaves? She's a liquid radiance, delicate, dissolving beside the oak. She's vulnerable, she needs its strength—

NATALYA PETROVNA: Is there a metaphor here? *(Laughs.)*

RAKITIN: *(Shrugs.)* Perhaps.

NATALYA PETROVNA: All right, let's play your little game, Michel. How suavely you speak of nature—so suavely, in fact, that nature herself should be grateful. You court nature the way a perfumed marquis on high red heels courts a pretty peasant girl. The only problem is nature can't possibly appreciate your subtleties, just as the peasant girl can't appreciate the courtly courtesies of the marquis! Nature is far simpler, coarser—her needs are basic ...

RAKITIN: I know when I'm being called a fool.

NATALYA PETROVNA: *(Sighing.)* We are indeed fools. Here we sit, in the place where only a moment ago sat two lovely young creatures. I doubt they speak in metaphors—

RAKITIN: Belyayev and Verochka? Ah! Now I understand. You envy their youth, their spontaneity—

Katya emerges from the raspberry bushes.

NATALYA PETROVNA: What do you have there, Katya? Raspberries?

KATYA: Yes, mistress.

NATALYA PETROVNA: Show me. *(Katya approaches her.)* Luscious-looking raspberries! How rosy ... and your cheeks are rosier still.

KATYA: Would you like some, mistress?

NATALYA PETROVNA: Never mind, dear, run along. *(Katya curtsies and exits. Natalya Petrovna sighs.)*

RAKITIN: There goes another young creature. *(Natalya Petrovna stands.)* Where are you going?

NATALYA PETROVNA: I want to see what Verochka's doing. It's time she went inside. Anyway, I don't much care for our conversation. We'll see each other soon. Friends?

RAKITIN: Always ... *(Presses her hand.)*

NATALYA PETROVNA: Good-bye. *(She opens her parasol and exits stage left.)*

RAKITIN: *(Paces.)* What's the matter with her? I've never seen her like this. Is she tiring of me? I never deceived myself, but I'd hoped ... or do I dare to? My situation

63

is contemptible ... this tutor ... she speaks of him so often ... I see nothing special in him. He's just like any other student. Can she really...? No, impossible! Ah! Here comes the "raw youth"[20] himself.

Enter Belyayev from stage left.

Ah, Aleksey Nikolayevich! Out for a bit of fresh air?

BELYAYEV: Yes, sir.

RAKITIN: It's awfully hot, but here, under the shade of the lime trees, it's bearable. *(A pause.)* Have you seen Natalya Petrovna?

BELYAYEV: I did, just now. She and Vera Aleksandrovna went inside.

RAKITIN: Didn't I just see you and Vera here a little while ago?

BELYAYEV: Yes, sir. We were taking a walk.

RAKITIN: Ah! So, how do you like country life?

BELYAYEV: Very much. Only the shooting's not so good. Tell me, where can I get gunpowder around here?

RAKITIN: In town, I should think.

BELYAYEV: Actually, it's not for shooting, it's for making fireworks.

RAKITIN: Really?

BELYAYEV: It's Natalya Petrovna's name-day next week, I've been told, so that would be just the right occasion. And I've already picked the right spot—down by the pond.

RAKITIN: Natalya Petrovna will be very pleased. She likes you, Aleksey Nikolayevich, I must say.

BELYAYEV: I'm flattered. What time is it, please?

RAKITIN: *(Looking at his watch.)* One thirty.

BELYAYEV: Kolya is so long at his piano lesson. I'll bet he's dying to be outdoors, running around …

RAKITIN: Nevertheless, one must study, Aleksey Nikolayevich.

BELYAYEV: Of course, you're right; no one should be as lazy as I am.

RAKITIN: Your free spirit is precisely what's so appealing about you.

BELYAYEV: To whom, for example?

RAKITIN: To Natalya Petrovna, for example.

BELYAYEV: Natalya Petrovna? But I don't feel free around her at all.

RAKITIN: Really? Why?

BELYAYEV: *(Distracted.)* Sounds like a corncrake calling in the garden.

RAKITIN: Where are you going?

BELYAYEV: To get my gun. *(He starts off, as Natalya Petrovna enters.)*

NATALYA PETROVNA: Where are you off to, Aleksey Nikolayevich?

BELYAYEV: I—

RAKITIN: To get his gun. He heard a corncrake in the garden.

NATALYA PETROVNA: Don't shoot—it might frighten Babushka—

BELYAYEV: As you wish.

NATALYA PETROVNA: *(Laughing.)* Aren't you ashamed, Aleksey Nikolayevich? "As you wish"—Why do you talk like that? Mikhail Aleksandrovich and I will have to see to your education, that's all. You will permit us, won't you?

BELYAYEV: I … it would be an honor …

NATALYA PETROVNA: We're old folks, he and I, whereas you're young. You'll see how good this arrangement will be. You'll look after Kolya, and I—we'll look after you.

BELYAYEV: I'd be most grateful.

NATALYA PETROVNA: By the way, what have you done with your kite?

BELYAYEV: I took it inside. I thought you didn't like it.

NATALYA PETROVNA: You were mistaken. Never mind. Kolya must be finished with his lesson now. Let's go get him and Vera and the kite— we'll fly it in the meadow.

BELYAYEV: With pleasure.

NATALYA PETROVNA: *(Holds out her hand.)* Here, take my arm.... How awkward you are! *(Laughing.)* Come! *(They exit quickly stage left.)*

RAKITIN: *(Gazes after them.)* What eagerness, what gaiety ... I've never seen such a look on her face. A complete transformation! Could it be? Impossible! But that smile, that warm, tender glance ... God spare me the jealousy!

Enter Shpigelsky and Bolshintsov from stage left.

RAKITIN: Hello, gentlemen. I didn't expect to see you today, Doctor.

SHPIGELSKY: Neither did I, actually. I dropped in on Bolshintsov, and he was already in his carriage on the way over here. So I simply turned around and came back with him!

BOLSHINTSOV: *(Timidly.)* Are we not disturbing you? We can come back another time—

RAKITIN: Not at all. You're most welcome.

SHPIGELSKY: The servants said that everyone's in the garden.

RAKITIN: Didn't you see Natalya Petrovna?

67

SHPIGELSKY: No. We didn't come from the house. Afanasy Ivanovich wanted to go mushrooming in the woods.

BOLSHINTSOV: *(Bewildered.)* Who, me? Since when?

SHPIGELSKY: *(Conspiratorially, to Bolshintsov.)* We all know how much you love the brown-caps. Where is Natalya Petrovna?

RAKITIN: She invited everyone for a walk. They're going to fly a kite—

SHPIGELSKY: Well, in that case we won't keep you.

RAKITIN: Good-bye for the moment, gentlemen. *(Exits.)*

SHPIGELSKY: Good-bye.

BOLSHINTSOV: What's all this talk about mushrooms, Ignaty Ilyich? What mushrooms?

SHPIGELSKY: Oh. So you'd rather I said you were too shy to go in, and asked to go the long way around, instead?

BOLSHINTSOV: True, but still, mushrooms? Why mushrooms?

SHPIGELSKY: Look, it was your idea to come here in the first place! Now don't mess it up!

BOLSHINTSOV: I'll try not to, I promise. Only tell me, I beg of you—did Natalya Petrovna give any indication what her response might be?

SHPIGELSKY: My dear friend! From your estate to here is roughly ten miles—and every mile you've asked me the same question. So here's the answer, and this is the last time I'll repeat it. Ready? Natalya Petrovna said: "I—"

BOLSHINTSOV: *(Listening attentively, nodding eagerly.)* Yes.

SHPIGELSKY: "Yes"? What do you mean, "yes"? I haven't told you anything yet! She said: "I don't know Bolshintsov, but he seems to be a good man. On the other hand, I have no intention of forcing Vera on him. So let him pay a call, and if he wins"—

BOLSHINTSOV: *(Eagerly.)* "Wins"? Did she say "wins"?

SHPIGELSKY: "If he wins her affections, I won't stand in the way"—

BOLSHINTSOV: Is that what she said?! "Won't stand in the way"?

SHPIGELSKY: *(Exasperated.)* Yes, yes, yes. "Won't stand in the way of their happiness."

BOLSHINTSOV: Huh.

SHPIGELSKY: "Their happiness." Get it? So here's the thing, Afanasy Ivanovich: your task now is to convince Vera Aleksandrovna that marrying you would make her happy. In other words you have to win her affections.

BOLSHINTSOV: *(Blinking.)* Yes, yes, "win" … right. I agree.

69

SHPIGELSKY: You insisted I bring you here today. So let's see what you can do.

BOLSHINTSOV: Yes, of course, we must do something, we must win. Right. The only thing is, Ignaty Ilyich, since you're my very closest friend, I must reveal one of my weaknesses. Yes, I asked you bring me here today—

SHPIGELSKY: Not "asked"—let's be clear—demanded—

BOLSHINTSOV: I know. It's just that, you see …well, at home I felt prepared, so to speak, but now I'm overcome with, er, shyness.

SHPIGELSKY: Why?

BOLSHINTSOV: It's … ah … risky.

SHPIGELSKY: What?

BOLSHINTSOV: Risky. Very risky. I must confess, Ignaty Ilyich—

SHPIGELSKY: Well?

BOLSHINTSOV: I must confess that … well, when it comes to the ladies, in general, I've had, shall we say, little experience with the opposite sex. And I openly admit, Ignaty Ilyich, that I simply can't imagine what one might say to such a person—not to mention alone, and especially to a young lady.

SHPIGELSKY: You amaze me. I don't know what one *can't* say to a member of the opposite sex, especially to a young lady, and especially alone.

BOLSHINTSOV: Well, you, of course. What am I compared to you?! And that's why I'm appealing to you, Ignaty Ilyich. Couldn't you help me out, please? Tell me how to start a conversation, give me a little "opener," then I'll be all right on my own. As for my expression of eternal gratitude, well … *(lowering his voice)* you can expect a troika.[21]

SHPIGELSKY: *(Feigning nonchalance.)* Oh, stop. Look, Afanasy Ivanovich—no doubt you're a splendid fellow, a man of stellar qualities—

BOLSHINTSOV: Please—

SHPIGELSKY: Plus the fact that you're the owner of three hundred serfs—

BOLSHINTSOV: Three hundred twenty.

SHPIGELSKY: You own them outright.

BOLSHINTSOV: I have no debts, not even a kopek.

SHPIGELSKY: You see. I told you that you were an excellent fellow and a suitor of great promise. And yet you say you've had little experience with the ladies?

BOLSHINTSOV: *(Sighing.)* That's the problem. If I may say so, Ignaty Ilyich, I've been afraid of the female sex since childhood.

SHPIGELSKY: Well, that's not necessarily a flaw in a husband—on the contrary, in some cases it might be an asset. More important, however, your appearance, though quite pleasant in general, isn't very striking—and that's a prerequisite nowadays.

BOLSHINTSOV: *(Sighing.)* I see ...

SHPIGELSKY: And then, there's your age ... Not one of your stronger suits, either. But that's not what counts. You have other fine qualities to offer, Afanasy Ivanich, like your 320 serfs. If I were you, I'd simply say to Vera Aleksandrovna—

BOLSHINTSOV: *(Lowering his voice.)* In private—

SHPIGELSKY: Of course in private! "Vera Aleksandrovna!" *(Bolshintsov listens attentively, mouthing the following words Shpigelsky is speaking.)* "I love you, and ask for your hand in marriage. I'm a harmless, goodhearted man—and not a poor one. You'll have complete freedom, and I'll do my best to satisfy your every whim. And I would beg you to pay me a little more attention than you have thus far, and give me a response whensoever you wish. I am prepared to wait—indeed, I consider it a privilege to do so."

BOLSHINTSOV: *(Uttering the last few words aloud.)* "To do so." Good, good, good ... I'm in complete agreement. Only here's the thing, Ignaty Ilyich—it seems that you used the word "harmless," meaning ... what?

SHPIGELSKY: Well, aren't you ... harmless?

BOLSHINTSOV: I suppose so ... But wouldn't it be better to say, for example—

SHPIGELSKY: Yes?

BOLSHINTSOV: Well, maybe, you're right, "harmless" will do.

SHPIGELSKY: Now listen, Afanasy Ivanich: the briefer you are, the better it will go, believe me. The main thing is, don't push. Vera Aleksandrovna is still very young, you might frighten her. *(Looks around.)* Here they come.

BOLSHINTSOV: *(Urgently.)* Vera Aleksandrovna knows nothing yet? Really?

SHPIGELSKY: Of course not!

BOLSHINTSOV: I'm counting on you. *(Blows his nose.)*

Enter Natalya Petrovna, Vera, Kolya, and Belyayev carrying the kite; behind them Rakitin and Lizaveta Bogdanovna.

NATALYA PETROVNA: Hello, Doctor, I wasn't expecting you today, but I'm delighted. Hello, Afanasy Ivanich!

(Bolshintsov bows, embarrassed.)

SHPIGELSKY: This gentleman insisted on bringing me along.

NATALYA PETROVNA: *(Laughing.)* Then I'm much obliged to him.

KOLYA: *(Fidgeting.)* When are we going to fly the kite, *Maman?*

NATALYA PETROVNA: Whenever you like. Let's go down to the meadow, Aleksey Nikolayevich. You, too, Vera. *(To the others.)* You don't mind, do you?

RAKITIN: Why would we?

NATALYA PETROVNA: Come!

Natalya, Vera, Belyayev and Kolya exit.

SHPIGELSKY: Afanasy Ivanovich, offer your arm to Lizaveta Bogdanovna.

BOLSHINTSOV: *(Hastily.)* With the greatest of pleasure.

SHPIGELSKY: Let's watch them fly the kite, shall we?

BOLSHINTSOV: *(As they walk, to Lizaveta Bogdanovna.)* Today, ah, the weather, one might say, is, er, lovely.

LIZAVETA BOGDANOVNA: *(Amused.)* Indeed, it is.

SHPIGELSKY: *(To Rakitin.)* You and I need to talk, Mikhail Aleksandrovich. *(Rakitin laughs.)* What's the matter?

RAKITIN: *(Laughing.)* Oh, nothing … funny how we've fallen behind. We're the rear guard now, as they say.

SHPIGELSKY: But that can easily change, you know. The rear guard can easily become the front one.

RAKITIN: How?

SHPIGELSKY: Simply by changing direction …

They all exit.

Scene Three

The next morning. The drawing room again, as in Act One. Rakitin and Shpigelsky enter from the outer hall.

SHPIGELSKY: So, Mikhail Aleksandrovich, help me, please.

RAKITIN: How can I help you, Ignaty Ilyich?

SHPIGELSKY: Just put yourself in my place. Of course none of this is my concern, I'm just trying to be of assistance. Kindness will be the death of me!

RAKITIN: *(Laughing.)* Not in the immediate future, let's hope.

SHPIGELSKY: *(Laughing too.)* Who knows. It's all very awkward, to say the least. I've brought Bolshintsov down here, but Natalya Petrovna still hasn't given me an answer with regard to his proposal to Vera.

RAKITIN: His what? So that's why she was asking me about him.

SHPIGELSKY: When? What did she say?

RAKITIN: Nothing. It sounds incredible!

SHPIGELSKY: Meanwhile, Bolshintsov is giving me no rest.

RAKITIN: Between you and me, Bolshintsov is a fool, and you're on a fool's errand.

SHPIGELSKY: That's not exactly news, is it?

RAKITIN: What possessed you to get involved in this in the first place?

SHPIGELSKY: The man wouldn't leave me alone.

RAKITIN: Is that the true reason?

SHPIGELSKY: Look—he's my oldest friend.

RAKITIN: *(Dubious.)* Well, that's something.

SHPIGELSKY: All right. I don't want to mislead you. The fact is … one of my trace-horses has gone lame, so he's promised me—

RAKITIN: Another?

SHPIGELSKY: —a whole troika, since you're asking.

RAKITIN: You should have told me this in the first place.

SHPIGELSKY: So I thought it was worth a try. In any event, I would have never agreed to be a go-between, if Bolshintsov weren't a good man. I mean, really, he's an innocent, straight from the garden of Eden. His intentions are entirely honorable.

RAKITIN: Yes, and his horses are good too.

SHPIGELSKY: True. *(Takes snuff and offers it to Rakitin.)* Would you care for some?

RAKITIN: No, thanks, Doctor.

SHPIGELSKY: So that's the story. If he's suitable, fine, if not—let them say so, and that's that.

RAKITIN: But where do I come in? I don't really see what I can do.

SHPIGELSKY: We all know very well that Natalya Petrovna respects you and values your opinion. So be a good friend, put in a good word.

RAKITIN: Come on, Doctor. Do you really think he'd make an appropriate husband for Verochka?

SHPIGELSKY: The important thing in marriage is a solid character. And who could be more solid than Bolshintsov? *(Listens.)* I think Natalya Petrovna's coming ... my dear, dear friend! The two trace-horses are chestnut, and there's a bay in between! Please, do your best!

RAKITIN: *(Dubious.)* Well—

SHPIGELSKY: I'm counting on you. *(Exits.)*

Natalya Petrovna enters.

NATALYA PETROVNA: Oh, it's you. I thought you were in the garden.

RAKITIN: You don't seem pleased—

NATALYA PETROVNA: Are you alone?

RAKITIN: The doctor just left. Is he out of favor too?

NATALYA PETROVNA: I deserve your reproach. Yes, I admit it, I behaved badly yesterday. But believe me, Michel, whatever I may say or do, there's no one I depend on as I do you. *(Lowering her voice.)* No one I love, as I love you. Don't you believe me?

RAKITIN: You're agitated. What's the matter?

NATALYA PETROVNA: Listen, Michel. I want to be open with you—I owe you that. Perhaps I shall upset you a bit, but I know it will upset you more if I keep things from you. I must confess that this young student—Belyayev—has made a rather strong impression on me—

RAKITIN: I knew it.

NATALYA PETROVNA: So you've noticed?

RAKITIN: Since yesterday.

NATALYA PETROVNA: Ah!

RAKITIN: The other day, you may recall, I spoke of a change in you. At the time, I didn't know how to explain it. But yesterday, after our talk, and then in the meadow … if only you could see yourself! I didn't recognize you—you were like another woman. Even now your face lights up at the memory of it.

NATALYA PETROVNA: The fellow dazzles me with his youth—that's all. I never was young, Michel—you know my story. The novelty of it has gone to my head like wine, and I know, I know it will pass as quickly as it has come. Only don't turn away from me. Help me.

RAKITIN: *(Aside.)* This is cruel. *(To Natalya Petrovna.)* You don't see what is happening to you, Natalya Petrovna. You say it's not worth talking about, and yet you ask for help.

NATALYA PETROVNA: You hate me for this, don't you?

RAKITIN: For God's sake, what do you want me to say?

NATALYA PETROVNA: I see I've offended you.

RAKITIN: Never mind.

NATALYA PETROVNA: *Give me your hand. (He doesn't.)* Why, you're jealous!

RAKITIN: I have no right to be, truly. *(Withdrawing.)* Better let's talk about Bolshintsov. The doctor is expecting your answer concerning Vera.

NATALYA PETROVNA: You're still angry with me.

RAKITIN: Me? Oh, no. I feel sorry for you.

NATALYA PETROVNA: And now you're purposely changing the subject? All right, then, this Bolshintsov business is very annoying. Who asked the doctor to interfere?

RAKITIN: He assured me that you're considering Bolshintsov's proposal—

NATALYA PETROVNA: I haven't promised anything. In fact, I don't know what I'm going to do. Anyway, what does it matter! Shpigelsky has his hand in all sorts of affairs, so he can't expect everything to go his way.

RAKITIN: He only wants an answer.

NATALYA PETROVNA: Actually, I still haven't spoken with Verochka about it.

RAKITIN: I'll go get her for you now.

NATALYA PETROVNA: Wait—you just said you felt sorry for me.

RAKITIN: I thought we changed the subject.

NATALYA PETROVNA: But what did you mean by it? Come on, Michel …

RAKITIN: *(Coolly.)* Never mind. Am I to go get her?

NATALYA PETROVNA: *(Annoyed.)* Yes, do. *(Rakitin exits into the study. Natalya Petrovna sits, picks up a book, opens it, and lets it fall into her lap.)* It's time to put an end to this. (Vera enters from the study.)

VERA: *(Hesitantly.)* You sent for me, Natalya Petrovna?

NATALYA PETROVNA: Ah! Verochka! Yes, I asked to see you.

VERA: Are you well?

NATALYA PETROVNA: Of course. Why?

VERA: I just thought—

NATALYA PETROVNA: No, I'm fine. It's the heat, that's all. Sit down. *(Vera sits.)* Are you busy right now, Vera?

VERA: Not really.

NATALYA PETROVNA: I sent for you, because I need to have a talk with you ... a serious talk. You see, my dear, until now I've always looked upon you as a child; but you're eighteen, you're sensible, and it's time you thought about your future. You know that I love you as a daughter; my home will always be yours. Tell me—wouldn't you like to be mistress, the mistress, I mean, of your very own house?

VERA: What do you mean, Natalya Petrovna? I don't understand.

NATALYA PETROVNA: I have received a proposal for you hand in marriage.

VERA: *(Amazed.)* What?!

NATALYA PETROVNA: You didn't expect it, I see—and I confess it seems strange to me, too. As far as I'm concerned, you're too young to marry. I only consider it my duty to inform you. Vera ... what is it? You're trembling ... surely you're not afraid of me, Vera?

VERA: I am in your power, Natalya Petrovna.

NATALYA PETROVNA: In my power, you say? What do

you take me for? Let me see you smile. There, that's better. *(Natalya Petrovna draws her close.)* Vera, my child, think of me as a mother, or better yet, an older sister, and let's talk about these things, shall we?

VERA: I'd like to.

NATALYA PETROVNA: Good. *(Hugs her.)* So, imagine that one fine day your sister says to you: "Vera, you have a suitor!" Well? What would your answer be?

VERA: Who is this suitor?

NATALYA PETROVNA: Ah! So you are curious. Haven't you guessed?

VERA: No.

NATALYA PETROVNA: You only just saw him earlier today. He's not handsome, and he's not young, either.... It's Bolshintsov.

VERA: *(Incredulous.)* Afanasy Ivanovich?

NATALYA PETROVNA: Yes ... Afanasy Ivanovich.

VERA: *(Stares, then bursts out laughing.)* You're joking!

NATALYA PETROVNA: No. But I see that Bolshintsov is wasting his time. If you'd burst into tears at the sound of his name, he might have a chance, but you're laughing! He's only got one choice—to go on his way, poor man.

VERA: Forgive me, but really, I had no idea. Do people actually marry at his age?

NATALYA PETROVNA: What do mean? He's not even fifty! And that's a fine age for marriage.

VERA: But he has such a strange face … *(Laughs again.)*

NATALYA PETROVNA: Never mind, let's not talk of him anymore. He's history. Anyway, it's understandable that a child your age couldn't be attracted to a man like Bolshintsov. You'll want to marry for love, not for convenience, right?

VERA: Of course! Didn't you marry Arkady Sergeyevich for love?

NATALYA PETROVNA: *(Quickly.)* Of course. Ah, Vera. I called you a child just now, but sometimes "out of the mouths of babes," as they say, comes the truth. So it's settled, yes? We're good friends, and we'll never hide anything from one another. Now, Verochka, what if I were to ask you, confidentially: Is it only because Bolshintsov is old and unattractive that you don't want to marry him?

VERA: Surely that's enough, isn't it?

NATALYA PETROVNA: I'm not disputing that. But is there no other reason?

VERA: I don't know him at all.

NATALYA PETROVNA: Really? In that case I would advise you to think it over. It wouldn't be easy to fall in love with Bolshintsov, I understand that. But I repeat, he's a good man. Of course if you loved someone else—now that's another story. But your heart hasn't spoken to you yet, has it?

VERA: *(Hesitant.)* What?

NATALYA PETROVNA: You love no one else?

VERA: I love you, and Kolya, and Anna Semyonovna, and—

NATALYA PETROVNA: I'm not talking about that kind of love. I mean, for example, among the young men you may have seen here, or at other gatherings, isn't there one who has attracted you?

VERA: Not really …

NATALYA PETROVNA: What about Rakitin?

VERA: I like Mikhail Aleksandrovich very much—

NATALYA PETROVNA: Yes, like an older brother. *(Casually.)* Oh, and what about Belyayev?

VERA: *(Embarrassed.)* Aleksey Nikolayevich? I like him.

NATALYA PETROVNA: Yes, he's a good fellow. But he's so shy with everyone.

VERA: Not at all—he's not shy with me.

NATALYA PETROVNA: Really!

VERA: He talks to me. Perhaps, you think he's shy, because … because he's afraid of you. He hasn't gotten to know you yet.

NATALYA PETROVNA: And how do you know he's afraid of me?

VERA: He told me so.

NATALYA PETROVNA: Ah! So he's more open with you than with others?

VERA: I don't know how he is with others, but with me ... perhaps it's because we're both orphans. Besides, I'm just a child in his eyes.

NATALYA PETROVNA: I like him too. He has a very good heart.

VERA: Oh, the kindest! If only you knew! Everyone in the house loves him. He's so friendly. He's always ready to help. The other day he carried a beggarwoman in his arms from the highway to the hospital. He picked a flower for me once from such a high precipice that I couldn't bear to watch—I was afraid he would fall, but he's so agile! You saw for yourself yesterday in the meadow, how agile he is.

NATALYA PETROVNA: Yes ...

VERA: Remember when he was chasing the kite, how he leapt across the ditch?

NATALYA PETROVNA: And he picked a flower for you from a dangerous height? He's obviously very fond of you.

VERA: He's so good-natured. He's always in a good mood.

NATALYA PETROVNA: It's strange, though. Why isn't he that way with me—

VERA: He doesn't know you yet. But wait ... I'll tell him that he has no need to be afraid of you—right? You're so good ...

NATALYA PETROVNA: Thank you. I'm glad you think so.

VERA: He'll listen to me, even though I'm younger than he is.

NATALYA PETROVNA: I didn't know you were that friendly with him. Vera, be careful, please. He's an excellent young man, of course. But, you know, people will imagine things. Don't be angry with me, my dear. It's the duty of the older generation to admonish the young. Though perhaps I don't need to tell you this—perhaps you simply like him, and nothing more?

VERA: He—

NATALYA PETROVNA: There you go, looking at me like that again! Vera, come close ... *(She strokes Vera's hair gently.)* What if your sister, a true sister, were to whisper in your ear: "Verochka, you're not in love with anyone, are you?" How would you respond? Your eyes want to tell me something ... Do you love him? Say it: Do you?

VERA: *(Burying her face.)* I don't know what's the matter with me ...

NATALYA PETROVNA: Poor child! You're in love. You're in love ... and he?

VERA: Why are you asking me this? I don't know. Perhaps ... I don't know ... Natalya Petrovna, what's the matter with you?

NATALYA PETROVNA: The matter? Nothing. Why? Nothing.

VERA: You're so pale—what's the matter?

NATALYA PETROVNA: No, don't. It's nothing. It will pass. See, it already has.

VERA: Allow me, please, to call someone—

NATALYA PETROVNA: No need. Actually, I'd like to be left alone now. All right? We'll talk more later. Go.

VERA: You're not angry with me, are you, Natalya Petrovna?

NATALYA PETROVNA: Angry? Not at all. On the contrary, I'm grateful for your trust. Only please leave me for now.

VERA: *(Close to tears.)* Natalya Petrovna—

NATALYA PETROVNA: Leave me, please. *(Vera exits quickly.)*

NATALYA PETROVNA: *(Alone.)* Now it's clear to me. These children love one another. Good for them. God grant them happiness! *(Laughs.)* What have I come to? Why am I doing this? Trying to marry that poor girl off to an old man! Using the doctor ... Am I jealous of Vera? Am I in love with him myself, is that it? My God, it's as if I've been poisoned ... What could he see in me, anyway? He's young, she's young, while I.... What is happening to me? I'm in love! This can't be. He must go away. Yes. Rakitin, too. I'll come to my senses.... I'll fall into Arkady's arms, I'll beg him to save me ... but is there no other way? This girl—she's just a child. She may be mistaken, he may not love her, after all ... so I'm still hopeful, is that it? And for what? God, don't make me hate myself!

RAKITIN: *(Entering, agitated.)* Natalya Petrovna ...

NATALYA PETROVNA: Oh. It's you.

RAKITIN: Vera Aleksandrovna told me you're not well—

NATALYA PETROVNA: I'm fine.

RAKITIN: No, Natalya Petrovna, you're not. Look at you.

NATALYA PETROVNA: Does it matter? What do you want?

RAKITIN: *(With emotion.)* I've come to beg your forgiveness. Half an hour ago I was unspeakably stupid and rude. Forgive me. Here I am, your constant friend, a man who asks nothing more than to serve you, support you ... don't deny me your trust, use me as you will and forget everything that may have offended you.

NATALYA PETROVNA: *(Distracted.)* Yes, yes ... oh, forgive me, Rakitin, I haven't heard a word you were saying.

RAKITIN: I asked for your forgiveness, Natalya Petrovna. I asked you if you would permit me still to be your friend.

NATALYA PETROVNA: *(Abruptly.)* Rakitin, tell me, what's happening to me?

RAKITIN: You're in love.

NATALYA PETROVNA: *(Repeating.)* I'm in love ... but it's madness, Rakitin, it's impossible! Can such a thing happen?

RAKITIN: You're in love. Don't fool yourself.

NATALYA PETROVNA: So what can I do?

RAKITIN: I'm prepared to tell you, Natalya Petrovna, if you promise me—

NATALYA PETROVNA: What?

RAKITIN: —that you won't misinterpret my intentions, that you believe my desire to help you is completely without self-interest.

NATALYA PETROVNA: Tell me then.

RAKITIN: All right, listen: he must go away. He must. I won't speak about ... about your husband, about your duty. Those words would be inappropriate, coming from my lips. But these children love one another. Imagine what it would mean to put yourself between them. It would destroy you!

NATALYA PETROVNA: He must go away ... and what about you? You'll stay?

RAKITIN: I must go away too. For your peace of mind, your happiness, he and I both must go away forever. There's no other way to save you.

NATALYA PETROVNA: Then what is there to live for?

RAKITIN: Has it really gone that far? You'll get over this, Natalya Petrovna, believe me. It will pass.

NATALYA PETROVNA: No, I mean it. What is there to live for, if everyone is leaving me?

RAKITIN: What about your family? Listen, if you like, after he goes I can stay behind for a few days, so that you—

NATALYA PETROVNA: *(Sharply.)* Ah! Now I understand. You're counting on force of habit. You're hoping that I'll come to my senses, that after he leaves, I'll turn to you, right?

RAKITIN: *(Taken aback.)* Natalya Petrovna, I'll leave today, at once, you'll never see me again— *(Starts to leave.)*

NATALYA PETROVNA: Michel, I don't know what I'm saying ... you see what a state I'm in. Forgive me.

RAKITIN: *(Consoling.)* Natalya Petrovna—

NATALYA PETROVNA: Oh, Michel, I'm utterly miserable. Help me, I'm lost without you. *(They embrace.)*

At this moment, the door to the outer hall opens, and Islayev and Anna Semyonovna enter.

ISLAYEV: I've always been of the opinion ... *(Stops in amazement at the sight of Rakitin and Natalya Petrovna. She exits quickly)*

ISLAYEV: What does this mean? What's going on here?

RAKITIN: *(Embarrassed.)* We were just—

ISLAYEV: Natalya Petrovna's unwell ... is that it?

RAKITIN: Not really, but—

ISLAYEV: Why did she rush out all of a sudden? She was crying, wasn't she? You were consoling her. What's happened?

RAKITIN: Nothing, truly.

ANNA SEMYONOVNA: What do you mean "nothing"? I'll go and see—

RAKITIN: *(Stops her.)* No, please, better leave her in peace just now—

ISLAYEV: But what's it all about? Tell us!

RAKITIN: Nothing, I assure you. Listen, I promise to explain it to you—I give you my word. But for now, please, if you trust me, don't ask—and try not to disturb Natalya Petrovna.

ISLAYEV: All right. But it certainly is strange. This has never happened before with Natasha. It's quite out of the ordinary.

ANNA SEMYONOVNA: What could have made Natasha cry? And why has she left us? Are we strangers?

RAKITIN: We didn't finish our conversation, that's all. I ask you both to leave us alone for just a little while.

ISLAYEV: Really! So there's some sort of secret between you?

RAKITIN: In a way. But you'll know about it soon, I promise.

ISLAYEV: Let's go, Mama, we'll leave them alone. Let them finish their mysterious conversation.

ANNA SEMYONOVNA: But—

ISLAYEV: Didn't you hear him? He promises to tell us everything.

RAKITIN: Rest assured—

ISLAYEV: Oh, I'm very assured. Let's go, Mama. *(They both exit.)*

RAKITIN: *(Goes to the door and calls out.)* Natalya Petrovna, come back, I beg you.

NATALYA PETROVNA: *(Entering.)* What did they say?

RAKITIN: I had to promise to explain everything tomorrow.

NATALYA PETROVNA: So what are you going to tell him?

RAKITIN: I'll think of something. But let's not worry about that just now. Let's take advantage of this respite. You see it can't go on like this, don't you agree?

NATALYA PETROVNA: Agree? About what?

RAKITIN: The necessity of our departure. There's no point to delay it. If you'll allow me, I'll talk to Belyayev right away. He's good fellow; he'll understand.

NATALYA PETROVNA: *(Agitated.)* Rakitin, if you utter one word about me, or from me, to Belyayev, I shall never forgive you.

RAKITIN: In that case, I won't. I'll leave this place without even saying good-bye to him. I won't impose my services upon you any longer.

NATALYA PETROVNA: *(Embarrassed.)* So now you think perhaps I've changed my mind about his leaving? On the contrary, I'm so convinced of the necessity, as you say, of his departure, that I intend to dismiss him myself.

RAKITIN: What?

NATALYA PETROVNA: Yes, at once.

RAKITIN: Right now?

NATALYA PETROVNA: Right now. I'll dismiss him and it will be forgotten, like a bad dream. We'll have a conversation and get it over with. Forgive me, please, and send him to see me.

RAKITIN: *(Formally.)* Very well. I will do as you wish.

NATALYA PETROVNA: Thank you, Michel.

RAKITIN: Spare me your thanks, at least. *(Exits.)*

NATALYA PETROVNA: *(Alone, after a pause.)* He's an honorable man. And he's right. Belyayev must go. He must ... How my head aches. Shall I put it off till tomorrow? No, better to end it once and for all ... Just one last effort, and then I'm free ... how I yearn for peace. *(Belyayev enters from the outer hall.)*

BELYAYEV: Mikhail Alekseyevich told me that you wanted to see me?

NATALYA PETROVNA: Yes. We need to clarify things.

BELYAYEV: I'm at your service.

NATALYA PETROVNA: Allow me to say, Aleksey Nikolayevich, that I'm somewhat displeased with you.

BELYAYEV: *(Surprised.)* May I ask, for what reasons?

NATALYA PETROVNA: Hear me out. I ... honestly don't know where to start. However, I must warn you, that my displeasure is not due to any deficiencies on your part. On the contrary, I'm very pleased with your care of Kolya.

BELYAYEV: Then what could it be?

NATALYA PETROVNA: No need to be alarmed. It's not a grave matter. You're young; you've probably never stayed with strangers before. You couldn't have foreseen—

BELYAYEV: I don't understand—

NATALYA PETROVNA: You want to know what it is, don't you? I understand your impatience. All right, then, I must tell you that Verochka …has told me everything.

BELYAYEV: *(Bewildered.)* Vera Aleksandrovna? What has she told you? And what does it have to do with me?

NATALYA PETROVNA: So you really don't know. Can't you guess?

BELYAYEV: I haven't a clue.

NATALYA PETROVNA: Really? Do you think you can convince me that you haven't noticed that child's feelings for you?

BELYAYEV: For me? I'm at a loss for words. I always thought that, as far as Vera Aleksandrovna is concerned, I've behaved quite appropriately—

NATALYA PETROVNA: —as you do with everyone else, is that what you're trying to say? In any case, whether you're unaware—or simply pretending to be—the fact is that the girl is in love with you. She confessed it to me herself. So now I'm asking you, as an honorable man, what are your intentions?

BELYAYEV: *(In disbelief.)* My intentions?

NATALYA PETROVNA: That's right.

BELYAYEV: This is quite unexpected, Natalya Petrovna ...

NATALYA PETROVNA: I see I haven't presented this well at all. You think I'm angry at you, whereas I'm only ... a little upset. Come, let's sit. *(They both sit.)* You see, Aleksey Nikolayevich, Vera is an orphan, she's my ward. I'm responsible for her, for her future, for her happiness. She's still young, and I'm convinced that the feeling you've inspired in her will soon pass. At her age, love does not last long. But please understand that it's my duty to warn you. It's dangerous to play with fire. And I don't doubt that, knowing her feelings, you'll change your behavior towards her. You'll avoid meetings and walks in the garden—won't you? I'm counting on you.

BELYAYEV: Truly, Natalya Petrovna, I don't know what you're trying to say.

NATALYA PETROVNA: Oh, believe me, I'm not asking for a confession, there's no need for that. I can tell from your behavior what the situation is. However, I must say that Vera felt you were not quite indifferent to her.

BELYAYEV: *(After a pause.)* Natalya Petrovna, I see that I can't remain in your house any longer.

NATALYA PETROVNA: *(Sharply.)* You might have waited for me to say that myself!

BELYAYEV: You have been open with me, so allow me to be open with you. I don't love Vera Aleksandrovna—at least not in the way you suggest.

NATALYA PETROVNA: But I didn't—

BELYAYEV: And if Vera Aleksandrovna cares for me, if—as you say—she senses that I in turn care for her, too, then I wouldn't want to deceive her. I'll tell her the truth myself. But after such declarations, I'm sure you'll understand, Natalya Petrovna, that it will be difficult for me to remain here. My situation would be too awkward. I can't begin to tell you how sorry it will make me to leave your home, but there is no other choice. I'll always remember you with gratitude. And now allow me please to leave. I'll come to bid you a proper farewell later.

NATALYA PETROVNA: Clearly, you find it easy to leave us.

BELYAYEV: Not at all.

NATALYA PETROVNA: I'm not accustomed to detaining people against their will ... please understand, I'm finding this very unpleasant.

BELYAYEV: *(After a moment.)* Natalya Petrovna, I don't want to cause you the slightest unpleasantness. I'll stay.

NATALYA PETROVNA: Ah! ... I didn't expect you to change your mind so fast. I'm grateful, but ... allow me to think it over. Perhaps you're right—perhaps it would be better for you to go. I'll think it over and let you know. Will you allow me to leave you in uncertainty till this evening?

BELYAYEV: I shall wait as long as you like. *(Bows, and turns to go.)*

NATALYA PETROVNA: Promise me—

BELYAYEV: What?

NATALYA PETROVNA: I believe you intend to talk about this to Vera ... I don't know if that would be appropriate. However, I'll leave it to you to decide. Good-bye for now.

Belyayev bows for a second time, and exits.

NATALYA PETROVNA: *(Alone.)* What a relief! He doesn't love her. So now what? Instead of sending him away, I'm keeping him here? That poor girl—I tricked her into a confession. Well, it can't be undone, can it? And he—how boldly and bravely he spoke. What a man! He must go. If he stays, I feel it might go too far. He must go, or else I'll won't survive! I'll write to him before he has the chance to see Vera. He must go! *(She exits quickly.)*

Scene Four

A corner of the garden, a few hours later. Stage right, there is small terrace with columns and a door into the main house. In a corner there are several shovels, watering cans and flower pots. It is early evening, with an intermittent, light rain. The last rays of a setting sun cast deep shadows.

KATYA: *(Enters from the house.)* Where can he be? They told me he'd gone out to the conservatory. Hmmm. I'll wait here until he returns. *(Sighs.)* They say he's leaving. How can we live without him? ... The poor miss! How she begged me to find him. And why shouldn't I help her? Let her have a last talk with him. Ooo, it's hot today! I think I feel a drop of rain. *(She suddenly withdraws.)* Oh, no. They're not coming this way, are they?

Katya tries to run off but doesn't reach the door before Shpigelsky and Lizaveta Bogdanovna enter. Katya hides behind a column.

SHPIGELSKY: Ah—the perfect spot. Let's wait here till the rain stops.

LIZAVETA BOGDANOVNA: Good idea.

SHPIGELSKY: Where are we?

LIZAVETA BOGDANOVNA: A hidden garden on the side of the house. No one ever comes here.

SHPIGELSKY: Let's sit, shall we? *(They sit on a bench.)* I must admit, Lizaveta Bogdanovna, that the rain has come at a most disadvantageous moment. It has interrupted our *tête à tête* at its most delicate point.

LIZAVETA BOGDANOVNA: *(Subtly.)* And what point is that?

SHPIGELSKY: I'm about to get to it. Anyway, no one can stop us from resuming our conversation here.

LIZAVETA BOGDANOVNA: It's been quite an afternoon around here.

SHPIGELSKY: So you said.

LIZAVETA BOGDANOVNA: Anna Semyonovna's completely out of sorts. She even had dinner alone in her room.

SHPIGELSKY: You don't say!

LIZAVETA BOGDANOVNA: This morning she found Natalya Petrovna with Mikhail Aleksandrovich—in tears. Of course he's just like one of the family, but even so.... Anyway, he's promised to explain everything.

SHPIGELSKY: Ah! Well then, she needn't worry. In my view Mikhail Aleksandrovich has never been a dangerous person.

LIZAVETA BOGDANOVNA: Why do you say so?

SHPIGELSKY: Because he's such a smooth talker. Some break out in a rash, while others break out in run-on sentences. Don't be afraid of the babblers, Lizaveta Bogdanovna. It's the quiet ones who are dangerous.

LIZAVETA BOGDANOVNA: Tell me, is Natalya Petrovna really ill?

SHPIGELSKY: No more ill than you or I.

LIZAVETA BOGDANOVNA: She didn't touch a thing at dinner.

SHPIGELSKY: Illness isn't the only cause of appetite loss.

LIZAVETA BOGDANOVNA: Do you know what, Ignaty Ilyich? I think Natalya Petrovna ... Well, she's been paying Belyayev a lot of attention lately, hasn't she?

SHPIGELSKY: I'd better have a talk with her. Let's hope she won't bite me. If I'm not wrong, I think she still needs me. Rakitin, I noticed, looks gloomy, too—

LIZAVETA BOGDANOVNA: Yes, he's not quite himself.

SHPIGELSKY: Hm. And what about Vera Aleksandrovna and Belyayev?

LIZAVETA BOGDANOVNA: Everyone seems out of sorts today. I have no idea what the problem is, truly.

SHPIGELSKY: You're very observant, Lizaveta Bogdanovna. I like that in a woman. Never mind them, though. Let's talk about our little matter instead. The rain still hasn't stopped. Shall we, then?

LIZAVETA BOGDANOVNA: What would you like to ask me, Ignaty Ilyich?

SHPIGELSKY: Oh come on, Lizaveta Bogdanovna, no need for pretense, is there? After all, we're not exactly young! All this standing on ceremony—it doesn't suit you. Let's talk practically, as befits our years. Here's the matter: we like one another—at least I assume you like me—

LIZAVETA BOGDANOVNA: Actually, I—

SHPIGELSKY: All right, all right, whatever. Let's say we like each other. And we'd make a fine match in other respects, too. Of course, under these circumstances I'm compelled to say that I'm not especially well-born, like all these other fancy folk, but then again neither are you. Nor am I rich—and if I were, I wouldn't be here, now, would I? *(Chuckles.)* But I've got a decent medical practice, not all my patients die on me. You say you've got fifteen thousand rubles of your own—and that's not so bad, is it?

LIZAVETA BOGDANOVNA: *(Startled.)* How did you know that?!

SHPIGELSKY: Never mind. Besides, I imagine you're getting tired of being a companion, fussing over some old lady, yessing her all the time—it can't be much fun.

LIZAVETA BOGDANOVNA: It's not …

SHPIGELSKY: For my part, I'm not exactly tiring of the bachelor life, but I'm growing older and my cooks are robbing me blind. So you see, things are pointing in the right direction, if you know what I mean. But here's the difficulty, Lizaveta Bogdanovna, we really don't know each other all that well, or shall I say, you don't know me. Whereas I know you. I understand your character.

LIZAVETA BOGDANOVNA: *(Wryly.)* Really? I'm impressed.

SHPIGELSKY: I'm not saying you're not without faults. You've been single for too long, forgive me for saying so, but that's not the end of the world. In the hands of a good husband, a wife is as soft as wax, as they say.

LIZAVETA BOGDANOVNA: *(Amused.)* You think so, Doctor? I wouldn't be too sure …

SHPIGELSKY: Never mind, forget I said that. Still, I'd like you to get to know me before the wedding, so you don't reproach me afterward. I wouldn't want to deceive you.

LIZAVETA BOGDANOVNA: Good idea.

SHPIGELSKY: I suppose you think I'm a cheerful sort, entertaining and so on, right?

LIZAVETA BOGDANOVNA: I wouldn't go that far. At this point, I'd say you seem agreeable—enough, that is, for me to be curious—

SHPIGELSKY: Just because I play the fool for others, tell them funny stories, humor them, wait on them hand and foot, people think I'm a cheerful type. To tell you the truth, if I didn't need these people, I wouldn't even look at them. I know that, behind their perfumed manners and simpering smiles, they look down in me.

LIZAVETA BOGDANOVNA: *(Amused.)* Really? What makes you think that?

SHPIGELSKY: I remember once, at one of their fancy dinners, just for the fun of it, a high-and-mighty young landowner sitting next to me plucked a radish off his plate and stuck it in my hair.

LIZAVETA BOGDANOVNA: *(Delighted.)* He didn't!

SHPIGELSKY: He did. I rose from the table, removed the vegetable from my person, and challenged him to a duel!

103

LIZAVETA BOGDANOVNA: *(Laughing.)* What happened?

SHPIGELSKY: Nothing much. The host made the landowner apologize. But I had my moment.

LIZAVETA BOGDANOVNA: Ignaty Ilyich, you surprise me! I'm doubly impressed.

SHPIGELSKY: I knew you'd be. Actually, to your point, I'm not particularly agreeable, and I'm not all that nice, either. The point is, I don't also want to pretend to be someone I'm not. My life hasn't amounted to that much. I'm a mediocre doctor—I won't hide it from you—and once we're together, if you ever take ill, I wouldn't treat you myself. As for my temperament, I really should warn you, Lizaveta Bogdanovna—at home I'm demanding. I don't get cross, as long as all my needs are met. I like to be fed well and have my routines respected. At the same time, I'm not jealous and I'm not stingy. In my absence you can do whatever you like. As for romantic love, forget it, there's no point even in talking about it. On the other hand, there are other advantages to cohabitation. Oh—and I'm not judgmental. There. That's my proposal. So what do you say?

LIZAVETA BOGDANOVNA: Er ... after that presentation, what can I say, Ignaty Ilyich?

SHPIGELSKY: Not tempting enough for you?

LIZAVETA BOGDANOVNA: Well, since you ask—

SHPIGELSKY: Please don't forget that another man in my place would say nothing about his faults, would be relieved you hadn't noticed, and then after the wedding, well, then it's too late. But I'm too proud to do that.

LIZAVETA BOGDANOVNA: *(Amused.)* Really?

SHPIGELSKY: Don't look at me like that. I'm not going to lie to my future wife. For now, consider the proposition I'm honored to present you, think it over in private, and let me know your decision. As far as I can tell, you're a sensible woman. By the way, how old are you?

LIZAVETA BOGDANOVNA: Who, me? Forty.

SHPIGELSKY: That's not true. You're every bit of fifty.

LIZAVETA BOGDANOVNA: All right, I'm forty-six.

SHPIGELSKY: Well, that's not forty. Anyway, that's not old, not for a married woman.

LIZAVETA BOGDANOVNA: Glad you think so.

SHPIGELSKY: And you shouldn't take snuff, either.

LIZAVETA BOGDANOVNA: Why not? You do.

SHPIGELSKY: That's different.

LIZAVETA: BOGDANOVNA: *(Wryly.)* Oh, really? Why?

SHPIGELSKY: *(Stands.)* Well. It appears the rain has stopped.

LIZAVETA BOGDANOVNA: *(Also stands.)* Yes, it has. All finished?

SHPIGELSKY: I am. So you'll give me your answer in a day or two?

LIZAVETA BOGDANOVNA: We'll see.

SHPIGELSKY: I like that! Sensible, very sensible! Think it over. Good. That's over with. Let's go inside.

LIZAVETA BOGDANOVNA: *(Gives him her arm.)* As you wish.

SHPIGELSKY: By the way, I haven't kissed your hand. It's what's done, isn't it? So, here goes! (Kisses her hand.) There.

LIZAVETA BOGDANOVNA: Is that "what's done"? Really?

SHPIGELSKY: What do you mean?

Lizaveta Bogdanovna suddenly grabs Shpigelsky and kisses him hard on the mouth.

SHPIGELSKY: *(Gasping.)* Good God! What are you doing?

LIZAVETA BOGDANOVNA: Just thought we'd get to know one another a little better. Wasn't that your suggestion?

SHPIGELSKY: *(Shaken.)* But—

LIZAVETA BOGDANOVNA: We'll resume this little *"tête a tête,"* as you suggest, tomorrow or the next day. By the way, it'll be my turn to interview you—before I give you my final answer, that is. I have a few questions—

SHPIGELSKY: *(Dumbfounded.)* About what?

LIZAVETA BOGDANOVNA: You'll see. Oh, and since you brought it up, just so you know, I'm a terrible cook, so you'd better find a new one for our household, or else learn to cook yourself.

SHPIGELSKY: Wait—

LIZAVETA BOGDANOVNA: And sorry about the snuff, but it stays. I drink, too, did you know that? Don't worry, only brandy, and only after dinner, well maybe sometimes in the afternoon—

SHPIGELSKY: *(Bewildered.)* Please, stop—

LIZAVETA BOGDANOVNA: Furthermore—oh never mind, let's save it for tomorrow. You'll have something to look forward to. Meanwhile, you'd better have that talk with Natalya Petrovna. Let's hope she won't bite you, too. *(Laughing, she leads him into the house.)*

KATYA: *(Emerging discreetly from behind the column, laughing.)* Ha! Good for her! That doctor's a nasty piece of work. ...blah, blah, blah! Who'd accept a proposal like that?! She's smart to straighten him out, before it goes any further. What's so good about being a doctor's wife, anyway? Never mind. The grass is shimmering after the rain. So fresh and fragrant, like wild cherry.... Ah, here he comes. *(Belyayev appears at the door to the garden.)* Aleksey Nikolayevich!

BELYAYEV: Is that you, Katya?

KATYA: Come outside. I've got something to tell you.

BELYAYEV: All right. *(Enters.)*

KATYA: You didn't get wet?

BELYAYEV: No, I was sitting in the greenhouse. How pretty you look today! *(Katya smiles, lowering her eyes. He takes a peach out of his pocket.)* Would you like a peach?

KATYA: *(Refusing.)* Eat it yourself.

BELYAYEV: But I didn't refuse when you offered me raspberries yesterday. Take it—I picked it for you, truly, I did.

KATYA: Oh, thank you. *(Takes the peach.)*

BELYAYEV: That's better. Now what did you want to tell me?

KATYA: The young mistress, Vera Aleksandrovna, asked me to find you. She wishes to see you.
BELYAYEV: I'll go to her at once.

KATYA: No—she wants to come here. She needs to have a talk with you.

BELYAYEV: *(With some surprise.)* Here?

KATYA: No one ever comes here. You won't be disturbed. She loves you very much, Aleksey Nikolayevich.

BELYAYEV: Katya, please—

KATYA: She's so good. Shall I go get her?

BELYAYEV: Yes, of course.

KATYA: Is it true what they're saying, Aleksey Nikolayevich? You're going away?

BELYAYEV: Me? No ... who told you that?

KATYA: You're not going away, then? Well, thank God! *(With some confusion.)* We'll be back in a minute. *(Exits into the house.)*

BELYAYEV: *(Alone.)* How extraordinary! I must admit, I never expected anything like this. *(Pulls a scrap of paper from his pocket.)* From Natalya Petrovna. "Don't leave, don't decide anything until I speak with you." About what? What foolish thoughts fill my head! I must admit this is all very embarrassing. I can't get over that conversation with her. And now Vera wants to see me ... she's a dear, sweet child.... What should I say to her? It's all so strange. *(Vera and Katya appear at the door. He quickly hides the note.)*

KATYA: Don't be afraid, miss; go to him; I'll wait outside. *(She exits into the house.)*

BELYAYEV: Vera Aleksandrovna, you wanted to see me. Come, sit down. *(Takes her hand and leads her to the bench.)* There, that's better. Now tell me, what did you want to talk about?

VERA: I came to ask your forgiveness, Aleksey Nikolayevich.

BELYAYEV: For what?

VERA: I heard that you had an unpleasant conversation with Natalya Petrovna. And that you're leaving ... that is, you're being asked to go.

BELYAYEV: Who told you this?

VERA: Natalya Petrovna ... I met her after your conversation with her. She told me that you didn't want to stay here yourself. But I was under the impression that you've been dismissed.

BELYAYEV: Tell me, does anyone else know about this in the house?

VERA: Only Katya. I had to tell her. I wanted to see you, to beg your forgiveness. You can't imagine how badly I feel. I'm the cause of it all, Aleksey Nikolayevich; I alone am to blame.

BELYAYEV: You?

VERA: I never would have dreamed that Natalya Petrovna ... But I forgive her, just as you must forgive me, too. This morning I was a foolish child, but now—

BELYAYEV: Nothing's been decided yet. I may very well be staying.

VERA: Look how you've changed since yesterday. Now I see—Natalya Petrovna has told you everything.

BELYAYEV: What do you mean?

VERA: I see it. She wanted to trap me, and, fool that I am, I fell right into her net. But she gave herself away. I'm not a child anymore. Oh, no!

BELYAYEV: What are you trying to say?

VERA: Aleksey Nikolayevich, do you really want to leave us?

BELYAYEV: Yes.

VERA: But why? *(Belyayev is silent.)* Won't you answer me?

BELYAYEV: You're right. Natalya Petrovna told me everything.

VERA: Like what, for example?

BELYAYEV: Vera Aleksandrovna, please … I just can't say it—

VERA: Perhaps she told you that I love you?

BELYAYEV: Yes.

VERA: But it's not true.

BELYAYEV: What?

VERA: I never said that! Oh, how cruelly she has treated me! And you're going away because of this?

BELYAYEV: Vera Aleksandrovna, give me your hand. Listen, there must be no misunderstanding between us. I love you like a sister; I love you because nobody could help loving you. Never in my life have I been in such a situation. I can't bear to hurt you. I'm not going to pretend—I know that you've grown fond of me. But what can come from this? I'm only twenty-two, and I haven't got a kopek. Please, don't be angry with me. I really don't know what to say.

VERA: I don't blame you, Aleksey Nikolayevich. It's all my fault, and I've been punished for it! And I don't blame her either: she's a good woman, but she can't help herself ... she's lost.

BELYAYEV: Lost?

VERA: Natalya Petrovna loves you, Belyayev.

BELYAYEV: What?

VERA: She's in love with you.

BELYAYEV: What are you saying?

VERA: I've aged years today. I'm not a child anymore, believe me. She actually was jealous—of me! How do you like that?!

BELYAYEV: It can't be!

VERA: Yes, it can. Why else did she decide to marry me off to that man, whatever his name is, Bolshintsov? Oh yes, she loves you, it's all too clear.

BELYAYEV: Vera Aleksandrovna, you're mistaken, I assure you.

VERA: No, I'm not mistaken. Trust me, I'm not. If she doesn't love you, then why has she tormented me like this? What have I ever done to her? Jealousy is an excuse for anything. And now, she's sending you away—why? Because she thinks that we ... well, she needn't worry! You can stay!

BELYAYEV: She hasn't asked me to leave yet, Vera Aleksandrovna. I already told you that it hasn't been decided.

VERA: Really?

BELYAYEV: Yes. But why do you look at me like that?

VERA: Ah! I understand ... yes.... She's still hoping that—

Natalya Petrovna appears, unseen, at the door to the garden.

BELYAYEV: What?

VERA: It's all clear to me. She's come to her senses, she sees I'm no danger to her! I mean really, what am I compared to her? A foolish girl—

BELYAYEV: How could you think—

VERA: Anyway, who knows? Perhaps you love her, too.

BELYAYEV: Who, me?

VERA: Yes, you. Why are you blushing?

BELYAYEV: Please, stop—

VERA: Do you love her? Could you? You haven't answered my question.

BELYAYEV: What do you want me to say? You're in a state. Calm down, for God's sake!

VERA: Am I not even worthy of a serious response? You just want to get rid of me, so you're consoling me! *(Sees Natalya Petrovna in the doorway.)* Oh!

NATALYA PETROVNA: I came to get you, Verochka.

VERA: You came all the way out here—just for me?

NATALYA PETROVNA: Yes. You've been reckless, Verochka. I've warned you about this. And you, Aleksey Nikolayevich, you've forgotten your promise. You've deceived me.

VERA: Enough, Natalya Petrovna, please, stop this! You're talking to me like a child. Today I am a woman—as much a woman as you are.

NATALYA PETROVNA: Vera—

VERA: He hasn't deceived you … nor did he arrange a tryst with me. He doesn't love me, you know that, so there's no need to be jealous.

NATALYA PETROVNA: Vera!

VERA: And stop manipulating. It won't do any good. I see right though it now, believe me. I'm not your ward, Natalya Petrovna, whom you watch over like an older sister. I'm your rival.

NATALYA PETROVNA: Vera, you're forgetting yourself—

VERA: Perhaps I can speak because there's nothing I want any longer, because you've had the pleasure of walking all over me. And you've succeeded. But you've overestimated your power. I don't intend to lie to you, as you have to me. I've told him everything.

NATALYA PETROVNA: What could you possibly tell him?

VERA: Why, everything I've been able to see. Tell me I'm wrong. Tell me you don't love him. He told me he doesn't love me! *(She stops suddenly.)* Forgive me ... I ... I have no idea what's come over me, forgive me please, have mercy ... *(Bursts into tears and rushes off.)*

BELYAYEV: I can assure you, Natalya Petrovna—

NATALYA PETROVNA: Stop, Aleksey Nikolayevich. It's the truth. Vera is right. It's time I stopped deceiving. I've wronged her, I've wronged you—you've every right to despise me. Besides, this will be the last time I see you, speak to you. I love you.

BELYAYEV: *(Shocked.)* You ...what?!

NATALYA PETROVNA: *(Calm, controlled.)* Yes. I love you. I've loved you since the first day you came here, but I didn't know it until yesterday. I don't intend to justify my behavior. Yes, I was jealous of Vera. Yes, I intended to give her away to Bolshintsov, to separate her from me and from you. Yes, I took advantage of my age and my position to unearth her secret, and in the process I gave myself away. I love you, Belyayev—and it's my pride that drives me to confess it. This farce I've been playing revolts me. Perhaps if all this hadn't happened, you'd have fallen in love with Verochka. I have only one excuse, Aleksey Nikolayevich. All this has been beyond my control.... You're not responding? Never mind, I understand. Anyway, what's the point in dissembling, when there's no one to fool anymore? It's all over now. I won't keep you any longer. Farewell. We weren't destined to know one another. But at least I hope you won't see me as the manipulative, cunning creature you took me for. Farewell.

BELYAYEV: I can't go— not like this! Listen, Natalya Petrovna. You don't want me to leave with unfavorable memories, and I in turn don't want you to think of me as a man who ... My God! I don't know how to say it, Forgive me—I don't know how to talk to a woman like you. Until now, I've only known ... ordinary women. How could I, a simple fellow, barely educated, even dream of meaning anything to you? Think who you are and who I am! How could I even imagine ... look at me in this old coat, and you in your sweet-scented dresses. Good God! Yes, I was afraid of you, I'm afraid of you now. I look upon you as a being of a high order—and meanwhile you say that you love me. You, Natalya Petrovna! Love me!... I feel my heart beating as never before. I—I just can't go away like this, say whatever you like!

NATALYA PETROVNA: *(To herself.)* What have I done!

BELYAYEV: I can't express what's going on inside me. I can't answer for anything—

NATALYA PETROVNA: *(Weakly.)* You must go, Belyayev ...

BELYAYEV: Only today, when we met before dinner, I felt for the first time something rare, extraordinary, like a hand clutching my heart—

NATALYA PETROVNA: Enough, Belyayev, enough. We mustn't even think of it. Remember that we're speaking for the last time—and that you're leaving tomorrow.

BELYAYEV: Oh, yes! I'll leave tomorrow! I don't want to prolong it. I'm going, no matter what. Meanwhile, I'll remember this moment forever, standing here, looking at you, hearing you say—

NATALYA PETROVNA: It's for the best that we stop this at once. Give me your hand—and farewell.

BELYAYEV: *(Takes her hand.)* Natalya Petrovna, I don't know how to say good-bye. My heart is so full ... God grant you— *(Stops and presses her hand to his lips.)* Good-bye. *(He starts to go into the house.)*

NATALYA PETROVNA: Belyayev—

BELYAYEV: Yes?

NATALYA PETROVNA: Stay.

BELYAYEV: What?

NATALYA PETROVNA: Stay, and let God be our judge! *(They rush into a passionate embrace.)*

Rakitin appears at the threshold of the garden door.

RAKITIN: We've been looking for you everywhere, Natalya Petrovna—

NATALYA PETROVNA: *(Regaining her composure.)* Ah, it's you. *(Belyayev turns to go.)* You're going, Aleksey Nikolayevich. Don't forget your promise. *(Belyayev bows and exits.)*

RAKITIN: Arkady is looking for you. I confess, I didn't expect to find you here. But as I was passing—

NATALYA PETROVNA: You heard our voices. Aleksey Nikolayevich had to talk some things over. It seems to be that kind of a day, but now we can go inside.

RAKITIN: May I ask …What is your decision?

NATALYA PETROVNA: *(Feigning surprise.)* What decision? Everything is as it should be. It's all over, it's passed. Why? You haven't spoken with Arkady, have you?

RAKITIN: No. I haven't thought of what to tell him yet—

NATALYA PETROVNA: Good. What do they want from me? They watch my every step. As for you, Rakitin, I'm ashamed, truly—

RAKITIN: Don't be. These things happen. And clearly our Belyayev is a novice! Anyway, in time, you'll learn to play your parts.

NATALYA PETROVNA: What do you mean?

Enter Islayev and Shpigelsky.

ISLAYEV: Ah, here they are! Well, well, well! What's this? A continuation of today's conversation? It must be on a very important matter.

RAKITIN: I happened to run into Natalya Petrovna—

ISLAYEV: An odd place to do so, don't you think? Do you want to go back in the house, Natasha? Tea's ready. It'll be dark soon.

NATALYA PETROVNA: *(Takes his arm.)* Let's go.

ISLAYEV: *(Looks around.)* This place can be converted into a nice sitting area, don't you think? Shall we put in a terrace? For secret trysts?

NATALYA PETROVNA: *(Embarrassed.)* Let's go in.

ISLAYEV: Tea-time, everyone! *(Exits with Natalya Petrovna.)*

SHPIGELSKY: *(To Rakitin.)* Give me your arm, Mikhail Aleksandrovich. It seems we're meant to bring up the rear again …

RAKITIN: Oh, Doctor, how sick and tired I am of you.

SHPIGELSKY: If only you knew what trouble I'm in, you'd have pity on me, too.

RAKITIN: What is it now?

SHPIGELSKY: You'll find out soon enough.

RAKITIN: Whatever it is, Doctor, you deserve it.

SHPIGELSKY: Apparently. *(Both exit into the house.)*

Scene Five

The next morning. The drawing room again, as in Scenes One and Three. Islayev sits at the table looking through papers. Early sunlight streams through the windows.

ISLAYEV: *(Suddenly.)* Forget it! I can't work today. I can't get it out of my head. Never have I been so upset, never. Matvey!

MATVEY: *(Enters.)* What may I do for you, sir?

ISLAYEV: Call the foreman. And tell the workers at the dam to wait for me. Go on.

MATVEY: Yes, sir. *(Exits.)*

ISLAYEV: *(Shuffles through papers.)* How do I handle it? That's the problem.

ANNA SEMYONOVNA: *(Enters.)* Arkady—

ISLAYEV: Ah, it's you, Mama. How are you feeling?

ANNA SEMYONOVNA: *(Sits.)* I'm well, thank God. *(Sighs audibly.)* Thank God, I'm well.

ISLAYEV: What's the matter?

ANNA SEMYONOVNA: As if you didn't know—

ISLAYEV: What do you mean?

ANNA SEMYONOVNA: I'm your mother, Arkady. You're a grown man, of course, and a sensible one, too. But still, I'm your mother. That's a weighty word—"mother."

ISLAYEV: Please explain.

ANNA SEMYONOVNA: You known what I'm hinting at, my dear. Your wife, Natasha—she's a wonderful woman, of course, and her conduct until now has been exemplary. But she's still young, Arkady, so young! And youth—

ISLAYEV: I understand. You think her relationship with Rakitin—

ANNA SEMYONOVNA: Heaven help us! I thought nothing of the kind.

ISLAYEV: You didn't let me finish. You think her relationship with Rakitin isn't altogether ... clear. Mysterious conversations, tears—it all must seem strange to you.

ANNA SEMYONOVNA: Has he finally told you what these talks are all about? He hasn't said a word to me. *(Annoyed.)* Although I must say he's had the opportunity.

ISLAYEV: I haven't asked him—and he appears to be in no hurry.

ANNA SEMYONOVNA: So? What are you planning to do?

121

ISLAYEV: Why, nothing.

ANNA SEMYONOVNA: Nothing? What do you mean?

ISLAYEV: Just what I said. Nothing.

ANNA SEMYONOVNA: I must admit, this surprises me. Of course, you're the master of the house, you know what's best. But think of the consequences—

ISLAYEV: There's no need to worry, Mama, really.

ANNA SEMYONOVNA: My dear, I'm a mother. I came to you to offer my services—

ISLAYEV: No! Don't interfere ... please.

ANNA SEMYONOVNA: As you wish, Arkady. Not another word about it. I've done my duty, and now I'll keep my mouth shut. But I'm warning you—you're too trusting, my dear. You judge everyone by your own standards!

ISLAYEV: *(Impatiently.)* Mama—

ANNA SEMYONOVNA: All right, I'll be quiet! Still, a mother is ... a mother. I was brought up with values, and tried to instill them in you. Never mind, I'll disturb you no longer—I'm going. You know best. *(Exits.)*

ISLAYEV: What makes the people who love you want to rub salt in your wounds? And yet they're convinced they're helping! How am I to handle this? *(Rings.)* Subtlety isn't my one of my strong suits.

Enter Matvey.

MATVEY: I did what you asked, sir. May I be of any further assistance?

ISLAYEV: Do you know if Mikhail Aleksandrovich is home?

MATVEY: He is, sir. I just saw him playing billiards.

ISLAYEV: Please tell him to come see me.

MATVEY: Very well, sir. *(Exits.)*

ISLAYEV: I'm not used to crises of this kind. I may have a strong disposition, but this I can't take.

Enter Rakitin.

RAKITIN: You called?

ISLAYEV: Yes ... Misha, you owe me something.

RAKITIN: I do?

ISLAYEV: Have you forgotten your promise? It's about Natasha's tears, and all that. When Mama and I stumbled on you—don't you remember?—you said that you shared a secret, and that you'd tell me.

RAKITIN: A secret? Is that what I said?

ISLAYEV: You did.

RAKITIN: But what secret could there be? We had a talk, that's all.

ISLAYEV: About what? And why was she crying?

RAKITIN: You know, Arkady ... there are moments in the life of a woman, even the happiest—

ISLAYEV: Rakitin, stop, we can't do this. I can't bear to see you in this situation. Your confusion upsets me more than it does you. *(He takes his hand.)* We're old, old friends. You've known me since childhood. I've never fooled you, and you've always been straight with me. So allow me to ask you one question. And I give you my word that I won't doubt the honesty of your reply. You love my wife—don't you?—in a way that's hard to admit to her husband?

RAKITIN: Yes, I love your wife ... in that way.

ISLAYEV: Thank you for your honesty, Misha. You're a good man. So now, what's to be done? Sit, let's talk this over. *(Rakitin sits.)* I know Natasha; I know her value. But I know my value, too. I'm not your equal—no, don't interrupt me, please. You're smarter, certainly more charming. I'm a simple man. Natasha loves me—I think, but after all she has eyes, and she must be attracted to you. Anyway, I noted your mutual attraction some time ago. But I was always so sure of you both, as long as nothing came out in the open. Ugh! I don't know how to put things. But then, after that scene yesterday, and the other one in the evening ... and there are others involved—Mama, that troublemaker Shpigelsky—

RAKITIN: You're quite right, Arkady.

ISLAYEV: That's not the point. What should we do? I'm a simple man, Misha, but this much I know—it's wrong to ruin another person's life, and sometimes it's a sin to insist upon one's rights. My conscience tells me that. Let them be free, right? Give them their freedom! Only one needs to think it over. It's too important.

RAKITIN: *(Rising.)* I already have.

ISLAYEV: What?

RAKITIN: I'm going away. I must.

ISLAYEV: Really? Just like that?

RAKITIN: Yes.

ISLAYEV: Perhaps you're right. We'll miss you terribly, but I think it's best. You're a threat to me, my friend. I don't think I could bear to live without Natasha.... These last few days, I've seen a change in her—a deep, abiding agitation. It frightens me. Am I wrong?

RAKITIN: No.

ISLAYEV: There, you see! So you'll go away?

RAKITIN: Yes.

Enter Matvey.

MATVEY: The foreman is here, sir.

ISLAYEV: Let him wait! *(Matvey exits.)* You won't be away for long, will you? That would be nonsense!

RAKITIN: I don't know, honestly. For a while, I think.

ISLAYEV: I never thought we'd ever have a conversation like this, you and I.

RAKITIN: *(Pressing his hand.)* You'll let me know when I may return.

ISLAYEV: No one could take your place, truly! Certainly not Bolshintsov!

RAKITIN: There are others.

ISLAYEV: Who? Belyayev's a nice boy, of course. But you can't talk about him in the same breath.

RAKITIN: You think so? You don't know him, Arkady. I suggest you take a closer look at him. He's quite an interesting young man.

ISLAYEV: So, my friend, it's settled. You're going away. Meanwhile, I'll reassure Mama. God bless you, Misha! You've lifted a weight from my heart. *(Hastily embraces him.)*

Enter Belyayev.

ISLAYEV: Ah, it's you! Hello, Belyayev.

BELYAYEV: Good morning, Arkady Sergeyevich.

ISLAYEV: Where's Kolya?

BELYAYEV: He's with Herr Schaaf.

ISLAYEV: Good! Well, I'm off, gentlemen. Haven't been anywhere this morning—not to the dam, not to the construction site. Haven't even glanced at my papers. *(Gathers them under his arm.)* Good-bye! Matvey! Matvey! *(Exits)*

BELYAYEV: How are you feeling today, Mikhail Aleksandrovich?

RAKITIN: Well, thank you, as usual. And you?

BELYAYEV: Quite well.

RAKITIN: That's obvious!

BELYAYEV: Why?

RAKITIN: From the look on your face, and the new coat you're wearing today. Charming. Oh, by the way, Aleksey Nikolayevich, if there's anything you need, I'm going to town tomorrow.

BELYAYEV: Really?

RAKITIN: Yes, and from there to Moscow.

BELYAYEV: To Moscow? But I thought you said yesterday that you were planning to stay another month or so.

RAKITIN: Yes, but circumstances have arisen—business, you know ...

BELYAYEV: Are you going for long?

RAKITIN: I don't know ... perhaps.

BELYAYEV: May I ask—does Natalya Petrovna know of your intentions?

RAKITIN: Why do you ask?

BELYAYEV: Oh, nothing.

RAKITIN: Aleksey Nikolayevich, as you can see, there's no one here but ourselves, so must we keep playing this little farce?

BELYAYEV: What are you talking about?

RAKITIN: Really? You don't understand why I'm going away?

BELYAYEV: No.

RAKITIN: That's strange. However, I'm prepared to believe you. Perhaps you really don't know the reasons. Shall I tell you why?

BELYAYEV: Please do.

RAKITIN: Here's the situation—and I do ask for your discretion. You just found me with Arkady Sergeyevich. I had a rather meaningful conversation, the outcome of which was my decision to depart. And do you know why? I'm telling you this, because you're a good man. He seemed to think that I ... well, that I was in love with Natalya Petrovna. What do you think of that?

BELYAYEV: What can I say?

RAKITIN: Tell me, what would you have done in my place? Of course, his suspicions are unfounded, that goes without saying, but still they bothered him. Sometimes, for the peace of mind of a friend, an honorable man must be ready to sacrifice ... certain pleasures. So that's why I'm leaving. I'm sure you approve of my decision, don't you? And you'd do the same in my place. You'd go away too, wouldn't you?

BELYAYEV: Perhaps.

RAKITIN: I'm pleased to hear it. Of course I won't deny that my departure has its comical side. It's as if I consider myself a danger. But you see, Aleksey Nikolayevich, a woman's honor is such an important thing. I've known women, pure and innocent in heart, who give way to a sudden passion, and then who knows? Extreme caution in such cases can't hurt.

BELYAYEV: I wouldn't know ...

RAKITIN: By the way, Aleksey Nikolayevich, perhaps you still imagine that love is the greatest joy on earth?

BELYAYEV: I'm not experienced in such matters, but I imagine that to love a woman and be loved in return is a great joy.

RAKITIN: Keep your illusions, if you can, my friend! In my experience, Aleksey Nikolayevich, any kind of love, happy or unhappy, is a disaster if you give yourself to it completely. Just wait! You'll find out what burning hatred lurks behind the most ardent love. You'll find out what it means to be enslaved—and how humiliating that slavery is. You'll think of me when you yearn for peace, like a sick man yearns for health. And you'll discover what a price you pay for so little. But why am I telling you all this? You won't believe me.

BELYAYEV: Thank you for the lesson, Mikhail Aleksandrovich, although it wasn't necessary.

RAKITIN: Forgive me. I was just talking—

BELYAYEV: About anyone in particular?

RAKITIN: Oh, nobody. Anyway, who am I to give advice?

BELYAYEV: On the contrary—

RAKITIN: So you don't need anything from town?

BELYAYEV: Nothing, thank you. I'm sorry you're leaving.

RAKITIN: Thank you. Believe me, I am too. I'm glad to have met you. *(Presses his hand.)*

Natalya Petrovna and Vera enter from the study.

NATALYA PETROVNA: Hello, gentlemen.

RAKITIN: *(Awkwardly.)* Hello, Natalya Petrovna. Hello, Vera Aleksandrovna. *(Belyayev bows.)*

NATALYA PETROVNA: *(To Rakitin.)* What have you been doing?

RAKITIN: Nothing, really.

NATALYA PETROVNA: Vera and I have been walking in the garden. It's such a lovely day. The scent of the lime trees is so sweet. *(To Belyayev.)* We were hoping to see you here.

RAKITIN: So! You've been admiring the beauties of nature this morning. Aleksey Nikolayevich can't go into the garden. He's wearing a new coat—

BELYAYEV: *(Embarrassed.)* It's the only good one I've got, and it might get torn—

RAKITIN: Oh yes, I forgot to tell you, Natalya Petrovna, I'm going away today—

NATALYA PETROVNA: *(Agitated.)* Going away? Where to?

RAKITIN: To town ... on business.

NATALYA PETROVNA: Not for long, I hope.

RAKITIN: For as long as it takes.

NATALYA PETROVNA: Then come back as soon as you can. *(To Belyayev.)* Aleksey Nikolayevich, were those your sketches that Kolya was showing me?

BELYAYEV: Oh, those ...they're nothing, really.

NATALYA PETROVNA: On the contrary, they're lovely. You have talent.

RAKITIN: I see you're discovering new talents in Belyayev every day.

NATALYA PETROVNA: Perhaps. And that's his good fortune. *(To Belyayev.)* You've got other drawings, most likely—you must show them to me.

RAKITIN: I think it's time to pack ... good-bye. *(Goes to the door.)*

NATALYA PETROVNA: You'll come to say good-bye ...

RAKITIN: Of course.

BELYAYEV: Mikhail Aleksandrovich, wait, I'll go with you. I'd like a few words.

Both exit into the outer hall. Vera is visibly shaken.

NATALYA PETROVNA: Vera ... what's the matter?

VERA: Nothing.

NATALYA PETROVNA: Don't be like this, Vera, for God's sake ... Verochka ... forgive me, please don't cry. *(Kneels.)* I kneel before you, I'm guilty. Can't you forgive me?

VERA: *(Through tears.)* Get up, please ...

NATALYA PETROVNA: I won't get up, Vera, not until you forgive me. You've been hurt, I know, but it's not any easier for me. You've done no wrong, while I—

VERA: You're so sweet today, so kind—

NATALYA PETROVNA: That's because I feel so guilty.

VERA: Is that only reason?

NATALYA PETROVNA: What other reason could there be?

VERA: Natalya Petrovna, don't torture me—

NATALYA PETROVNA: What do you mean?

VERA: You're kind to me today, because you feel loved.

NATALYA PETROVNA: Vera!

VERA: Well, isn't it the truth?

NATALYA PETROVNA: We're equally unhappy, you and I, believe me.

VERA: He loves you!

NATALYA PETROVNA: Vera, what's the point? Rather than tormenting each other, hadn't we better think of how to get out of this difficult situation, to save ourselves? Have you forgotten who I am? What's the use ... you're not listening.

VERA: He loves you.

NATALYA PETROVNA: He's going away, Vera—

VERA: I can't bear this anymore—

ISLAYEV: *(Offstage.)* Natasha, Natasha, where are you?

NATALYA PETROVNA: *(Calling to Islayev.)* I'm here. What is it? *(To Vera.)* Wait for me here. *(She exits.)*

VERA: *(Alone.)* He loves her! And I must stay in her house. It's too much.

Shpigelsky puts his head through the door. He approaches Vera on tiptoe.

SHPIGELSKY: Ah, Vera Aleksandrovna!

VERA: Oh, it's you, Doctor.

SHPIGELSKY: You look pale, my dear—are you ill?

VERA: It's nothing.

SHPIGELSKY: Let me check your pulse. Hmmm ... I wish you'd listen to me, my dear. You know I have your best interests at heart.

VERA: Ignaty Ilyich—

SHPIGELSKY: My goodness, what a look ... what is it?

VERA: This gentleman, Bolshintsov, your acquaintance—is he a good man?

SHPIGELSKY: He's an excellent fellow—the most honorable of men, the paragon of virtue.

VERA: He's not bad-natured?

SHPIGELSKY: He's kindness itself. He's not a man, he's a lump of dough. You only need to take him and mold him. You couldn't find a better man with a candle in broad daylight.

VERA: Will you vouch for him?

SHPIGELSKY: *(A hand on his heart, raising the other.)* As I would for myself.

VERA: In that case you can tell him ... that I'm prepared to marry him.

SHPIGELSKY: *(Amazed.)* Really?

VERA: But as soon as possible—do you hear?

SHPIGELSKY: *(Elated.)* Tomorrow, if you like! Well done, Vera Aleksandrovna! Here's to you! I'll gallop over to see him at once. He'll be thrilled! What an unexpected turn of events! He worships the ground you walk on—

VERA: Don't say that, Ignaty Ilyich.

SHPIGELSKY: As you wish, Vera Aleksandrovna, as you wish. You'll be happy with him, you'll see, you'll have me to thank. All right, I'll be quiet. So may I tell him then?

VERA: You may.

SHPIGELSKY: Very good, indeed. Astonishing, in fact! I'll never understand women, but what does it matter? I'm off. Good-bye! Astonishing! *(Exits.)*

VERA: *(Alone.)* Anything, anything in the world, except stay here ... I've made up my mind. I will no longer remain in this house. I can't bear seeing her bask in that glow of happiness.

Belyayev appears in the doorway to the outer hall.

BELYAYEV: Vera Aleksandrovna, are you alone?

VERA: *(Startled.)* Yes.

BELYAYEV: I'm glad. I've come to say good-bye.

VERA: Good-bye?

BELYAYEV: Yes, I'm leaving.

VERA: You too?

BELYAYEV: Yes. *(Agitated.)* I can't stay here. My presence has already caused so much harm. I've disturbed your peace of mind, Natalya Petrovna's—and I've destroyed old friendships as well. Because of me, Rakitin is going away and you've quarreled with your guardian. It's time to put an end to all this. After I go, I hope there will be order here once more. I don't want to deceive you, Vera Aleksandrovna, I'm frightened of staying here. I can't answer for what might happen. Above all, I couldn't stay here, not with you both—

VERA: Oh, you needn't worry about me! I'm not staying here long, either.

BELYAYEV: Why not?

VERA: That's my secret. But I won't stand in your way, don't worry.

BELYAYEV: I just had a long talk with Rakitin. You can't imagine how bitterly he spoke. And he was right to make fun of my jacket. Yes, I must go. Believe me, Vera Aleksandrovna, I'm counting the moments till I'm sitting in that cart, racing along the high road, the wind in my face. I'm suffocating here, I need the open air. I'm sad, and at the same time light-hearted, like one who's setting out on a long, exhilarating journey. Yes, I'm off, to Moscow, I'll work—

VERA: So you love her, Aleksey Nikolayevich. You love her, and yet you're leaving anyway.

BELYAYEV: Enough, why go on? I shall never forget you, Vera Aleksandrovna. I'm very fond of you, believe me. Give this to Natalya Petrovna. *(Hands her a letter.)*

VERA: A note?

BELYAYEV: Yes. I can't say good-bye to her face.

VERA: So you're going right now?

BELYAYEV: At once. I've told no one about this, except Mikhail Aleksandrovich. He approves. Give her this note and say ... never mind, don't say anything. What for? *(Listens.)* They're coming. Good-bye. *(Rushes out.)*

Natalya Petrovna enters.

NATALYA PETROVNA: Verochka ... what's the matter? *(Vera silently hands her the note.)* A note? From whom?

137

VERA: Read it.

NATALYA PETROVNA: You're frightening me. *(Reads the note silently.)*

VERA: Natalya Petrovna—

NATALYA PETROVNA: He's gone! He didn't even want to say good-bye ... but to you he did.

VERA: He doesn't love me.

NATALYA PETROVNA: He had no right to run away like that. Who gave him permission to leave? It's contemptible, that's what it is.

VERA: Natalya Petrovna, you said yourself he had to go. Remember?

NATALYA PETROVNA: It's better for you now. He's gone, and now we are equals.

VERA: Natalya Petrovna, you just told me: rather than torture one another, hadn't we better think of how to get out of this difficult situation ... to save ourselves? Well, now we are saved.

NATALYA PETROVNA: Ah.

VERA: I understand you, Natalya Petrovna. Don't worry, I wouldn't burden you any longer with my presence. We cannot live together.

NATALYA PETROVNA: What are you saying, Verochka?

Do you really want to leave me? We're saved now. It's all over. Everything will be as it was.

VERA: No, it can't, Natalya Petrovna.

Islayev enters from the study.

ISLAYEV: *(To Vera, in a low voice.)* Does she know he's leaving?

VERA: *(Perplexed.)* Yes, she does.

ISLAYEV: Natasha ... *(Takes her hand.)* Are you all right, my darling? You ought to lie down.

NATALYA PETROVNA: It's nothing, Arkady.

ISLAYEV: But you're pale. Rest a while.

NATALYA PETROVNA: All right.

ISLAYEV: Want me to come along?

NATALYA PETROVNA: That won't be necessary.

Rakitin enters from the hall.

RAKITIN: Here I am, Natalya Petrovna—

ISLAYEV: Ah, Misha! Come here! *(Aside.)* Why did you have to tell her now? Didn't I ask you not to? What was the hurry? I found her in such a state—

RAKITIN: I don't understand.

ISLAYEV: You told Natasha you were going away.

RAKITIN: So that's what you think is upsetting her?

ISLAYEV: Sh! She's looking at us. *(Aloud.)* Aren't you going to lie down, Natasha?

NATALYA PETROVNA: Yes, I'm going.

RAKITIN: Good-bye, Natalya Petrovna! *(She goes to the door.)*

ISLAYEV: Natasha, did you know that here stands the finest of men—

NATALYA PETROVNA: *(Suddenly.)* Yes, I know, he's a splendid man— so are you all, all splendid men. *(She exits quickly. Vera exits after her. Islayev sits in silence at the table and leans on his elbows.)*

RAKITIN: *(To himself.)* Four years of love, and that's the good-bye I get. Well, what do you expect, fool? *(To Islayev.)* So, Arkady, good-bye.

ISLAYEV: *(In a choked voice.)* Good-bye, friend. It isn't easy. I never expected this. It's been like a sudden storm on a clear day. But it shall pass. So thank you— you're a true friend.

RAKITIN: *(Abruptly.)* Good-bye.

Rakitin starts toward the hall, and meets Shpigelsky, who is entering)

SHPIGELSKY: What's happening? They told me Natalya

Petrovna is ill.

ISLAYEV: Who told you?

SHPIGELSKY: Her maid—

ISLAYEV: It's nothing, Doctor. I think it's best not to disturb Natasha now.

SHPIGELSKY: Well, fine! *(To Rakitin.)* They say you're going into town?

RAKITIN: Yes, on business.

SHPIGELSKY: Ah! On business ...

Anna Semyonovna, Lizaveta Bogdanovna, Kolya, and Schaaf burst into the room from the outer hall.

ANNA SEMYONOVNA: What's going on? What's the matter with Natasha?

KOLYA: They said Mama fainted! What's wrong, Papa, tell me!

ISLAYEV: Nothing's wrong, nothing at all ... I just saw her ...

ANNA SEMYONOVNA: Really, Arkady, they told us Natasha was ill—

ISLAYEV: *(Impatiently.)* It's all under control, Mama.

ANNA SEMYONOVNA: But why are you getting angry? We're concerned.

ISLAYEV: I'm assuring you that there is nothing the matter with her. I should be asking what's the matter with all of you instead?!

RAKITIN: So, it's time for me to go.

ANNA SEMYONOVNA: You're going away?

RAKITIN: Yes.

ANNA SEMYONOVNA: Ah! So now I understand.

KOLYA: Papa—

ISLAYEV: What is it?

KOLYA: Why has my tutor left?

ISLAYEV: Who, Belyayev? I didn't know he'd gone!

KOLYA: He hugged me, put on his cap, and left. And it's time for my Russian lesson.

ISLAYEV: He'll be back soon, most likely. In the meantime, we can send someone to look for him.

RAKITIN: *(Aside, to Islayev.)* Don't send for him, Arkady. He's not coming back.

Anna Semyonovna tries to eavesdrop; Shpigelsky whispers to Lizaveta Bogdanovna.

ISLAYEV: What does that mean?

RAKITIN: He's gone away too.

ISLAYEV: Gone away ... but where to?

RAKITIN: To Moscow.

ISLAYEV: To Moscow? But why? Has everyone lost their mind today?

RAKITIN: *(To Islayev.)* Between us, Vera has fallen in love with him. And being an honorable man, Belyayev decided to go. Now you understand—

ISLAYEV: Who, me? I understand nothing. My head is spinning! What's there to understand? They're flying off like partridges and all because they're honorable men? All of a sudden, on the very same day?

ANNA SEMYONOVNA: What? Belyayev is going too, you say? But why? Bring him back, Arkady, you must, for Kolya's sake, bring him back—

ISLAYEV: *(Agitated.)* Never mind, Mama, never mind! Mr. Schaaf, be so kind as to give Kolya his lesson, instead of Belyayev. Now, please.

SCHAAF: *Ja wohl!* Right avay! *Schnell!*[22] *(Takes Kolya by the hand.)*

KOLYA: But Papa—

ISLAYEV: Go, go! *(Schaaf takes Kolya out.)* As for you, Rakitin, I'll see you off. I'll have my horse saddled, and wait for you at the dam. And meanwhile, Mama, please, for God's sake, don't disturb Natasha—you too, Doctor ... Matvey! Matvey! *(Rushes off.)*

Anna Semyonovna sits with an air of dignity. Lizaveta Bogdanovna takes her place behind her. Katya waits by the door, unsure of what to do.

SHPIGELSKY: *(To Rakitin.)* So, Mikhail Aleksandrovich, will it please you to take a drive on the high road in my brand new troika?

RAKITIN: Ah! So you've got your horses already?

SHPIGELSKY: *(Discreetly.)* I had a little talk with Vera Aleksandrovna, and it's all settled. Will you allow me?

RAKITIN: Why not? *(Bows.)* Farewell, Anna Semyonovna.

ANNA SEMYONOVNA: Good-bye, Mikhail Aleksandrovich. I wish you a happy journey.

RAKITIN: I humbly thank you. Good bye, Lizaveta Bogdanovna. *(He bows and exits.)*

SHPIGELSKY: *(Kisses Anna Semyonovna's hand.)* Good-bye, dear lady ...

ANNA SEMYONOVNA: Ah! So you're going too, Doctor?

SHPIGELSKY: Yes. Patients to see ... you know. Besides, as you can tell, my presence here is no longer needed. *(Bows, winks slyly at Lizaveta Bogdanovna, who winks back.)* Good-bye, for now ... *(Rushes off after Rakitin.)*

ANNA SEMYONOVNA: *(To Lizaveta Bogdanovna.)* And what do you think of all this, my dear?

LIZAVETA BOGDANOVNA: It's all very interesting, Anna Semyonovna.

ANNA SEMYONOVNA: Did you hear that Belyayev is going away?

LIZAVETA BOGDANOVNA: Actually, I won't be staying much longer, either, Anna Semyonovna ...

ANNA SEMYONOVNA: What?

LIZAVETA BODGANOVA: As a matter of fact—*(Jumps up.)* Doctor, wait for me! I'm riding in that troika too! *(She exits quickly.)*

Anna Semyonovna looks around in astonishment.

ANNA SEMYONOVNA: Everyone's going. Poor Kolya. Who is left to teach him now? Who?

End of Play.

Notes

(1) Preference: a three-handed game, similar to whist

(2) "Hartz" ("Hearts"): Schaaf speaks with a pronounced German accent.

(3) *"Monte-Cristo se redressa haletant"* (French). Translation: "Monte Cristo jumped up, panting." From Alexandre Dumas père's novel *The Count of Monte Cristo*.

(4) *"Und"* ("and," in German). Schaaf intersperses his dialogue with German words (like *"gut"* ["good"], etc.).

(5) "Babushka" (Russian): Grandmother

(6) *"Maman"* (French): Mother

(7) *"Natürlich"* (German) : naturally (in the sense of "of course")

(8) "Another man's soul is a dark, dark forest." A Russian proverb.

(9) *"Ce que vous êtes pour moi"* (French) "What you mean to me"

(10) *"Wie gehts?"* (German) "How are you?"

(11) "*Kommen Sie, Mein Herr*" (German): "Come, sir"

(12) "*Morgen*" (German): "tomorrow."

TROIKA

(13) *"Morgen, morgen, nur nicht heute, sagen alle faule Leute ..." (German).* The opening lines of a poem by Christian-Felix Weise (1726–1804), that became a well-known proverb.

(14) *"Natürlich, Gnadige Frau ... Es ist unerhört"* (German). "Of course, dear lady ... This is unheard of."

(15) *"Mon enfant, vous feriez bien de mettre une autre robe pour le diner ..."* (French). "My child, you'd better put on another dress for dinner"

(16) "Michel" (French); the French equivalent of Rakitin's first name, "Mikhail"

(17) *"On n'entre pas comme cela dans une chambre ...Cela ne convient pas"*: (French) "One doesn't enter a room like that. It won't do."

(18) *"Vera, allez en avant avec monsieur"* (French): "Vera, go on ahead with the gentleman"

(19) "It's not the fire ..." A Russian folksong. ("Pitch" is used to preserve wood when making wheels, buildings, etc.)

(20) Rakitin refers to Belyayav as a "raw youth." The reference is to Dostoevsky's novel of that name (1875) about a young intellectual who espoused a nihilistic ideology popular in the 1860s in Russia.

(21) Troika: a vehicle (carriage) pulled by three horses.

(22) *"Schnell"* (German): "Quickly"

Carol Rocamora

Pronunciation

(Note: Accented syllable is highlighted in boldface **CAPS**)

Characters names:

Arkady Sergeyevich Islayav
    *(Ar-**KA**-dy Ser-**GE**-ye-vich Is-**LA**-yev)*
Natalya Petrovna (
    *Na-**TA**-lya Pye-**TROV**-na)*
Vera Aleksandrovna
    *(**VYE**-ra Alek-**SAN**-drov-na (**VYE**-roch-ka)*
Anna Semyonovna Islayeva
    *(**A**-na Sem-**yon**-ov-na Is-**LA**-ye-va*
Lizaveta Bogdanovna
    (Lee-za-**VE**-ta Bog-**DA**-nov-na)
Schaaf
    (**SHAF**)
Mikhail Aleksandrovich Rakitin
    *(Mi-kha-**IL** A-lek-**SAN**-dro-vich Ra-**KI**-tin)*
Aleksey Nikolayevich Belyayev
    (A-lek-**SEY** Ni-ko-**LA**-ye-vich Bel-**YA**-yev)
Afanasy Ivanovich Bolshintsov
    (A-fa-**NA**-sy I-**VA**-no-vich Bol-shin-**TSOV**)
Ignaty Ilyich Spigelsky
    (Ig-**NA**-ty Il-**YICH** Shpi-**GEL**-sky)
Kolya
    (**KO**-lya)
Matvey
    (Mat-**VEY**)
Katya
    (**KA**-tya)

Others names/words:

Babushka (**BA**-boosh-ka)
Krinitsyn (Kri-**NIT**-syn)
Mama (**MA**-ma) (Russian)
Maman (Ma- **MAN**) (French)
Michel (Mee-**SHEL**) (French)
Papa (**PA**-pa) (Russian)
Perekusov (Pe-re-**KU**-zov)
Protobekasov (Pro-to-be-**KA**-sov)
Verenitsyn (Ve-re-**NIT**-syn)

Rasputin's Brother

Inspired by the Trilogy of Aleksandr Sukhovo-Kobylin

Cast of characters

Lydia Petrovna (Lidochka), a lovely young girl of marriageable age
Pyotr Andreyevich Muromsky, her well-meaning father, a wealthy landowner
Anna Andreyevna Atuyeva, Lydia's aunt, Muromsky's sister
Tishka, a tipsy servant
Mikhail Vasilyevich Krechinsky, a ne'er-do-well opportunist
Fyodor, Krechinsky's ancient servant
Vladimir Dmitrevich Nelkin, an upright young nobleman
Ivan Ivanich Popov, a rogue, Krechinsky's sidekick
Timofey Timofeyevich Shebnev, a merchant
Blekh, a pawnbroker
Artemisa, Krechinsky's luscious young mistress
Policemen

Appearing in Act Two, can be double-cast (see casting grid, page 266):

Kandid Kastorich Slinkov, a State Councilor
The Very Important Person
Constable Klop
Clerks
Petitioners

(note: an ensemble of ten actors can play all of the above roles)

ACT ONE

Moscow, 1850s

Scene One: Muromsky's Moscow flat

> Lights come up on in the well-appointed drawing room of Muromsky's Moscow flat. Enter Tishka, a servant, humming a traditional Russian tune, carrying a stepladder. He is slightly drunk. He sets the ladder down. Clumsily, he climbs the ladder to the top and starts hammering a bell on the wall. Enter Atuyeva.

ATUYEVA: Tishka! What are you doing?

TISHKA: What you told me to do, Madam.

ATUYEVA: Namely?

TISHKA: Hang the bell, Madam. Don't ask me why—

ATUYEVA: But I *shall* ask you why, Tishka, and you'd better know the answer. We live in Moscow now, not the country; you're a footman here, not a porter, and in Moscow, a footman announces the guests. So listen up. When a lady comes calling, ring the bell twice.

TISHKA: *(Trying to concentrate.)* Yes, Madam.

ATUYEVA: If it's a gentleman, ring once.

TISHKA: Got it, Madam.

ATUYEVA: If it's any woman other than a lady, don't ring.

TISHKA: Whatever you say, Madam.

ATUYEVA: If it's a merchant, don't ring either.

TISHKA: As you wish, Madam.

ATUYEVA: Do you understand, Tishka?

TISHKA: Every word, Madam ... so ring first, and then announce?

ATUYEVA: What an idiot! Of course!

TISHKA: I'm on it, Madam.

ATUYEVA: And it's *Madame*, not Madam.

TISHKA: I'll try to remember that, Madam.[1]

ATUYEVA: Hopeless. Now climb up that ladder and start hammering. *(He does.)*

TISHKA: *(Positions the bell.)* Here?

ATUYEVA: A bit higher.

TISHKA: *(Climbing one step higher.)* Here?

ATUYEVA: No ... wait ... lower! You're drunk again, Tishka, aren't you?

TISHKA: I do my best, Madam.

ATUYEVA: *(Irked.)* For God's sake, get on with it!

Tishka holds a nail in place, strikes it with all his might, hits his own finger instead, and tumbles from the ladder, producing a crashing noise.

Muromsky hurries in.

TISHKA: Owwww!

MUROMSKY: What's going on here?!

ATUYEVA: Tishka's drunk again! It just won't do, not in Moscow—

TISHKA: Truly, master, I was only trying to hang that bell—

MUROMSKY: Bell? What bell?

TISHKA: The bell Madam asked me to install—

MUROMSKY: A bell? In the parlor?

ATUYEVA: In Moscow you see them in all the best houses, brother!

MUROMSKY: That's idiotic!

ATUYEVA: We live in Moscow now, and we must live *comme il faut*.[2]

MUROMSKY: It sounds like a fire alarm to me! Never mind, what's the use—

157

ATUYEVA: And since we're giving a soirée—

MUROMSKY: Soirée? Who said anything about a soirée?

ATUYEVA: It's only a little ball, Pyotr, like the one we had the other night—

MUROMSKY: You told me that was the last one—

ATUYEVA: Impossible; society demands it.

MUROMSKY: What are you doing to me, sister? You drag me to Moscow, you set up house, and money starts flowing like the Volga! Night after night, ball after ball! You dress my servants like mannequins, and you turn that idiot, Tishka, a simple country cobbler, into a ridiculous footman. And now you've put up a bell!

ATUYEVA: How else can Tishka announce the guests?

MUROMSKY: I'll tell you how—he can call out: 'Here come the parasites!"

ATUYEVA: What do you know about society, brother?

MUROMSKY: Enough that I don't want to know any more!

ATUYEVA: You've buried yourself in country life, running an estate, farming—

MUROMSKY: Yes, and if I hadn't, you couldn't be giving these balls.

ATUYEVA: But that's your duty. You have a daughter of

marriageable age!

MUROMSKY: So what must I do? Stand at the door and cry "Come in!" to all the passersby? So that they can eat us out of house and home, drink us dry, and mock us behind our backs?

ATUYEVA: That's better that than wasting your time with the peasants!

MUROMSKY: At least something comes of it. What comes of your bell-ringing?

ATUYEVA: We're not beggars.

MUROMSKY: We will be, if this keeps up!

ATUYEVA: Pyotr, please, it's for Lidochka—

MUROMSKY: But that's just my point! What kind of life is this for her? Rising at noon, shuffling through calling cards, chasing around town.... What are you teaching her? To babble away in French, *comme il faut*?

ATUYEVA: She'll be passed over, ignored, if you don't allow her to—

MUROMSKY: She's a well-born girl—some decent fellow will come along and marry her.

ATUYEVA: And she'll be buried alive in the country—

MUROMSKY: Spend a lot of money, put on airs, and you'll pay for it later, you'll see. Ah, here she is now, my little princess!

Enter Lydia.

LYDIA: Good morning, Papa.

MUROMSKY: *(Delighted.)* My only child! *(Embraces her.)*

LYDIA: Good morning, Auntie.

MUROMSKY: And how was the ball last night?

LYDIA: Divine, Papa, how we danced!

ATUYEVA: With Mikhail Vasilyevich!

MUROMSKY: Krechinsky?

LYDIA: Yes, Papa!

MUROMSKY: Isn't he a little old for the mazurka? He must be almost forty!

ATUYEVA: Nonsense!

LYDIA: He's a wonderful dancer, Papa.

ATUYEVA: And he knows *everyone*!

MUROMSKY: I don't know what you see in this Krechinsky. They say he hangs around clubs, plays cards, and has debts, huge ones. No daughter of mine will marry anyone with debts.

ATUYEVA: It's that Nelkin again, whispering in your ear. Hmmph!

MUROMSKY: You'd never catch Nelkin playing cards.

ATUYEVA: You and your Nelkin! He'll never be accepted in society. He doesn't know anyone, he cowers in the corner at balls, he's an awful dancer—

MUROMSKY: Enough of this talk, sister. You'll make a fool of yourself in that society of yours, you'll stumble and fall and bring her down with you! *(He exits.)*

ATUYEVA: He's gone—tell me everything!

LYDIA: It was wonderful, Auntie, we danced and talked and—

ATUYEVA: He's so clever when he's speaking French. When says *"sacre bleu,"*[3] it's thrilling!

LYDIA: Auntie, I—I don't know how to tell you—

ATUYEVA: What, my sweet?

LYDIA: *(Ecstatic.)* Oh, Auntie, he proposed to me!

ATUYEVA: *(Delighted.)* Krechinsky? Really?

LYDIA: He says he loves me very much, and—

ATUYEVA: And?

LYDIA: Of course I said to him: *"Parlez à ma tante et papa."*[4]

ATUYEVA: You did the right thing, my dear, *comme il faut*.

LYDIA: Oh, Auntie! *(Throws her arms around her.)* I love him! He's so handsome, so clever! Only Papa doesn't like him. You heard him. He wants me to marry Nelkin. And I wouldn't marry anyone without Papa's consent, of course.

ATUYEVA: The only reason your father wants you to marry Nelkin is because he lives in the country, and has an estate right next to ours.

LYDIA: Papa says Nelkin's a good man.

ATUYEVA: *(Sighs.)* If you marry Krechinsky, think of the household he'll set up for you in Moscow, the life you'll lead in society—

LYDIA: As long as he loves me, Auntie.

ATUYEVA: I'll have a talk with your father at once, darling. Leave it to me. *(Tearfully.)* I only want to see you happy, as your poor mother would have wanted.

Tishka enter, rings the bell, and stands there, mute.

ATUYEVA: Tishka, you fool! How many times do I have to tell you? Ring and announce, ring and announce!

TISHKA: I was just about to, Madam ... only I forgot his name ...

Muromsky rushes in.

MUROMSKY: My God, is there a fire? Get rid of that thing, sister, or else—

TISHKA: *(Suddenly.)* I remember! *(Earnestly.)* Vladimir Dmitrevich Nelkin.

Enter Nelkin. He bows to the ladies and shakes Muromsky's hand.

MUROMSKY: Welcome, dear fellow—we've missed you!

NELKIN: Good morning, Pyotr Andreyevich. What a striking bell you have, Anna Andreyevna!

MUROMSKY: *(To Atuyeva.)* You see?

NELKIN: There was a ball last night at the princess's, and they had the same sort of contraption. When it started clanging, I almost fell down a flight of stairs!

MUROMSKY: I can't stand those affairs.

NELKIN: Nor can I! I feel quite ill at ease. I spent the whole evening in the corner. Lydia Petrovna didn't notice me—she was dancing all night with Krechinsky.

ATUYEVA: What a man of the world! *Charmant!*

NELKIN: But one hears so little good about him.

ATUYEVA: What do you mean?

NELKIN: The gambling, the debts, he's the talk of Moscow—

ATUYEVA: Forgive me, Vladimir Dmitrevich, but I am tired of hearing these tales of yours. You don't really know Moscow, so you just pick up whatever anyone tells you and repeat it. That is not *comme il faut*.

MUROMSKY: To hell with your *comme il faut*, sister. How I miss the country ...

NELKIN: Are you going back to the estate soon? It's almost summertime, and there's planting to be done.

MUROMSKY: I've already given orders to spread the manure. After all, without manure you wouldn't be able to give any of your parties, sister, would you?

Tishka enters and rings the bell. They all jump.

MUROMSKY: Good God!

TISHKA: *(Announcing diligently.)* Mikhail Vasilyevich Krechinsky.

Krechinsky makes a flamboyant entrance. He is dressed like a dandy, sporting a walking stick and gloves. Tishka bows awkwardly and exits, walking backward.

KRECHINSKY: Good morning, Pyotr Andreyevich! *(Bows.)* Mesdames.

NELKIN: *(Aside.)* Ha! First thing in the morning, and he's already here.

KRECHINSKY: What have we here, Anna Andreyevna? A church bell?

ATUYEVA: *(Flustered.)* Oh dear, don't you approve?

KRECHINSKY: It's a fine bell, Anna Andreyevna, only you ought to hang it near the staircase—that's where they hang the bell in the best of houses—

MUROMSKY: That's the spirit, Mikhail Vasilyevich! Hey, Tishka!

Tishka enters.

MUROMSKY: Take that damn thing out of here and hang it near the staircase! *(Tishka hesitates.)* Go on! *(Tishka removes the bell and exits.)*

KRECHINSKY: *(Familiarly.)* Didn't we have a wonderful time at the ball last night, Lydia Petrovna?

LYDIA: *(Enthralled.)* Oh, yes!

KRECHINSKY: *(To Muromsky.)* How charming Lydia Petrovna looked ...

LYDIA: Mikhail Vasilyevich chose my entire ensemble.

ATUYEVA: What exquisite taste he has!

LYDIA: Everyone admired it!

KRECHINSKY: What can I say—I have a talent for appearances.

NELKIN: *(Aside.)* And how deceiving they are ...

KRECHINSKY: Speaking of appearances, you must come visit my estate.

MUROMSKY: So you *do* have an estate in Simbirsk, then?

KRECHINSKY: Of course.

MUROMSKY: But I heard you didn't care for the country ...

KRECHINSKY: Who told you that? I adore it!

NELKIN: *(Aside.)* Here we go ...

KRECHINSKY: *(Waxing poetic.)* The air, the peace, the quiet ... I walk through the fields and the forests, and I think: "This is mine, all mine. Even the blue horizon is mine!"

MUROMSKY: *(Sighing.)* I feel exactly the same way.

KRECHINSKY: When I rise in the morning, I head straight for the meadows. Then on to the greenhouses—

MUROMSKY: —and the threshing floor?

KRECHINSKY: —and the threshing floor. I raise livestock, too!

MUROMSKY: *(Impressed.)* You do?

KRECHINSKY: Of course. When you visit, I'll make you a gift of my prize steer!

MUROMSKY: My dear Mikhail Vasilyevich, I couldn't accept such a gift!

KRECHINSKY: I insist! Yes, country life ... It makes one

feel ... what? So alive ... *(Sighs.)* Still, for me, there is one thing lacking.

MUROMSKY: What is that, Mikhail Vasilyevich?

KRECHINSKY: Come now, Pyotr Andreyevich! You don't know?

MUROMSKY: Not really.

KRECHINSKY: A wife! A wife to share all that beauty with me.

MUROMSKY: Well, of course!

KRECHINSKY: But what kind of wife—that's the question! *(Gazes at Lydia.)* Fair, modest, gentle ... after a vigorous day's work, you come home, you take her lovely little face in your hands ... "Greetings, little wife," you say, "How about some tea?"

NELKIN: *(Aside.)* I don't believe this.

KRECHINSKY: The samovar's boiling in the cozy parlor. There sits an aged father, hair as white as snow. On his knee, a grandson. A scene of pastoral bliss! *(To Lydia, softly.)* And you, Lydia Petrovna, do you love country life?

LYDIA: *(Enthralled.)* Oh I do, very much.

ATUYEVA: *(Surprised.)* Since when?

KRECHINSKY: I knew you would. *(Sighs.)* Forgive me, I digress. We're in the city now. *(Impulsively.)* Pyotr Andreyevich, how about a ride in my new carriage?

167

NELKIN: *(Aside.)* Carriage? How is he paying for that?!

LYDIA: *(Clapping.)* A carriage ride? How lovely!

ATUYEVA: You'd better dress for the occasion, brother—people are out and about this afternoon.

MUROMSKY: Why not? We'll show them what country folk look like!

LYDIA: Come, Papa! *(Laughing, grabs his arm. They exit.)*

Nelkin sits, anxiously awaiting Lydia's return. Krechinsky leads Atuyeva downstage.

KRECHINSKY: *(Unheard by Nelkin.)* So, Anna Andreyevna, what do you think?

ATUYEVA: Of what?

KRECHINSKY: Of my little ode to country life.

ATUYEVA: Tell me the truth—do you really love the country?

KRECHINSKY: What do *you* think? I can't stand it!

ATUYEVA: *(Sighs.)* It gives my brother such pleasure when people praise it.

KRECHINSKY: Exactly! And why not make an old man happy? After all, he's a landowner, and landowners can't see beyond their cattle sheds and fertilizers.

ATUYEVA: This morning he was going on about manure! I mean, really—

KRECHINSKY: You need someone around here who is worldly, *comme il faut.* Your household would be the envy of Moscow.

ATUYEVA: *(Sighing.)* I know …

KRECHINSKY: *(Impulsively seizing Atuyeva's hand.)* Then help me, Anna Andreyevna, I beseech you!

ATUYEVA: What do you mean? How?

KRECHINSKY: I'm asking for the hand of your niece, Lydia Petrovna.

ATUYEVA: *(Moved.)* Lidochka's happiness and welfare is more important to me than anything in this world. And I believe that she'll be happy with you.

KRECHINSKY: *(Kissing her hands.)* I'm most grateful.

ATUYEVA: You must have Pyotr Andreyevich's consent, you know …

KRECHINSKY: I know. *(Aside.)* That's the fly in the ointment, isn't it?

ATUYEVA: What's that?

KRECHINSKY: *(Solemnly.)* I was only saying that parental blessing is the foundation upon which all else rests.

ATUYEVA: True …

KRECHINSKY: How do we broach the matter with him, then?

ATUYEVA: He'll want time to think it over.

KRECHINSKY: I see. In that case, we must improvise ... *(Aside.)* I'm due at the races in an hour. I have a big bet on with the Prince. So let's move things along—

ATUYEVA: Excuse me?

KRECHINSKY: I'm counting on you, Anna Andreyevna—my fate is in your hands.

ATUYEVA: I'll do my best, Mikhail Vasilyevich.

KRECHINSKY: *(Aside, to the audience.)* Ta da! A cool million, falling right into my lap. Now, how to pull it off ... watch this ...

Muromsky returns, adjusting his tie. He wears a frock coat and carries a top hat.

MUROMSKY: Here I am, Mikhail Vasilyevich—all set!

KRECHINSKY: Pyotr Andreyevich! Before we take our carriage ride, please, let me talk frankly. I don't like to beat around the bush. Last night I proposed to your daughter, and I've just had a talk with Anna Andreyevna. She's given me her full support—

ATUYEVA: *(Taken aback.)* I—

KRECHINSKY: —and now I stand before you. The decision is yours.

MUROMSKY: *(Flustered.)* My—my dear sir, this is a bit sudden. Give me some time to consider your proposal.

KRECHINSKY: I would have thought you've had plenty of time to think it over.

MUROMSKY: What do you mean?

KRECHINSKY: As you know, for several months I've been coming to your home—

MUROMSKY: But I never dreamed—

KRECHINSKY: The fault is yours, Pyotr Andreyevich. You really were obliged to think about it. After all, an honorable man doesn't frequent the home of a respectable family and risk compromising a lovely young lady—not without a special agenda.

NELKIN: *(Aside.)* Can you believe this?

MUROMSKY: *(Embarrassed.)* Yes, of course, I see—

KRECHINSKY: Therefore I shall ask you not to postpone your decision.

MUROMSKY: *(Hesitantly.)* I ... I don't know—

KRECHINSKY: May I ask what concerns you? My current circumstances?

MUROMSKY: Well, if you really must know, that's part of it.

NELKIN: *(Aside.)* Hah!

KRECHINSKY: You see for yourself—my estate, my carriage—I'm not concealing anything. And you might notice that I haven't asked about your daughter's dowry.

MUROMSKY: Dowry? Hold on, man, you go too fast! A father has to have some ... ah ... certainties first, so to speak.

KRECHINSKY: Perhaps, then, you've heard that my affairs aren't quite in order?

NELKIN: *(Aside.)* Hah!

MUROMSKY: I must confess, I have heard such talk.

KRECHINSKY: Tell me, Pyotr Andreyevich. Is there anyone living in Moscow whose affairs *aren't* unsettled? We're *all* unsettled, we who live in the capitals! What about your own affairs since you came to live in Moscow?

MUROMSKY: My God! An utter mess!

KRECHINSKY: Exactly. We country folk have one nemesis: city life.

MUROMSKY: How true ...

KRECHINSKY: *(Improvising.)* And that's why I'm leaving Moscow.

MUROMSKY: You're returning to the country?

KRECHINSKY: Why of course.

ATUYEVA: *(Gasps.)* What?

MUROMSKY: *(Moved.)* You love the country that much?

KRECHINSKY: *(Emotional.)* Ah, Pyotr Andreyevich! How could you doubt it? Your daughter and I love each other deeply, and we shall love living in the country. We shall be with you always, we'll never leave your side. We shall till the soil together!

NELKIN: *(Aside.)* I can't take much more of this!

Lydia rushes in, bonnet in hand.

LYDIA: What is it? Has something happened? *(Looks at Krechinsky then at Muromsky.)* Oh Papa, has he asked you yet?

MUROMSKY: *(With emotion.)* My darling child—

LYDIA: Dear, dear Papa! Please say yes!

MUROMSKY: Wait—this is all too fast. I haven't had a chance to think about it—

ATUYEVA: What is there to think about, brother?

MUROMSKY: Perhaps you're right. *(Sighs.)* Here, Mikhail Vasilyevich, here is her hand, the hand of my only daughter, my treasure, but promise me one thing—

KRECHINSKY: Whatever you wish!

MUROMSKY: *(Choked with emotion.)* You know ... the cozy parlor, the white-haired old man, the grandson on his knee ...

KRECHINSKY: *(Takes Lydia's hand.)* How could you doubt it?

MUROMSKY: Then God grant it!

KRECHINSKY: Anna Andreyevna! Give us your blessings too.

ATUYEVA: *(In tears.)* Be happy, my children!

LYDIA: *(Kisses her aunt and her father.)* My heart is so full!

NELKIN: *(Aside.)* This is unbearable!

KRECHINSKY: Think of that cattle farm we'll set up together! And now, to the carriage!

LYDIA: *(Clapping her hands.)* I almost forgot!

KRECHINSKY: Only dearest Lydia Petrovna, forgive me, it must be a very short ride. I'm afraid I've been called away on urgent business.... Let's go, quickly!

They all rush off.

NELKIN: *(Alone, to the audience, clenching his fists.)* He may be clever, but he can't fool everyone! I'll have a look around, and when I find out what he's up to, I'll go straight to the old man!

Nelkin dashes off. Scene change. Music.

Scene Two

The next morning; the study of Krechinsky's Moscow flat

> *The study is luxuriously furnished but in great disarray. A settee, a desk with papers. A Chinese screen stands to one corner. Fyodor, an ancient servant, tidies the room.*

FYODOR: Oh, what trouble, what trouble we're in. You wouldn't believe it. No heat, rooms like ice, and what do you expect, with all his goings-on.... When we lived in St. Petersburg, good Lord, the money we had! Now he burns through rubles like kindling wood. Parties, drinking, gambling—you can't imagine! And women? Don't get me started! He used to have a country estate—now it's gone, along with his title. He lost his racehorses, his family silver, he even had to sell some of his clothes. Everything's gone, as if the earth swallowed it up! No friends left either, they all dropped him, save for Popov, that leech. Why the master keeps him around, I don't know, except to help him gamble back some of his losses …

> *A bell rings off stage.*

FYODOR: There he is now.

> *Enter Popov, in disarray, a crumpled hat on his head. He collapses in a chair.*

POPOV: *(Sighs deeply.)* It's a dog's life ...

FYODOR: How was your day, Ivan Ivanich? Was there a card game?

POPOV: Ooooooh yes, there was—there was a game, all right!

FYODOR: And what happened?

POPOV: You want to know what happened? I'll tell you what happened. I brought my own stacked deck and I tried to switch some cards and I got caught. And it was one smack after another! "You'll learn your lesson!" said one. *Pow!* "I'll split him like a log!" said another. *Whop!* A fist in the face, a kick in the belly, a crack on the shins—

FYODOR: *(Chuckling.)* Taught you a good lesson, did they?

POPOV: I appreciate your compassion, Fyodor. Perhaps you'll advise me, then, on what to tell your master? I promised him I wouldn't return empty-handed!

FYODOR: He's not up yet, sir. Had quite a time himself last night.

POPOV: Good. I'll sneak out the back door, and try my hand again at a game. If he catches me empty-handed, I'll get another beating for sure—

FYODOR: Look sharp, sir, here he comes!

POPOV: Omigod! *(He dives behind the Chinese screen.)*

Enter Krechinsky, wearing a lounging robe, along with Artemisa, clad in a revealing dressing gown. Krechinsky sits on the settee; Artemisa drapes herself on it, beside him.

FYODOR: Good morning, sir. Did you sleep well last night?

KRECHINSKY: Mmmm, yes—well, as a matter of fact, no—

FYODOR: So—"yes and no," sir? Sorry to hear it.

KRECHINSKY: That damned Popov—I was waiting for him to return from his card game. When he didn't come back, I became, er, otherwise engaged—

ARTEMISA: *(Laughs.)* You were, dearie, weren't you?

KRECHINSKY: Yes, Artemisa, my sweet. So now tell me, Fyodor, is he in?

FYODOR: Who?

KRECHINSKY: Popov, that rogue—

FYODOR: Popov, Popov … let me think … I'm trying to remember …

As they speak, Popov is tiptoeing offstage. Krechinsky spots him.

KRECHINSKY: There you are, you rogue! Not so fast—

POPOV: *(Stops in his tracks.)* Why, Mikhail Vasilyevich! What a coincidence!

KRECHINSKY: Where do you think you're going?

POPOV: Nowhere at all, heh-heh! Just thought I'd get a breath of fresh—

KRECHINSKY: Well? Hand it over!

POPOV: *(Innocently.)* Hand what over?

KRECHINSKY: Don't play games with me, you devil, you played cards last night. So where are your winnings? Hand the money over, come on!

POPOV: *(Rummages through his pockets, forcing a grin.)* Let me see ... heh-heh ... it must be here somewhere ... now that's strange—

ARTEMISA: *(Helpfully.)* Shall I help you look for it, Ivan Ivanich, golubchik?[5]

KRECHINSKY: Just a moment, my angel. *(Fiercely.)* You lost, didn't you, dunce?

POPOV: Me? Now where did you get such an idea?!

KRECHINSKY: *(Raises a hand in threat.)* Don't try to bluff me, blockhead!

POPOV: *(Whining.)* Why do you keep picking on me day after day?

KRECHINSKY: Because you're a leech, that's why! Because you don't earn your keep! I'm not a charity, you poacher. So tell me—did you win or not?

POPOV: Hmmm ... let me try to remember.... As a matter of fact—no!

KRECHINSKY: All right, then hand over what you took *to* the game!

POPOV: That's what I'm trying to tell you, Mikhail Vasilyevich: it's gone ...

KRECHINSKY: What do you mean "gone"?

POPOV: They took it, all of it! *(Cowering)* Don't get angry, please!

ARTEMISA: Poor Ivan Ivanich ...

KRECHINSKY: Just a moment, my lovely! *(Fiercely.)* I get it, misery! They took your money and *then* they gave you a beating. I ought to shake you till your teeth rattle!

POPOV: *(Cringing.)* Please, Mikhail Vasilich, save your energy—they've given me a good shaking already, that'll hold me for a while!

KRECHINSKY: I don't care where you find it, just go out and get some money. My whole future depends on three thousand rubles—

ARTEMISA: Can I help, Misha?

KRECHINSKY: Of course, my pet, but first, go into the parlor, Fyodor will serve your coffee in there—*(Through clenched teeth.)* Won't you, Fyodor?

FYODOR: Yes, sir—

KRECHINSKY: How many times do I have to remind you? Call me 'Your Honor'!

FYODOR: I try to remember, sir, really I do, but first of all, I'm old, and second of all, you're not a judge, so—

KRECHINSKY: All right, all right. *(To Artemisa, sweetly.)* Go on, my lovely—

ARTEMISA: Don't be too long ... Good day, Ivan Ivanich! *(Blows him a kiss.)*

Artemisa exits, Fyodor shuffles off after her.

POPOV: But Mikhail Vasilich—

KRECHINSKY: Did you hear me? Go get some money! Pawn your soul, steal if you have to! If you come home empty-handed again, I'll wring your neck like a chicken!

POPOV: What, may I ask, is the urgency?

KRECHINSKY: I'll tell you what the urgency is. I'm going to get married to Muromsky's daughter, that's what! She's a great catch, I got her father's blessings, and the wedding's in ten days! Now what do you say to that?

POPOV: *(Uncertainly.)* Congratulations?

TROIKA

KRECHINSKY: Idiot! Don't you see? With the dowry Muromsky'll give me, I'll get 1500 serfs. That's worth a million alone. Plus whatever else comes with it—a country estate, a town house, furniture, carriages, servants—oh, and an obedient wife ... Don't worry, Popov, I'll reward you, I'll give you two hundred thousand —enough to last you all your days ... And the rest I'll cash in and gamble and make millions!

POPOV: *(Rubbing his hands together, excited.)* Two hundred thousand? Woo hoo!

KRECHINSKY: But first you have to bring me ready cash. If I don't pay off my creditors, word will get around, and that will be the end of my engagement. The old man will never let me marry her! *(Popov by the collar.)* Do you understand? I'm desperate! I need that money! Now!

POPOV: *(Agitated.)* I hear you—see? My teeth are chattering! Right away! *He dashes off.*

KRECHINSKY: *(Alone.)* He'll pull it off, I know him. Mmmm, that million ... I can almost taste it! Once I'm married, I'll have real cash, I'll play and win a mountain of gold from all those aristocratic swine ... And I have no intention of living in the country with that old fool. I'll take off to St. Petersburg—that's where the real money is! Ha-ha!

Offstage a bell rings. Enter Fyodor.

FYODOR: Sir—Your Honor—Shebnev the merchant is here to see you—

KRECHINSKY: Fool, you should have told him I wasn't here.

FYODOR: He'd insist on waiting, sir—

KRECHINSKY: All right, all right, show him in.

Enter Shebnev. He is fashionably dressed, wearing a huge gold chain and a velvet vest.

KRECHINSKY: *(Charming.)* Good morning, Timofey Timofeyevich!

SHEBNEV: *(Cheerfully.)* Mikhail Vasilyevlich! I hope you're in good health?

KRECHINSKY: *(Feigning a cough.)* Just a bit under the weather ...

SHEBNEV: A slight chill, perhaps?

KRECHINSKY: To what do I owe the honor of your visit, Timofey Timofeyevich?

SHEBNEV: *(Amicably.)* I thought I might save you the trouble of coming to the club this morning, Mikhail Vasilyevich.

KRECHINSKY: How very thoughtful—

SHEBNEV: *(Cheerfully.)* There's a little balance due me after yesterday's card game—fifteen hundred rubles—I'm sure you recall ... would you care to settle it now?

KRECHINSKY: You needn't have inconvenienced yourself. I promised you yesterday, gentleman to gentleman, that I'd bring it to you in person.

SHEBNEV: *(Agreeably.)* No inconvenience at all. My pleasure!

KRECHINSKY: Quite honestly, Timofey Timofeyevich, I don't have the money just now. I'm expecting it any minute, and the moment I receive it, I'll bring it right over—

SHEBNEV: I'm afraid that it's due ... now ...

KRECHINSKY: I find this somewhat strange, Timofey Timofeyevich, truth be told. How can I give you what I don't have? What am I to do, bang it out of the table with my fist? *(Suddenly loses control and smashes the tabletop violently.)*

SHEBNEV: *(Pleasantly.)* As you wish. You won't be offended then, will you, Mikhail Vasilyevich, if I go straight to the club and enter your name in our little black book?

KRECHINSKY: *(Alarmed.)* Little black book?

SHEBNEV: *(Agreeably.)* Yes, that's the usual procedure ...

KRECHINSKY: But that means instantaneous disgrace! The entire club will know about it, and by tomorrow it will be all over town!

SHEBNEV: *(Nods his head sympathetically.)* I know, Mikhail Vasilyevich.

183

KRECHINSKY: But why today? Can't it wait? I need until tomorrow, at least—

SHEBNEV: In that case, then, I'm afraid I must inform you— gentleman to gentleman— that I'm off to the club, to enter your name in the—

KRECHINSKY: Why are you doing this, Timofey Timofeyevich? You'll ruin me!

SHEBNEV: The rules are the rules. *(Cheerfully.)* Good day, Mikhail Vasilyevich!

Shebnev bows and exits.

KRECHINSKY: *(Calling after him.)* Judas! He'll scrawl my name in the club book, and it'll be all over town like lightning. The marriage will go up in a puff of smoke! Poof! *(Throws off his dressing gown.)* It's stifling in here ... Everything depends on Popov. He's got to come up with that money! *(Sits at desk.)* How much do I need? Let's see ... a thousand to one jackal, five hundred to another, fifteen hundred to that wolf at the door ... and what do I have here? *(Rummages in the drawer.)* A miserable fifty rubles. Pathetic ... *(Despairing.)* I'll never raise enough for all of them.

A bell rings.

FYODOR: Sir, the coachman is at the door! He's asking for money.

KRECHINSKY: Tell him he'll get it, right in the neck! *(Counting.)* Fifty-one, fifty-two ... and what about the wedding? Good God! The florist, the caterer, the footmen, the—

A bell rings.

FYODOR: Mikhail Vasilyevich, the laundress is here. She wants her payment!

KRECHINSKY: To hell with her!

FYODOR: And the woodsman with the kindling has been waiting for hours.

KRECHINSKY: Why do you keep bothering me?

FYODOR: I'm running out of excuses, sir.

Fyodor shuffles out. Voices arguing are heard in the hallway. A bell rings.

KRECHINSKY: *(His head bent over the desk, not looking up.)* Go away!

Popov sneaks into the room and hides behind the screen. His hat is visible.

KRECHINSKY: *(Spotting his hat.)* You can come out now, you good-for-nothing …

Popov creeps out from behind the screen.

KRECHINSKY: Well? *(Popov hangs his head.)* I knew it! Come here …

Warily, Popov approaches. Krechinsky rises and grabs Popov by the lapels.

KRECHINSKY: *(Shaking him.)* I told you to bring me the money or else!

POPOV: But Mikhail Vasilich, they wouldn't let me play without security!

KRECHINSKY: *(Still shaking him.)* I ordered you to steal, you thief!

POPOV: Help!

KRECHINSKY: There's money hidden away in every house in Moscow! You just have to know where to find it ... *(Stops shaking Popov.)* Wait a minute! *(Releases him.)* Hidden away ... hidden away ...

Krechinsky rushes over to his desk and starts rummaging through all the drawers, papers flying everywhere, throughout Popov's following speech.

POPOV: Two beatings in twenty-four hours! What a day ... Some sit at life's banquet table, while others hide under it, waiting for crumbs ... *(Sighs.)* You won't find any money in there, my friend. Nor anywhere else ... What's he digging for?

Krechinsky suddenly extracts a large brooch.

KRECHINSKY: Eureka!!

POPOV: What's he got there?

KRECHINSKY: *(Hold the brooch up, laughing.)* Eureka!!

POPOV: I'll slip away while I'm still in one piece … *(Starts to tiptoe out.)*

Enter Fyodor.

FYODOR: *(Alarmed.)* What's the matter, sir?

KRECHINSKY: Don't worry, Fyodor, I'm fine … Hey, Popov!

POPOV: *(Stops in his tracks.)* Who, me?!

KRECHINSKY: Yes, you, jackass! Go to the florist in Petrovka Street, order three dozen camellias, white ones, got it? Bring them to me this minute! *(Paces, deep in thought.)*

POPOV: *(To the audience.)* Doesn't have a kopek, and he's ordering bouquets!

KRECHINSKY: *(To Popov.)* Are you deaf? Did you hear what I told you?

POPOV: *(Whining.)* But what am I going to do for money?

KRECHINSKY: Don't bother me with details!

POPOV: Be reasonable, Mikhail Vasilyevich!

KRECHINSKY: *(Rips the watch off his chain, throws it at Popov.)* Here's your money! And I want those flowers back here in five minutes, or else! Get going!

Popov dashes off stage left. Krechinsky sits at desk, picks up a pen.

KRECHINSKY: And now, to work! *(Dips pen in ink, writes..)* Hmmm …

FYODOR: Just look at him, like a hawk ready to swoop down on a mouse …

KRECHINSKY: *(Reads what he's written; crumples the paper, throws it over his shoulder.)* I need to write a letter that will make her veins throb … Hmm … This is what I call *real* work; look, I've started to sweat … "My tender angel, oh harbor of my soul, *(writes)* lend me one of your tiny wings" —oooh, that's good! *(Continues writing.)* "Send me your diamond brooch, I'll have it mounted in an exquisite setting, an enchanted vessel in which to sail forth on our wedding day, over the sparkling seas!" *(Folds letter, seals it.)* Yes, that's it! Not bad for a day's work! Now where is that jackass?

Popov rushes in stage left, breathless, carrying a giant bouquet.

POPOV: *(To the audience.)* Twenty-five rubles for this broom! Bah!

KRECHINSKY: At last! What kept you so long, fool?! Bring it over here, let's have a look at it. *(Popov shows him the bouquet.)* Not bad, it'll do. Well? Hand it over! *(Holds out his open hand.)*

POPOV: Hand what over?

KRECHINSKY: The change, idiot!

POPOV: *(Feigning ignorance.)* Change? *(Rummages in pockets.)* Change ... change ... oh, right ... here it is! Thirty rubles. *(Hands him the money.)*

KRECHINSKY: That's all? Never mind; listen carefully; this will be tricky. Here is a letter to Lydia Petrovna. You know where the Muromsky house is, don't you?

POPOV: The big white house with the grand pillars just around the corner?

KRECHINSKY: Right. Let me see ... *(Searches for his watch; realizes he's given it to Popov to pay for the flowers.)* Damn it, what time is it?

POPOV: Almost ten.

KRECHINSKY: Good—the old man won't be home now, he's riding around in his carriage with those miserable nags of his. Go straight to the house, and deliver the bouquet to Lydia Petrovna yourself. Wish her a good morning, you know, with a little finesse, just as I would—and then hand her this letter—

POPOV: Letter?

KRECHINSKY: What is this—an echo chamber? Don't ask questions, fool, just do what I say. Stand there while she reads the letter, be patient—and wait while she disappears, returns, and hands you her diamond brooch, just like that!

POPOV: *(Sputtering.)* Her d-d-d-iamond brooch? Mikhail Vasilyevich!

KRECHINSKY: Don't interrupt! I want to have it reset for the wedding, so take it from her, promise its safekeeping, and get your carcass back here immediately!

POPOV: But sir—

KRECHINSKY: Run!

POPOV: *(Excited.)* Like the wind, Mikhail Vasilyevich, like the wind! *(Takes the letter and rushes off stage right with a final leap.)*

KRECHINSKY: Yes, like the wind—the wind of diamonds, hearts, spades, and clubs! *(Laughs, and drops into the chair at his desk.)* And now, down to business. Fyodor!

Fyodor enters stage left.

KRECHINSKY: Where have you been, man, napping?

FYODOR: I've only got two legs, sir—

KRECHINSKY: So get a third! We've got work to do, now listen sharp! They're coming for champagne this evening—my fiancée, her father, and her aunt—so see to it that everything's just so.

FYODOR: How are we going to pay for the champagne, sir?

KRECHINSKY: Order it on credit from a shop in town I don't owe—

FYODOR: —if there is one, sir—

KRECHINSKY: Light the lamps—and the candelabra—

FYODOR: We've run out of oil, sir, and candles—

KRECHINSKY: *(Tosses him the remaining rubles.)* Then get some—oh, and straighten up the rooms, spray them with perfume, put up the decorations, coats of arms, the works. They'll be arriving at seven—

FYODOR: As you wish, sir. What should I do with Mademoiselle Artemisa? She's still having her coffee in the drawing room—

KRECHINSKY: Blast! I completely forgot—

Artemisa appears, still in a dressing gown.

ARTEMISA: Misha, darling, I've been waiting for you in the drawing room—

KRECHINSKY: Of course you have. Forgive me, my precious—

ARTEMISA: *(Alluringly.)* Won't you come and join me?

KRECHINSKY: Of course, my lovely, of course—I just have a little pressing business to do. Meanwhile, Fyodor will look after you—Fyodor, on your way back from the candle shop, stop in at the bakery and get mademoiselle her favorite croissants—

FYODOR: The *French* bakery, sir? But you know how much that costs—

KRECHINSKY: *(Under his breath.)* Charge it, fool! *(Aloud.)* You'd better hurry, Fyodor, Mademoiselle hasn't had her *petit dejéuner* yet, *(sweetly)* has she?

ARTEMISA: You're so sweet, Misha, no, I haven't. *Two* croissants, if you don't mind, Fyodor—oh, and with *confiture*[6] ... yum!

FYODOR: *Confi*—what?

KRECHINSKY: Jam, you fool! And tonight we're dining at the Slavyansky Bazaar!

ARTEMISA: Lovely!

FYODOR: But sir, I thought you just said that tonight your fiancée—

ARTEMISA: Who?

KRECHINSKY: *(Interrupting.)* Later, Fyodor, later—off with you!

Fyodor shuffles off, stage right.

KRECHINSKY: *(Approaching Artemisa, sweetly.)* And now, *cherie, alongez-vous*[7] on the divan in the drawing room, and I'll join you *tout de suite!*[8]

ARTEMISA: *(Giggling.) Oui, oui, tout de suite!* *(Kisses him, exits stage left.)*

KRECHINSKY: *(Alone.)* Damn it. Can't get any work done around here this morning. Where was I? Oh, yes.

(Rummages through his desk, finds two sheets of white paper.) Excellent, splendid ... now let's have them match exactly ...

Krechinsky cuts and shapes the paper with scissors, folds them into boxes, and fits lids on each of them while singing a song:

> Let's live our lives off of our wit
> Or else what is the point of it!
> Why live in poverty and woe?
> Oh, think how far a man can go!
> Just use your wits before you're old
> And fill your pockets full of gold.
> La la, la la, la la, la la ...
> Etcetera, etcetera ...

Popov rushes in, breathless, stage right.

POPOV: Victory, Mikhail Vasilyevich, victory! Ta da!

Popov holds the brooch high, claps his hands, dances a little dance, and then hands the brooch to Krechinsky.

KRECHINSKY: Ta da! The Rubicon is crossed!

POPOV: Aren't you going to ask me how I pulled it off?

KRECHINSKY: Don't bother me—I'm busy. *(He rummages in his desk.)*

POPOV: I arrived at the house, the door opened, and—

KRECHINSKY: Yes, yes, never mind, good job, but now, watch this! *Attention, s'il vous plaît!*[9] In my right hand I hold ... this gem, this beauty ... (*Holds up Lydia's diamond in his right hand.*) See how it sparkles in the light?

POPOV: (*Swooning.*) Oh, how it sparkles—

KRECHINSKY: And now ... (*He scoops up the other diamond brooch from the desk.*) *Voilà!* In my left hand I hold ... *this* gem, *this* beauty!

POPOV: Mikhail Vasilyevich—I don't believe my eyes ...

KRECHINSKY: Look how they *both* sparkle and gleam ...

POPOV: But I don't understand. Where did you get *two* brooches?

KRECHINSKY: Ah, that's another story. The lady in the other room could tell you—but don't ask her.

POPOV: Who?

KRECHINSKY: Artemisa, you idiot! It was a bauble given to her by a paramour in Paris. But it's fake—I checked it out, of course. She misplaced it a few days ago while she was, er, taking off her dressing gown, so I'm keeping it safe for her, so to speak—

POPOV: But—

KRECHINSKY: Now watch this ... ta da! (*He switches the brooches from hand to hand.*) Now tell me, Popov, which is which?

POPOV: Remarkable, Mikhail Vasilyevich ... I can't tell the difference!

KRECHINSKY: Exactly! *(Laughs.)* Yes, this will work like a charm ...

POPOV: What will work?

KRECHINSKY: And now, for my next conjuring trick—be right back!

Krechinsky flings on his cloak.

POPOV: But what about the brooch? I promised Lydia Petrovna to return it to her by this evening. She looked at me with such trusting eyes—

Krechinsky puts each brooch in a little white box, and stuffs them in his pockets.

KRECHINSKY: Don't you worry; leave it to me!

Enter Fyodor, carrying a parcel.

FYODOR: Here are the candles, the oil, and the croissants, sir ...

KRECHINSKY: Good—bring mademoiselle the candles, put the croissants in the—no, the other way around, you know what I mean—I'm in a rush, back in a moment—

FYODOR: But sir—

KRECHINSKY: And don't let this jackass out of your sight!

Krechinsky rushes out.

POPOV: *(Agitated.)* What's happening? Where'd he go?

FYODOR: *(Shrugs.)* Why, I imagine he's gone to pawn it.

POPOV: Pawn it? But the brooch has to be returned this evening, or else the police will come and throw us in jail! He's flown the coop, hasn't he, Fyodor? And so will I! *(Attempts to exit.)*

Fyodor picks up Krechinsky's walking stick and blocks Popov's path.

FYODOR: It's no use, sir. If he wants you to stay, you'll stay.

POPOV: Out of my way, old man!

Fyodor whacks Popov on the head with the walking stick.

POPOV: Ow! Ow!

FYODOR: Don't make me do it again, sir!

POPOV: Would you believe it? My third beating of the day!

Artemisa appears, stage left.

ARTEMISA: What's all the commotion? *(Sees Popov, holding his head, moaning.)* Oooooh ... having a bad day, golubchik?

FYODOR: Have you finished your breakfast yet, *Mademoiselle?*

ARTEMISA: Not yet …

FYODOR: The master will be so disappointed—

ARTEMISA: *(Tempting.)* Can I offer a croissant to Ivan Ivanich?

FYODOR: I'm afraid Ivan Ivanich is occupied at the moment. And anyway, the master bought them especially for you, Mademoiselle.

ARTEMISA: Then I'll gobble them right up—*(to Popov)* and you next! Boo!

POPOV: *(Jumps in fright.)* Aaaaah!

Artemisa runs off, laughing.

POPOV: *(Wringing his hands.)* God in heaven! My babies! Will I ever see them again? My babies, you are naked and cold—

FYODOR: I thought you were single, sir—

A bell rings.

POPOV: *(Terrified.)* Omigod! The police! They're here!

Krechinsky enters, flings his cape on the desk, removes his gloves with a flourish.

KRECHINSKY: Well done, Fyodor, well done, he's still here! *(To Popov.)* You're such a worrier, Ivan Ivanich. Yes, the police will catch up with us one day, and no, one can't avoid being sent to Siberia eventually, but everything in its own time. Meanwhile, here's something to keep you busy. *(Reveals a parcel..)* Here—open it, count all the money and lay it out in piles. I've got to pay my debts. After all, it's our duty. And here's the brooch—it has to be returned this evening to its rightful owner.

POPOV: *(Incredulous.)* Wha—?

KRECHINSKY: You see, Ivan Ivanich, this is how you get things done.

POPOV: *(Looking at the piles of money.)* I see stars before my eyes ... money ... more money ... *and* the brooch! *(Takes money and begins to count.)* One hundred ... two hundred ... four hundred ... nine hundred ... fourteen hundred—

KRECHINSKY: Keep counting ... you never stop talking, do you, Popov? It's that sentimental side of you.

POPOV: Good God! *(Kisses a pack of rubles.)* Perfume! I smell jasmine ...

Popov embraces Krechinsky and gives him a kiss on the cheek.

KRECHINSKY: Feeling better now?

POPOV: *(Sorting the money.)* My darlings, my doves!

KRECHINSKY: *(Picks up his cape.)* Never mix your metaphors. So, my prodigy, are you finished counting?

POPOV: In a minute, in a minute ...

KRECHINSKY: *(Takes one pack of money.)* I'll deliver this money myself to Shebnev; you take this pile *(gives him the other packs)* and get my watch out of pawn. Here's a list of my creditors. Be sure you don't leave anyone out.

POPOV: *(Takes the piles of money and wraps them carefully. Then stops.)* But wait—how is this possible? Isn't this money from Blekh, the pawnbroker?

KRECHINSKY: Good guess! Now watch this ... abracadabra! *(Produces a small white box, opens it, flashes the diamond brooch.)*

POPOV: But this is the very same brooch I got from Lydia Petrovna, right?

KRECHINSKY: Of course! And this evening we'll return it to her!

Krechinsky takes the pin from Popov and locks it in his desk drawer.

POPOV: But it can't be Lydia Petrovna's brooch! You pawned it for the money! You can't end up with both the money *and* the brooch, can you?

KRECHINSKY: You may be a hound dog, Popov, but you have no scent. Ha-ha-ha-ha-ha!

Krechinsky continues laughing as the lights change; music plays.

Scene Three

That evening at Krechinsky's flat

Bell rings. Enter Popov, followed by Fyodor. Popov hangs up his hat. He is dressed in an evening jacket; his hair is combed. Fyodor begins to light the candles.

POPOV: Ha-ha-ha-ha-ha-ha … it's just too much.… I can't stop laughing about it! What did he say? "Urethra"?

FYODOR: I believe it was "Eureka," sir …

POPOV: "Eureka," that's right, "Eureka"! I'll have to write that one down!

FYODOR: You do that, sir.

POPOV: Genius! Pure genius! And all in a matter of minutes!

FYODOR: Oh he's good, the master, he's good.

POPOV: How I wish I'd been there to see it! Mikhail Vasilich told me every detail! *(Rapidly, in one breath.)* He goes to the pawnbroker, shows him the brooch, Blekh holds it in the light, tests it on the scales, says, "Well, well," offers the master four thousand; the master says, "Ten thousand." Blekh says, "Five thousand." The master says, "Insulting!," grabs the brooch, puts it in the box, says, "I'm out of here," and makes for the door. Then Blekh says, "Eight," and the master says, "Deal!" Then Blekh says, "Wait." He turns his back; the master switches the boxes. Blekh turns around, hands over the money, and the master is gone in a flash! *(Exhales.)* Whew!

FYODOR: *(Shaking his head.)* Lord, Lord …

POPOV: He's a wizard! When I think of that Blekh, hunched over his little glass "treasure," his mouth watering, I can't stop laughing …

FYODOR: Don't strain yourself, sir—

POPOV: He pulled it off! Without a trace! And now he'll pay off his debts, plan a little wedding, get a big dowry, and start scheming for more. He'll build a mountain of gold higher than the Urals, eh, Fyodor? And he won't forget us, will he?

FYODOR: Let's hope not.

POPOV: He promised me two hundred thousand!

FYODOR: You know the old Russian saying: "The master promised me a sheepskin coat, and his word keeps me warm."

POPOV: Come again?

A bell rings.

POPOV: Oh ho, here he is! Greetings, o conjuror!

Enter Krechinsky. He hangs up his hat.

201

KRECHINSKY: What a day! I'm exhausted! *(Falls in chair.)* Is everything ready?

FYODOR: Yes, sir!

KRECHINSKY: *(To Popov.)* Did you do as I told you?

POPOV: Down to the last detail. Would you like the receipts?

KRECHINSKY: Absolutely! You don't expect me to operate on faith, do you? *(Takes receipts.)* Good ... Fyodor! Here, take these and lock them in the desk drawer.

POPOV: And here's your watch and chain, just as you ordered.

KRECHINSKY: *(To Popov.)* Good again. Now listen, you, when the guests arrive, keep the old man talking. I'll take the ladies aside and get this wedding tied up in a day. Only don't lie any more than you have to. You tend to get carried away—

POPOV: *(Hurt.)* Why are you always criticizing me? You never give me a word of praise. I bought a new jacket for the occasion, and you didn't even notice!

KRECHINSKY: Very nice. *(Looks at his watch.)* They'll be here any minute. See to it that everything's in order, Fyodor. And go look in the corridor—there's a portrait of some grim old general from the reign of Catherine the Great with a face like this. *(mugs.)* Dust it off and hang it in here over my desk. Family genealogy, you know ...

The bell rings.

KRECHINSKY: "Curtain up"! I'll go receive them. You, Popov, sit over here on the settee, look like someone important. Pick up the newspaper. *(Popov picks up a book, assumes an affected pose.)* The *newspaper*, idiot! ... stretch out a little ... *(Popov strikes an exaggerated pose.)* Hopeless! *(Exits.)*

POPOV: Two hundred thousand, my friend—and don't you forget it!

Enter Muromsky, Atuyeva, and Lydia, followed by Krechinsky, followed by Fyodor, who struggles to hang a huge portrait of a lugubrious general over Krechinsky's desk. This effort lasts quite a while.

MUROMSKY: What a splendid apartment you have here!

ATUYEVA: *Très elegant*! And what exquisite taste!

LYDIA: It's lovely ...

KRECHINSKY: It's only lovely since your arrival, *Mesdames*. *(Kisses their hands.)*

ATUYEVA: How charming you are, Mikhail Vasilyevich! I have only one regret—

KRECHINSKY: And what is that, Anna Andreevna?

ATUYEVA: That I'm not younger. If I were, I'd be in love with you myself!

KRECHINSKY: Then I regret that I'm not older! *(They share a laugh.)*

LYDIA: Mikhail Vasilyevich, may I ask you something? *(Beckons him aside.)*

KRECHINSKY: Why certainly—what is it?

LYDIA: *(Shyly.)* Do you really love me?

KRECHINSKY: Of course I do. Very much.

LYDIA: I want you to love me terribly, beyond measure, beyond reason *(lowering her voice),* just as I love you ...

ATUYEVA: *(Eavesdropping.)* What are you two whispering about?

LYDIA: Nothing, Auntie—

KRECHINSKY: *(Rushes over to Muromsky.)* Pyotr Andreyevich! Allow me to offer you a seat! What would you prefer—a high or low back, soft cushion or—

MUROMSKY: The divan is fine. *(Sits next to Popov.)*

KRECHINSKY: Allow me to present my dear friend, Ivan Ivanich Popov.

POPOV: *(Jumps up, bows, sputtering.)* An honor, sir, it's an honor ...

MUROMSKY: My pleasure.

They sit together awkwardly on the divan. Fyodor begins to serve champagne to the ladies, then to Muromsky and Popov. As Fyodor is very old, this is a precarious process, and the tray he is carrying with champagne glasses shakes violently.

MUROMSKY: May I ask, are you in the military or the civil service?

POPOV: Who, me? Ah … in the … in the … civil military service …

MUROMSKY: And do you live in Moscow, sir, or in the country?

POPOV: Yes …

MUROMSKY: Pardon?

POPOV: In Moscow, some of the time … *and* in the country … most of the time …

MUROMSKY: I see. And tell me, please, in what province is your estate?

POPOV: My estate? … My estate? Ah … in the … in the … *(searches desperately for a name)* Simbirsk province—that's it! Yes, the Simbirsk province.

MUROMSKY: Really? That's where my estate is too! That's odd … I know all the landowners in that province, and I've never heard your name mentioned.

POPOV: Really? Well … that's because my estate is actually … *not* there …

MUROMSKY: But I thought you said—

POPOV: It *was* there ... but then they ... er ... moved it.

MUROMSKY: They *moved* it? Extraordinary ...

POPOV: Yes ... it got ... er ... too big, so they just—*(Makes a big sweeping motion.)*

KRECHINSKY: *(Quickly.)* It's true, Ivan Ivanich's estate is in the Saratov district now—

MUROMSKY: *(Bewildered.)* Really? But how—

KRECHINSKY: Amazing, the things they can do nowadays. Ha-ha!

Krechinsky and Popov laugh. Muromsky, not wanting to be left out, joins in.

MUROMSKY: Ha-ha-ha! *(A pause.)*

KRECHINSKY: *(Diving in again.)* Ivan Ivanich is my neighbor, his grandfather knew my grandfather, you see, that portrait of him over there—

MUROMSKY: Ah, yes, very impressive—

KRECHINSKY: And now, ladies, I'll take you into the next room for a little game of billiards. *(Winks at Popov.)* I'll leave you to your scintillating conversation ...

Krechinsky exits with Lydia and Atuyeva. Popov mops his brow.

MUROMSKY: *(Indicating the portrait.)* Handsome man, our host's grandfather ... Is he living?

POPOV: Well ... no ... I mean ... yes ... It depends—

MUROMSKY: I see. You knew him, I assume?

POPOV: Oh ... ah ... yes, of course, of course!

MUROMSKY: Tell me about him ...

POPOV: Oh. Well, I was just a little boy at the time, but ... *(gathers confidence)* ... yes ... I remember him clearly. He was a small man, about so high *(indicates a man of very short height.)*

MUROMSKY: Really? In the portrait he appears to be quite a large man ...

POPOV: Oh *(looks at the portrait),* yes, you're quite right, actually, he was small when I first knew him, but then, as I grew, he grew too, quite rapidly in fact, to about "so" *(adjusts his hand higher)*—

MUROMSKY: Really? Only that tall?

POPOV: More like ... this, maybe? *(Adjusts his hand higher.)*

A bell rings.

POPOV: *(Aside.)* Saved by the bell!

Nelkin rushes in.

MUROMSKY: Ah, Vladimir Dmitrevich, dear friend! *(To Popov.)* Allow me to present Vladimir Dmitrevich Nelkin, my good neighbor and family friend. Meet Ivan Ivanich Popov. *(Nelkin and Popov exchange bows.)*

NELKIN: We've already had the honor—

MUROMSKY: Why are you so late, Vladimir Dmitrevich?

NELKIN: *(Agitated.)* I've been detained on a business matter of the utmost urgency! Where is everyone?

MUROMSKY: Inside, playing billiards.

NELKIN: Pyotr Andreyevich, I must have a word with you right away—

MUROMSKY: Do join us, Vladimir Dmitrevich, we've been having a pleasant chat—

NELKIN: *(Suspiciously.)* What did you say your name was?

POPOV: Who, me? Ivan Ivanich Popov. Heh-heh.

MUROMSKY: He's a close colleague of our host, Mikhail Vasilyevich. We're among friends here—

NELKIN: *(Darkly.)* Are you really? Take a look again, my friend—

MUROMSKY: Why, what do you mean?

NELKIN: You're in a den of thieves!

MUROMSKY: What are you saying?

NELKIN: Yes, thieves who are stealing your daughter—can't you see it?

MUROMSKY: Get hold of yourself, Vladimir Dmitrevich; you're talking about my future son-in-law!

NELKIN: No, you get hold of *your*self, my friend! You're standing on the edge of an abyss! Can't you see? They're stealing your daughter from right under your nose! And more!

MUROMSKY: Why are you talking like this, sir?

NELKIN: Tell me—where is your diamond brooch?

MUROMSKY: You mean Lidochka's pin? She has it, of course!

NELKIN: Are you certain of that?

MUROMSKY: Of course I'm certain!

NELKIN: I have news for you. She doesn't!

MUROMSKY: Nonsense!

NELKIN: Your daughter's brooch is no longer safe in your home, Pyotr Andreyevich—it's fallen into other hands.

MUROMSKY: Whose hands?

NELKIN: A pawnbroker's, that's whose!

POPOV: *(Aside.)* Uh oh—

MUROMSKY: That's ridiculous! Why, I saw it myself only yesterday!

NELKIN: I'm telling you that Krechinsky pawned your daughter's diamond brooch!

POPOV: *(Aside.)* Things are getting a little out of hand ... better let him know ... . *(He begins to tiptoe out.)*

MUROMSKY: *(Unconvinced.)* How did the brooch fall into Krechinsky's hands?

NELKIN: Ask *him*! *(Points to Popov, who is tiptoeing out.)*

MUROMSKY: *(Incredulously.)* Popov?

NELKIN: When I called on you this morning, I saw Lydia Petrovna hand Popov the brooch. *Aha*! I thought. "What's going on here? There's something tricky about this." Then Popov left, and I followed him. He brought it right to Krechinsky.

MUROMSKY: *(Barely able to speak.)* Then what?

NELKIN: Then Krechinsky took it to Blekh the pawnbroker and pawned it!

MUROMSKY: That can't be!

NELKIN: I just left him.

MUROMSKY: Who?

NELKIN: Blekh the pawnbroker. I'll take you there—he'll tell you himself!

MUROMSKY: *(Bewildered.)* What's going on here? Lidochka! Lidochka!

Lydia runs in from the other room with a billiard cue in her hand.

LYDIA: What is it, Papa? Why did you tear me away from the game?

MUROMSKY: Tell me, Lidochka, your diamond brooch—it's safe, isn't it?

LYDIA: Of course it is, Papa!

NELKIN: You're wrong, Lydia Petrovna—the brooch is gone!

LYDIA: Gone? What do you mean?

NELKIN: You gave it away!

LYDIA: *(Amazed.)* What are you talking about? This morning I sent it to Michel—he wants to have it reset for the wedding.

NELKIN: That's a lie!

LYDIA: But he has it! He just told me.

MUROMSKY: And?

LYDIA: He'll give it back to me, that's all!

NELKIN: I don't think so.

LYDIA: *(Heatedly.)* What do you mean? How dare you accuse my fiancé?

NELKIN: Lydia Petrovna! For God's sake, please don't get angry with me! I'd do anything for you, die for you ... but on my honor, I must tell the truth!

LYDIA: What's going on? Papa! I'm frightened!

Enter Atuyeva, Krechinsky, and Popov.

ATUYEVA: What's the matter, darling? What's happened? *(To Nelkin.)* Ah, it's you again! What are you up to now?

MUROMSKY: *(To Krechinsky, delicately.)* Forgive me, Mikhail Vasilyevich, we just need to have a little word together —the family, that is—

KRECHINSKY: Well, I'm about to join your family, so go right ahead!

MUROMSKY: I realize that. Still—

NELKIN: If we're going to speak openly, let's do it right now! We're talking about the diamond brooch.

KRECHINSKY: What diamond brooch?

MUROMSKY: Lidochka's—you took it from her earlier today, didn't you?

KRECHINSKY: *(Innocently.)* Yes, I'm sure she told you all about it.

MUROMSKY: So do you have it now or don't you?

KRECHINSKY: Aha ... so *that's* what this is all about! *(To everyone.)* Tell me, who has been putting lies in your heads? *(Points to Nelkin accusingly.)* This man?

NELKIN: *(Exploding.)* How dare you!

KRECHINSKY: *(With emotion.)* Pyotr Andreyevich, I have Lydia's diamond brooch! On my word!

MUROMSKY: I never doubted it for a moment. But Nelkin said that you are deceiving us, that you took the diamond brooch and pawned it!

KRECHINSKY: A despicable lie! I demand that you throw him out of your house immediately! As for the brooch *(takes it from the desk drawer)*— here it is, take it!

ATUYEVA: Give it to me! *(Grabs the brooch from Krechinsky.)*

All gather round her. General commotion and noise.

NELKIN: *(Shocked.)* What's this? It can't be!

ATUYEVA: *(Shows Nelkin the brooch.)* This is it, all right. Here, my darling, just as he promised! *(Hands the brooch to Lydia.)*

KRECHINSKY: Well, Pyotr Andreyevich?

MUROMSKY: *(To Nelkin, heatedly.)* You have deceived us, my friend!

NELKIN: *(Grabs Lydia's arm.)* Lydia Petrovna, listen to me, please!

KRECHINSKY: Don't touch her!

NELKIN: This can't be happening!

MUROMSKY: Please leave, Vladimir Dmitrevich. You have no further business here.

NELKIN: *(With dignity.)* At your service, sir. *(To Krechinsky.)* And if you demand satisfaction, I am ready to oblige you—to the death! *(Throws down a glove.)*

LYDIA: Vladimir Dmitrevich, how could you?

ATUYEVA: For God's sake, go away!

MUROMSKY: Gentlemen, please!

KRECHINSKY: Silence! Soooooo! You want to fight a duel, is that it? Fine, I accept! *(Throws down a glove too.)* Tomorrow, if you like. *(Calls out.)* Hey! Are there any servants around?

Fyodor shuffles in.

KRECHINSKY: *(To Fyodor.)* Take this man by the collar and throw him out!

NELKIN: Never mind, Fyodor, I know the way ... *(In great distress.)* Oh, truth! Where is thy power?! *(Exits.)*

POPOV: *(Calling after Nelkin.)* Good luck! Heh-heh.

KRECHINSKY: *(After a pause.)* Are you satisfied now, Pyotr Andreyevich?

MUROMSKY: *(Shaken.)* Poor man, he simply lost his mind!

KRECHINSKY: So now, let's wrap this up, shall we?

MUROMSKY: What do you mean?

KRECHINSKY: We've just had a scandal, and thanks to you, I've been compromised. With a blot on my reputation, what sort of husband would I be for your daughter now? Pyotr Andreyevich, I return your consent, and Lydia, I return your heart. Take them both, be happy, and forget about me.

LYDIA: What are you saying, Michel? My heart can't be returned—it belongs to you! Papa, say something, for God's sake! We're to blame for this.

MUROMSKY: *(Quickly.)* Please, Mikhail Vasilyevich—

KRECHINSKY: *(Feigning deep offense.)* How could you treat me this way, Pyotr Andreyevich? If some other gossip comes along tomorrow and tells you I'm a gambler, will you believe him too?

MUROMSKY: Mikhail Vasilyevich! What are you saying?

KRECHINSKY: I know the rules of middle class morality. But my pride forbids me to accept them. I don't need your brooch and I don't need your money. I throw them right in your face!

LYDIA: Michel! For God's sake, forgive him! If you love me even a little—

MUROMSKY: Mikhail Vasilyevich, I beseech you, forgive me!

KRECHINSKY: *(Aside.)* Uh oh, I know where that Nelkin is headed. I'd better speed things up here ...

LYDIA: *(Desperate.)* We'll do anything!

KRECHINSKY: *(After a moment.)* Very well, I forgive you, Pyotr Andreyevich—

MUROMSKY: *(Embracing Krechinsky, with emotion.)* Good man!

ATUYEVA: *(Also emotional.)* Thank you, Mikhail Vasilyevich!

KRECHINSKY: Let's have the wedding tomorrow! We'll end this once and for all.

LYDIA: *(With emotion.)* I'm yours, Michel!

MUROMSKY: If that's what you want, then it's tomorrow.

KRECHINSKY: And after that, we'll go to the country, to Streshnovo.

MUROMSKY: Absolutely, to Streshnovo!

KRECHINSKY: And you'll have nothing more to do with Nelkin.

MUROMSKY: Whatever you want, word of honor. Just one thing ... remember ... . *(His voice trembles.)* She's all I have ...

KRECHINSKY: *(Looks at his watch.)* It's late—time for you to go home. *(To Lydia.)* And tomorrow, you'll be mine, all mine ...

LYDIA: Oh yes, Michel, darling! Only tell me once more you love me!

KRECHINSKY: Don't you believe it?

LYDIA: I just want to hear the words. I can't explain—I'm afraid ...

KRECHINSKY: Afraid?

LYDIA: I'd give up everything for you ...

KRECHINSKY: No need, my angel, (*aside*) at least not yet ... *(Kissing her hand.)* And now, Pyotr Andreyevich—it's time for you to go home.

MUROMSKY: Yes.

KRECHINSKY: Be off! Please put Lydia Petrovna to bed—she needs her rest.

ATUYEVA: Of course.

KRECHINSKY: *(Tenderly.)* Lidochka! Tomorrow you'll be fresh-faced and rosy-cheeked and lovelier than springtime! My blushing bride ...

Bell rings, abruptly and loudly. Everyone freezes.

KRECHINSKY: *(Sharply.)* What's that?

Bell rings again. Voices offstage: "Open the door!," commotion.

KRECHINSKY: *(Shouting.)* Don't let anyone in, do you hear me?

Enter Fyodor.

FYODOR: Nelkin's back, sir. And he's got someone with him!

Banging on the door, commotion continues. More clanging of the bell.

KRECHINSKY: *(To Popov.)* Get rid of them!

POPOV: Right away! *(Dashes off, followed by Fyodor.)*

KRECHINSKY: So he's back, is he?

Krechinsky breaks an arm off a chair. Muromsky and Lydia try to restrain him.

LYDIA: Michel, what are you doing!

MUROMSKY: Calm down, for God's sake!

ATUYEVA: Mikhail Vasilyevich, please!

KRECHINSKY: I'll handle this!

Popov rushes in.

POPOV: *(Breathless.)* Omigod—there's a crowd out there!

KRECHINSKY: *(Threateningly.)* Get rid of them, though you die doing it!

More offstage voices, commotion. Enter Fyodor.

FYODOR: Mikhail Vasilyevich! The police are here!

KRECHINSKY: The police? *(Throws the arm of the chair away.)* It's over ...

Commotion. Sound of a crash. Nelkin rushes in, followed by Blekh and a policeman.

BLEKH: There he is! Thief! Thought you could pawn a piece of glass, did you? *(Krechinsky stands calmly, his arms folded across his chest. Popov hides behind him.)* He took my money! Grab him!

LYDIA: *(Shrieking.)* Aaaaaaaaah!

BLEKH: Grab him, I say!

POLICEMAN: Calm down! *(To Krechinsky.)* Your name, please?

KRECHINSKY: *(Proudly.)* Mikhail Vasilyevich Krechinsky.

POLICEMAN: *(To Popov.)* And yours?

POPOV: Who, me? I ... I have no name ...

KRECHINSKY: Ivan Ivanich Popov. (*Makes a sudden move to flee.*)

BLEKH: Stop him! Don't let him go!

POLICEMAN: (*Pulls out a nightstick and blocks Krechinsky's path.*) Stay where you are!

BLEKH: He's a thief, I tell you! Grab him! Eight thousand rubles I gave him for this piece of glass! It's a fake! *(Holds up the fake diamond brooch.)*

LYDIA: Please, sir, let him go! *(Reaches in her pocket; holds out her hand to Blekh.)* Here's the brooch that should have been pawned. Take it! It was a mistake.

MUROMSKY: *(Shocked.)* Lidochka!

ATUYEVA: *(Gasping.)* What are you doing?

BLEKH: *(Looks at the brooch and compares it to the other.)* Is this the real one? The *real* brooch? So it is! *(Kisses the real brooch.)* Thank heaven!

Lydia covers her face with her hands and sobs.

KRECHINSKY: *(To the audience.)* That was close!

Enter Artemisa. Sees Blekh holding up the two brooches.

ARTEMISA: Ah! There it is, Misha! I've been looking for it everywhere! Oh, how sweet, you made me another one!

They all freeze.

POPOV: *(Aside.)* Oh no, not her again!

LYDIA: *(Choking.)* Who ... who is this?

NELKIN: *(Shocked.)* Good God!

ATUYEVA: *(Horrified.)* Oh brother, what shall we do?

MUROMSKY: Hide, sister! Hide from the shame!

Lights. End of Act One. Intermission.

Act Two

Scene One

Evening of the following day. A jail cell in Moscow, stage left. Krechinsky is seated behind bars, smoking. Popov sits on a stool outside the cell. They are playing cards through the bars on a little fold-up board that Popov is balancing on his knees.

KRECHINSKY: Your turn.

POPOV: Er ... ah ... *(He puts down his hand.)* Three clubs.

KRECHINSKY: *(Nonchalantly puts down his hands.)* Four aces.

POPOV: (*Folding, defeated.*) Oh no, Mikhail Vasilyevich, not again ...

KRECHINSKY: *(Sighs.)* I can't help winning, can I? *(Stands, restless.)* What am I going to do, Popov—sit here and play cards with you forever, until they convict me? You're a terrible player. And you can't even pay up!

POPOV: *(Whining.)* You're hurting my feelings, boss, and anyway, if you paid me, at least I'd have something to lose to you!

KRECHINSKY: *(Starts to pace.)* I've got to get out of here. This is hurting my reputation, not to mention my career. Anyway, it's your fault I'm here in the first place—

POPOV: *(Offended)* But boss, I did everything you told me. And what about me? I've lost my livelihood, if you could call it that—

KRECHINSKY: Now, now, let's not be ungrateful. I would have given you your two hundred thousand, believe me, and still can, if only—

POPOV: If only what, boss? Looks like you're in a tight spot, if you ask me—

KRECHINSKY: Not so fast, not so fast, Ivan Ivanich, my lovely. Where's your faith, eh? *(Paces)* ... Hmmmm. ... Where is Artemisa?

POPOV: I don't know, sir. It was pandemonium at the Muromskys. I think she ran after Blekh—you know how she loves jewelry ...

KRECHINSKY: Quiet! *(Paces)* Don't interrupt me, I'm thinking ...

Enter a large constable with a nightstick and a large ring of keys hanging from his waist.

CONSTABLE: What's going on here? *(To Popov.)* You—what are you doing here? The prisoner isn't allowed any visitors!

POPOV: (*Leaping to his feet.*) I ...I ...Your Excellency, I mean, Your Officer, or whatever they call you, they told me I could come to visit my master to, er, comfort him, yes, that's right, to divert him in this, his darkest hour—

CONSTABLE: *(Suspiciously looking at the playing board.)* What's that?

POPOV: *(Folds it up and tries to hide it.)* Nothing. It's, er, a praying board, we were about to light candles and recite our—

KRECHINSKY: *(Smoothly.)* Now, now, Popov, let's not deceive this very kind constable, shall we? He's entitled to the truth. After all, he's an officer of the Tsar, and a fine one at that—

POPOV: (*Catching on.*) Yes, very fine, very fine indeed—

KRECHINSKY: The truth of it is, Officer, what is your name, sir?—

CONSTABLE: (*Mistrustfully.*) Klop ... Constable Klop—

KRECHINSKY:—the truth is, Constable Klop, we were playing a little game of poker to give homage to the Tsar, of course, since we know it's one of *his* favorite games too—

POPOV: It is; it truly is!

KRECHINSKY:—and my poor servant Ivan Ivanich here is so distressed—

POPOV: (*Faking tears.*) I really am!

KRECHINSKY: He fears this will be our last night together … actually, I'm just wondering, would you like to join us in a little game? This could be the last game I'll ever play—

POPOV: (*Faking tears.*) The very last …

CONSTABLE: (*Softening.*) Well, under the circumstances, I suppose—

KRECHINSKY: Excellent! Go on, Ivan Ivanich, give up your hand to our esteemed Constable Klop—

Popov gestures unctuously for Constable Klop to take a seat. He ceremoniously places the board on Klop's knees and hands him the deck of cards.

CONSTABLE: (*Shuffling the deck.*) Actually, I hear you're a pretty sharp player, Mikhail Vasilyevich. You've got quite a reputation, yes, indeed. They say you've won thousands at cards—

POPOV: (*To audience.*) Yes, and lost it too …

While the constable shuffles, Krechinsky signals to Popov to take the nightstick and bang the constable over the head. Popov violently signals "no" back. A lot of gesticulation ensues between them, out of the constable's view.)

KRECHINSKY: Take your hat off, please; make yourself comfortable.

CONSTABLE: (*Removes his hat and deals a hand to Krechinsky and himself.*) No harm done, I suppose. There aren't any rules against such diversions, especially since, as you say, this might be your last game. So, in service to the Tsar, your move, Mikhail Vasilyevich—

KRECHINSKY: No, yours, Constable, I insist …

CONSTABLE: Very good of you, Mikhail Vasilyevich, very good of you. (*Concentrates on his hand.*) In that case—

Popov stealthily removes the constable's nightstick from his belt and bops the constable on the head. The constable falls off the chair onto the floor, unconscious.

KRECHINSKY: (*Jumps up!*) Eureka!

POPOV: (*Horrified.*) Omigod! What have I done?!

KRECHINSKY: Good job, Ivan Ivanich! I may keep you after all. Now hurry, the keys—

POPOV: What will they do to me now?

KRECHINSKY: Stop blubbering, man—quickly, the keys!

Popov fumbles for the keys, tears them from the constable's belt, fumbles to open the door, and Krechinsky walks out of the cell.

KRECHINSKY: Whew! That was a close call. (*Dusts himself off, smoothes his hair.*) How do I look? It was pretty nasty in there.

POPOV: I'll go to prison for this, boss!

KRECHINSKY: No you won't! (*Looks at the inert constable.*) And now, his clothes—

POPOV: What do you mean?

KRECHINSKY: His clothes! A shame to waste the uniform of an officer of the Tsar—you never know when it might come in handy.

POPOV: (*Horrified.*) What?

KRECHINSKY: (*Annoyed.*) Do I have to do everything around here? (*Quickly turns the constable over, starts pulling off his jacket and belt.*) Take off your coat and give it to me—hurry!

POPOV: (*Shocked.*) What are you doing?

KRECHINSKY: (*Hands Popov the Constable's coat.*) Put this on!

POPOV: (*Obeying.*) But boss, we'll never get away with this!

KRECHINSKY: Why not? You'll be him and he'll be … you! Not exactly a fair trade, but never mind. Come on, quickly!

(*While Popov puts on the constable's uniform, Krechinsky dresses the inert constable in Popov's jacket and hat.*)

KRECHINSKY: This is hard work! (*Impatiently.*) Help me, won't you?

Popov aids Krechinsky in dressing the constable.

POPOV: (*Out of breath.*) Whew ... now what?

KRECHINSKY: I'm out of here. Give me a few hours to get lost, and meanwhile, find a nice big hole to hide him in, or an empty cell—if there is one. Then go down and report to the front desk that I've escaped.

POPOV: But what if he wakes up?

KRECHINSKY: Let's be sure he doesn't, then—at least not for a while.

Krechinsky produces a flask of vodka from his pocket, takes a swig, and then pours the rest of it down the constable's throat.

POPOV: (*Terrified.*) But he will wake up, eventually, won't he?

KRECHINSKY: By that time, I'll be long gone—

POPOV: And me?

KRECHINSKY: You? You'll go off duty and ... and ... just disappear in a puff of smoke! Poof! (*Terrified, Popov jumps; Krechinsky laughs.*)

POPOV: But sir, where will you go? Where will I find you?

KRECHINSKY: Don't worry so much! (*Pinches his cheeks.*) Tsk-tsk, you're such a worrier, Ivan Ivanich—you know you're really fond of me after all. Admit it! (*Kisses him. Then stands back and admires Popov in the constable's uniform.*) Not bad, Ivan Ivanich, the uniform actually suits you! An Officer of the Tsar! Hah! Good luck! (*Raises his flask in a toast.*) *Za vashe zdarovye!*[10] (*Drinks, laughs again. Hand the flask to Popov, who guzzles gratefully.*)

POPOV: Believe me, I need it!

KRECHINSKY: (*Winks at him.*) *Do svidanya!*[11] (*Runs off.*)

Popov stands for a moment, bewildered, contemplating the constable's inert body.

POPOV: He's left me holding the bag ... again ... (*Starts dragging the Constable.*) God, he's heavy!

(*Shaking his head, Popov drags the Constable's inert body offstage.*)

Music.

Scene Two

Lights up on the front door of Krechinsky's house, stage right. It is night. Nelkin approaches in a long coat. He knocks at the door.

NELKIN: Open up! Open up! I beseech you!

He continues to knock loudly. Fyodor opens the door; he is wearing a nightgown and nightcap, and carries a candle.

FYODOR: Who's there? What's happening?

NELKIN: Where is your master, Fyodor? I demand to see him!

FYODOR: (*Warily.*) My master? What do you mean? You know very well where he is … in prison!

NELKIN: Well, he's not!

FYODOR: (*Feigning surprise.*) What do you mean, sir? Of course he's in prison. Where else could he be?

NELKIN: Don't tell me you don't know.

FYODOR: (*Playing innocent.*) Know what, sir?

NELKIN: He's escaped, man!

FYODOR: Really!

NELKIN: (A*ngrily.*) Forgive me, Fyodor, but I don't believe you!

FYODOR: I won't take such an insult, sir, not at this or any hour! (*Tries to shut the door.*)

Nelkin puts his foot forward to block the door from closing.

NELKIN: No wait, please, Fyodor; I beg you; we're desperate—

FYODOR: What do you mean?

NELKIN: All right: whether you know it or not, your master has fled prison, the authorities are enraged, and now they're accusing Lydia Petrovna of aiding and abetting him in his flight!

FYODOR: They've *what*?

NELKIN: They came to arrest her, but her father, Pyotr Andreyevich, begged them not to, so they've arrested him instead!

FYODOR: (*Genuinely.*) Tsk-tsk, poor fellow ...

NELKIN: Lydia Petrovna is weeping, her aunt is hysterical, we don't know what to do! Please—where is your master? Is he hiding inside? I beg you, Fyodor, we're desperate. Only your master can save them—

FYODOR: (*Stubbornly.*) I've already told you, he's not here, he's not—

NELKIN: Please, Fyodor. I must convince Mikhail Vasilyevich to do the right thing, face the consequences and let my beloved's father go free—

FYODOR: Your beloved? I thought my master was going to marry Lydia Petrovna!

NELKIN: Never mind—please, just let me speak with him. We're wasting precious time!

FYODOR: (*Softening.*) All right, all right ... Yes, Mikhail Vasilyevich did stop by here a few hours ago ...

NELKIN: Then let me in, I beg you—

FYODOR: But then he left. He's not here, not anymore, I assure you—

NELKIN: Where did he go?

FYODOR: (*Stubbornly.*) *That* I cannot say, Sir, not even if you torture me.

NELKIN: (*Forcefully.*) Is your heart made of stone, man?

FYODOR: The truth is, I don't know where he is … he just said he was going someplace to "lay low for a while" … somewhere safe and "sequestered" … those were his words …

NELKIN: (*In despair.*) Where can I turn now? They're counting on me, Lydia Petrovna and Anna Andreyevna— (*Holds his head in his hands.*)

FYODOR: (*Pats Nelkin on the back.*) There, there, sir … perhaps, if you can find his sidekick—

NELKIN: Who, that rascal, Popov?

FYODOR: Just a suggestion … I haven't seen him since the master was, er, detained. Although I do hear he has a new job—

NELKIN: Who, your master?

FYODOR: No, Popov … and a good job too, so they say …

NELKIN: I'm off—and no matter what, I'll find him … O justice, where art thou? (*Runs off, leaving Fyodor shaking his head.*)

Lights out.

Scene Three

Lights up on the prison cell again, stage left. Muromsky sits behind bars on a stool, slumped, dejected. Sounds of mournful guitar music.

MUROMSKY: (*Humming along with the music.*) Streshnovo, my Streshnovo, I shall never seen thee again, thy gentle fields, thy golden pastures, thy flowing streams, thy—(*He weeps softly.*)

Enter Popov in a constable's uniform, trying to look official.

MUROMSKY: Constable, please, can you tell me, how long am I to be detained here?

POPOV/CONSTABLE: (*Trying to disguise his voice.*) I am an officer of the law, sir, I don't have that information.

MUROMSKY: Please, I must know, I need to gather my thoughts—

POPOV/CONSTABLE: I'm not supposed to talk to prisoners, sir. It's not in my job description!

MUROMSKY: Have a heart, man!

POPOV/CONSTABLE: (*To audience.*) Believe me, I used to, until Mikhail Vasilyevich cut it out, along with my wages! (*To Muromsky.*) Your lawyer can help you.

MUROMSKY: Since when, in this country, can a lawyer help anyone?

POPOV/CONSTABLE: He can represent you at your hearing—

MUROMSKY: (*With dignity.*) I plan to represent myself. I am an innocent victim, and my daughter is purer than driven snow. That villain Krechinsky and his worthless sidekick, Popov—

POPOV/CONSTABLE: (*Offended.*) Now wait just a minute—

MUROMSKY: They've gotten away with murder! They've deceived my daughter, sullied our name, and now they've run off. Meanwhile, the authorities have turned around, accused my daughter of complicity, and arrested me! What have I done to deserve this?

POPOV/CONSTABLE: (*Sympathetic.*) I see your problem—

MUROMSKY: The allegations are shocking! And anyway, I don't have the money to hire a lawyer—

POPOV/CONSTABLE: But sir, I thought you were a wealthy landowner—

MUROMSKY: Not any more. I've received a message from my sister, saying she had a visit from one the state councilors. Our case will be heard tomorrow in court. It has been suggested that—I can't even bear to say it—if she presents some kind of "gift to the court"—I think that's how he put it, and "discreetly," he said—then the charges might be dropped.

POPOV/CONSTABLE: (*Shocked.*) What?

MUROMSKY: I know, it's a disgrace to the Tsar, but what can we do! The State Councilor—Slinkov, I think his name is—said they are prepared to be flexible—

POPOV/CONSTABLE: What do you mean?

MUROMSKY: They'll take cash, jewels, bonds, whatever we are prepared to offer!

POPOV/CONSTABLE: (*In his own voice.*) The scoundrels!

MUROMSKY: I thought I'd never see this day. The shame of it ...

POPOV/CONSTABLE: (*To the audience.*) Why do other people find it so easy to raise money? Be honest, tell me—what am I doing wrong? (*To Muromsky again, in his own voice, with feeling.*) A bribe, that's what they want!

MUROMSKY: (Star*tled.*) Your voice is so familiar ...

POPOV/CONSTABLE: (*Again, in his own voice.*) A bribe, the devils! A bribe!

MUROMSKY: (*Bewildered.*) I've heard that voice before ...

POPOV/CONSTABLE: (*Quickly.*) No you haven't, sir, I'm not from these parts.

MUROMSKY: No, wait, yes, yes—oh no, it *can't* be!

POPOV/CONSTABLE: (*Trapped.*) I wouldn't jump to conclusions, sir—after all, you're on the wrong side of the bars to do that—

MUROMSKY: Omigod ... it's you! Propop, Plopov, whatever your name is, the sidekick of that criminal Krechinsky, the man who has ruined my daughter—

POPOV/CONSTABLE: (*Quickly.*) Now really, sir, you're being a bit too harsh; he didn't mean any harm, he just needed to raise a little quick cash. He planned to make your daughter very happy, I assure you—

MUROMSKY: (*Shouting.*) Guard! Guard!

POPOV/CONSTABLE: (*Alarmed.*) Calm down, Pyotr Andreyevich—anyway, *I'm* the guard!

MUROMSKY: *You?* What are *you* doing here?

POPOV/CONSTABLE: It's a long story, really, I don't want to bore you—

MUROMSKY: Bore me? What are you talking about! My life is at stake—my life! And my darling daughter's!

POPOV/CONSTABLE: I know, I know, it's gotten a little out of hand—

MUROMSKY: (*Suddenly*) Help me, please, Pop-whatever your name is, please find your master, ask him to do the right thing, turn himself in—

POPOV/CONSTABLE: Honestly, I don't know where he's gone to.

MUROMSKY: You're a resourceful fellow, try to find him, try—

POPOV: (*Flattered.*) You think so? You're appealing to my better side here ...

MUROMSKY: Save us, please! I'll do anything. If we survive, I'll let you live with us at Streshnovo, in the country—

POPOV: (*Aside, to audience.*) I don't like living in the country, do you? Too many mosquitoes—

MUROMSKY: For justice's sake, help us, please! Help an old soldier of the Tsar clear his family name, and the name of his innocent daughter!

POPOV/CONSTABLE: All right, all right, leave it to me! Only remember, I'm Constable Klop—not that Pop-fellow whose name you can't pronounce—got it?!

MUROMSKY: Thank you, Pop—er, Constable Klop—

POPOV: I'm off—like the wind! (*To audience.*) Now where could my master be hiding? You'd tell me if you knew—wouldn't you? (*Runs off with a little leap, leaving Muromsky sitting behind bars.*)

Music.

Scene Four

The parlor of the Muromsky home, stage right Lydia Petrovna and Anna Atuyeva sit at a little table, upon which sit two jewel boxes. They remove pieces of jewelry and count them. To one side stands Nelkin, to the other stands Slinkov, a state councilor.

SLINKOV: *(Pleasantly.)* We're so glad you're taking this course of action, Anna Andreyevna. It's a wise decision.

ATUYEVA: *(Counting in a broken voice.)* One pearl necklace, one pearl bracelet—

NELKIN: *(Sternly.)* Believe me, State Councilor Slinkov, never did I think the day would come when the noble name of Muromsky would be stained with such outrageous accusations.

SLINKOV: All the more reason, then, to offer these modest gifts. The court appreciates gestures like these. They help in the service of justice.

LYDIA: *(Calmly.)* One pair of diamond earrings, one emerald pin—

ATUYEVA: *(Crying out.)* But you can't, Lydia—

LYDIA: I must, Auntie. Anything to save Papa and the family name ...

SLINKOV: *(Discreetly inspecting the collection of jewels.)* Hmmm ... Might I suggest that a slightly more generous gift would speed the cause of justice ...

LYDIA: *(To Atuyeva, hesitantly.)* All I have left is mother's wedding ring. I can't bear to part with it—

NELKIN: *(To Lydia, with emotion.)* And you won't! *(Reaches into his pocket and draws out a large wad of rubles.)* Will this suffice, sir?

LYDIA: No, Vladimir Dmitrevich, you mustn't! You've done so much already!

SLINKOV: (*Suppressing his surprise and enthusiasm at the large amount of cash.*) Hmmmm ... I think this might help things along a bit. It certainly is worth a try.

ATUYEVA: (*Sharply*) A *try*? But I thought you said—

SLINKOV: Calm yourself, Madam, and leave it to me—

NELKIN: As difficult as this situation is, Anna Andreyevna, we have no choice but to trust the State Councilor. He has had extensive experience in these matters. (*Sharply.*) Isn't that right, sir?

SLINKOV: (*Nods, smiling slightly.*) Thank you. You might say so —

NELKIN: (*Continuing emphatically*)—and he has *assured* us that we are in good hands. (*Distastefully.*) So does this conclude our affairs?

SLINKOV: Give me a moment. (*He counts the jewels and the money.*)

NELKIN: (*To the audience, sardonically.*) Just to be sure that no stone is left unturned.

SLINKOV: Yes, Vladimir Dmitrevich, I believe everything is in order.

NELKIN: (*Places the jewels and money in a parcel, hands it to Slinkov.*) Remember, the good name of a loyal servant of the Tsar is at stake—as well as the honor of an young damsel in distress, for whom I would do anything—

SLINKOV: (*Smiling.*) Yes, very touching. Till tomorrow, then, at two o'clock sharp. The case will be heard in the highest court—

NELKIN: By whom?

SLINKOV: By the Highest of the High, of course! Who else!

Atuyeva and Lydia Petrovna look terrified.

ANNA: God help us!

SLINKOV: All done and dusted. (*Cheerfully.*) I'll be off, then. Good day, *mesdames, monsieur.* See you in court! (*Exits, whistling "Una furtive lagrima" from Donizetti's opera "L'elisir d'amore."*)

NELKIN: We must have faith, Anna Andreyevna, that justice will be served. (*To Lydia Petrovna.*) Have no fear, Lydia Petrovna, I'll be by your side at every moment ...

LYDIA: (*Bravely.*) I have faith; I have faith ...

Lights out. Ominous music.

Scene Five

The Courtroom

A high platform with a towering seat. Below it, stage right, a desk and chair. Below it, stage left, a bench, upon which four petitioners sit. On the upstage scrim, a huge image of the Tsar (Nicholas II) is projected. Behind the desk sits Slinkov, wearing a wig and a black robe. Ominous music plays. Enter Muromsky, escorted by Popov, still disguised as the constable.

SLINKOV: *(Announcing officiously.)* You are entering the offices of The Very Important Person ...

POPOV/CONSTABLE: (*Announcing Muromsky.*) The prisoner Muromsky has been summoned to see His Grace—

SLINKOV: *(Sternly.)* Be seated, and wait ...

Muromsky sits on the bench submissively. Slinkov rises and crosses to Muromsky. His demeanor is increasingly reptilian.

SLINKOV: *(In a low voice.)* His Grace is not in good humor today, I'm afraid.

MUROMSKY: What can I do? It's all in God's hands ...

SLINKOV: (*Still in a low voice.*) We'll do our best, Pyotr Andreyevich. Your family has presented the court with a small gift, so—

MUROMSKY: (*Holding his hands over his ears.*) Please do not speak to me of such things, sir. I'm an officer of the Tsar, with the highest integrity—

SLINKOV: *(Shrugs.)* As you wish. *(Raises his voice.)* You are entering the offices of the Very Important Person— here he comes. All rise!

There is a sound of a wind machine offstage, accompanying the entrance of the Very Important Person. (He walks on stilts covered by a long flowing black robe so the stilts are not visible to the audience. He towers over everyone.) The petitioners leap to their feet and bow obsequiously. Then they all begin waving their petitions in the air, shouting: "Your Excellency!" "Your Grace!" "Please hear my case!" "No, hear mine first!" etc.

SLINKOV: *(Authoritatively, pointing to Muromsky.)* You— remain here. All other petitioners: wait in the hall!

The petitioners bow obsequiously. They exit, still facing the Very Important Person, who takes his seat in a high chair behind the desk on the high platform.

VERY IMPORTANT PERSON: *(Waves his hand dismissively.)* That will be all. *(To Slinkov.)* Right. And what do we have on the docket today, State Councilor Slinkov?

SLINKOV: *(Discreetly.)* Your Excellency, before we proceed, may I have a word—

VERY IMPORTANT PERSON: *(Interrupting, indicating Muromsky.)* And who, may I ask, is this?

SLINKOV: *(Hands the Very Important Person some papers.)* A detainee, Your Grace, recently arrested in connection with the Krechinsky case—

VERY IMPORTANT PERSON: Ah-ha. *That* case! Murky business!

MUROMSKY: If you would only allow me to—

VERY IMPORTANT PERSON: (*To Slinkov.*) Where is his lawyer?

SLINKOV: The prisoner insists on representing himself.

VERY IMPORTANT PERSON: Ah-ha. Highly irregular, but we'll allow it. You may approach. State your name.

MUROMSKY: (*Rises, flustered.*) My name is Muromsky, Your Excellency. I mean, Your Honor, or rather—

SLINKOV: "Your Grace" will do.

MUROMSKY: Yes, of course, Your Grace. My name is Muromsky—retired captain Pyotr Andreyevich Muromsky of the Tsar's regimen.

VERY IMPORTANT PERSON: (*Places his pince-nez on his nose.*) Ah-ha. And what is it that you want from the court?

MUROMSKY: Justice, Your Grace. To hear my case and to offer justice!

VERY IMPORTANT PERSON: (*Consulting the papers.*) You have been charged with conspiracy to defraud a pawnbroker, Blekh, plus theft of a priceless article of jewelry—

MUROMSKY: But why would I conspire to steal from myself, Your Grace? The charges are absurd!

VERY IMPORTANT PERSON: *(Sternly.)* The court will not tolerate such slurs, Sir!

MUROMSKY: Then hear my case, I beg of you, Your Grace—

VERY IMPORTANT PERSON: Briefly, then; we haven't got all day—

MUROMSKY: You see, Your Grace, I have an only daughter, my life's treasure, the purest of angels. I raised her in a home befitting my name and station—

VERY IMPORTANT PERSON: *(Impatiently, to Muromsky.)* Just explain the case.

MUROMSKY: The case concerns the theft of a family heirloom by that scoundrel Krechinsky, who, in the guise of her fiancé, stole the priceless brooch from my trusting daughter, pawned it, and—

VERY IMPORTANT PERSON: You're wasting my time, Sir. *(To Slinkov.)* I'm confused. Didn't we arrest Krechinsky in connection with the theft?

SLINKOV: *(Nonchalantly.)* Indeed we did, sir, but it seems as if this Krechinsky has, er, gone missing—

VERY IMPORTANT PERSON: *(Staring over his half-glasses.)* Missing? What do you mean "missing"?

SLINKOV: That is to say, he's absented himself from his cell, sir—

243

VERY IMPORTANT PERSON: Escaped from the Tsar's prison? Impossible! We have the most loyal guards in our service!

SLINKOV: (*Defensively.*) Of course we do, but even so, he just somehow, ah, slipped away—

VERY IMPORTANT PERSON: (*Angrily.*) Where's the constable on duty?

POPOV/CONSTABLE: (*In a tiny voice.*) Er … here, sir?

VERY IMPORTANT PERSON: What happened, man? Speak up!

POPOV/CONSTABLE: Er … I … can't really say, sir!

VERY IMPORTANT PERSON: What do you mean?

POPOV/CONSTABLE: That is, I was guarding the prison with the utmost care. I'm very good at my job, Your Superiority, I assure you—

VERY IMPORTANT PERSON: (*Impatiently.*) Get to the point, man!

POPOV/CONSTABLE: And er … (*Gathering momentum, with relish*) someone must have come up behind me and (*gesticulates*) whomp! That's all I remember! (*Helpfully.*) Would you like to see the bump? (*Takes off his hat and bops himself on the head surreptitiously.*)

VERY IMPORTANT PERSON: (*Annoyed.*) This is highly irregular! (*To Slinkov.*) Start an investigation into this assault, Kandid Kastorovich. And meanwhile, decorate this constable—what did you say your name was?—for suffering a head wound in heroic service.

POPOV/CONSTABLE: (*To himself, searching*) Er, Krop ... Klub ...? (*remembering, suddenly*) *Klop*! Constable Klop—that's my name!

(Offstage, faint shouts are heard: "Help! Let me out! Let me out!")

VERY IMPORTANT PERSON: What's that?

POPOV/CONSTABLE: (*Alarmed, then composing himself.*) Pay that no mind, Your Holiness, I mean, Your Supremacy. Just a restless prisoner, that's all, heh-heh. Oh, and thanks for the decoration! (*To the audience.*) I'll bet it comes with a raise!

VERY IMPORTANT PERSON: (*Irritated.*) My patience is wearing thin. How is it that Muromsky is detained, if Krechinsky was the thief?

MUROMSKY: That's exactly what I want to know, Your Grace!

SLINKOV: (*Hastily.*) We went to Krechinsky's home, but his servant knew nothing of his whereabouts. We then went to the home of his fiancée, Lydia Petrovna, thinking she might be hiding him—

MUROMSKY: Outrageous! He deceived her, humiliated her!

SLINKOV: She said she had no idea where he was, but she seemed so shaken, that we suspected that she was colluding with Krechinsky in some way.

MUROMSKY: Preposterous!

VERY IMPORTANT PERSON: Quiet! *(To Slinkov.)* Continue, Councilor—

SLINKOV: Indeed, Your Grace, there are rumors that not only was she complicit in the theft, but also that she and Krechinsky may have been carrying on an illicit relationship, one which, how shall I put it, might now be bearing ... er ... fruit?

MUROMSKY: Monstrous!

VERY IMPORTANT PERSON: *(Suspiciously.) Fruit?* What kind of *fruit*?

SLINKOV: So, in accordance with the Tsar's order that no prison cell be left empty, we went to arrest her—

MUROMSKY: But of course I wouldn't allow it. I'd lay my life down for my darling child. So I told them to arrest me instead—

SLINKOV: We have our quotas, after all—

MUROMSKY: *(Bewildered, to Slinkov.)* But I thought you promised to help us—

SLINKOV: *(In a low voice.)* In due time ...

VERY IMPORTANT PERSON: I'm getting a headache from all this!

Commotion offstage. Lydia bursts into the courtroom, followed by a distressed Atuyeva and Nelkin. There is a shocked "Ah" from all.

LYDIA: *(Throwing herself on her knees before the Very Important Person.)* Your Grace, I beseech you, spare my father and hear my plea!

VERY IMPORTANT PERSON: Who is this individual?

LYDIA: Lydia Petrovna, Your Grace, daughter of Pyotr Andreyevich, the unjustly accused and the cruelly abused. My father is innocent, sir. Take me instead—

MUROMSKY: Lidochka!

VERY IMPORTANT PERSON: *(To Nelkin.)* And who are you?

NELKIN: A loyal friend of the Muromsky family, ready to lay down his life to restore their good name.

VERY IMPORTANT PERSON: *(To Atuyeva.)* And you?

ATUYEVA: The devoted sister of the unjustly accused, Your Grace. Most grateful for your mercy, and for your willingness to accept our small gift—

VERY IMPORTANT PERSON: *(Startled.)* Gift? What gift?

ATUYEVA: Why, the gift that your State Councilor Slinkov advised us to present to the court, in the name of justice!

VERY IMPORTANT PERSON: *Who?*

SLINKOV: *(Placating.)* I can explain, sir—

VERY IMPORTANT PERSON: *(To Slinkov.)* What is the meaning of this?

SLINKOV: (*In a low voice, to the Very Important Person.*) I was following the standard procedure, Your Grace, you know, 50/50, as always—

VERY IMPORTANT PERSON: (*Aloud.*) There must be some misunderstanding! Where is this "gift"?

SLINKOV: (*Innocently.*) Why right here, in the drawer, for safekeeping, just as always—

VERY IMPORTANT PERSON: Give it to me! (*Slinkov sheepishly produces the parcel, hands it to the Very Important Person, who snatches it from him.*)

VERY IMPORTANT PERSON: (*Sternly, to Muromsky.*) This will go badly for you, Retired Captain Muromsky! Not only is your daughter accused of complicity in a tawdry business, but now it appears that you have attempted to bribe the Highest Court—

MUROMSKY: I would never do such a thing!

NELKIN: Objection, Your Honor! Lydia Petrovna and Anna Andreyevna were doing what they were advised by your own state councilor, to give—

VERY IMPORTANT PERSON: Enough! I now charge you officially, Retired Captain Muromsky, with theft, collusion, and now bribery! (*To Popov/Constable.*) Take him away!

MUROMSKY: God help me! (*Clutches at his heart.*)

ATUYEVA: O, brother! (*Lydia swoons.*)

POPOV/CONSTABLE: (*Brightly.*) Your Grace, may I offer a helpful suggestion at this critical moment?

VERY IMPORTANT PERSON: *(Exasperated.)* Please do. This is mayhem!

POPOV/CONSTABLE: *(Unctuously.)* Clearly, the detainee is not qualified to represent himself in this complex case. I suspected as such, while I was guarding him closely, heh-heh. So in anticipation, I have taken the liberty of summoning a man of the cloth—

VERY IMPORTANT PERSON: Of the *what*?

POPOV/CONSTABLE: A man of "faith," sir, who can speak on the prisoner's behalf and infatuate, I mean, facilitate a hasty conclusion to this case.

VERY IMPORTANT PERSON: Where is this "man of faith," then? I can't take too much more of this.

POPOV/CONSTABLE: He's right outside in the waiting room—

SLINKOV: But Your Grace, my office hasn't been notified of this. The prisoner clearly states that he wanted to defend himself—

VERY IMPORTANT PERSON: I'll allow it. Anything to move this case along. (*To Popov/Constable.*) Send in this "man of the cloth."

Solemn, Russian chorus music plays. Enter Krechinsky, heavily cloaked in a monk's garb, his face hidden.

POPOV/CONSTABLE: May I present the most humble of monks, sir, who has left his lifetime sequestration of piety and prayer in the deepest depths of the Novodevichy Monastery to appear before you and serve the Tsar's court in the defense of the prisoner.

KRECHINSKY *(in disguise): (Bowing low.)* Your Esteemed, most Venerable, Grace.

SLINKOV: *(Suspiciously.)* May I advise Your Grace? This is highly irregular—

VERY IMPORTANT PERSON: *(To Krechinsky, in disguise.)* With all due respect, Father—or should I say Brother?—what would be your qualifications for representing the prisoner?

POPOV/CONSTABLE: Oh, well, that's easy, Your Grace, first of all, his name is ... er ... Brother Bogdan, isn't that right, Brother Bogdan?

Krechinsky nods.

POPOV/CONSTABLE: Second, he is known throughout the monastery and beyond for his knowledge of the sacred and secular law. He holds a law degree from, from, from Novodevichy University—

SLINKOV: Novodevichy University? Objection! Never heard of it!

POPOV/CONSTABLE: *(Quickly.)* And no wonder, that's because it's a *secret* university of the law—

SLINKOV: *(Incredulous.)* A "secret" law school?

POPOV/CONSTABLE: Yes, buried so deep in the cataracts—I mean the catacombs— of the Novodevichy Monastery that no one can find it.

SLINKOV: Why?

POPOV/CONSTABLE: Er, well, that's because, well, because it's available to its resident monks only. It's a highly competitive law school, you know. In fact, the standards are so high, they've only had one graduate!

SLINKOV: *(Dryly.)* And that's Brother Bogdan?

POPOV/CONSTABLE: *(Emboldened.)* Right! Third—and most important—in addition to being a devout man of faith and of the law, our esteemed Brother Bogdan possesses the most extraordinary qualification of all, known only to a chosen few …

VERY IMPORTANT PERSON: *(Suspiciously.)* And that would be…?

POPOV/CONSTABLE: But first, the Court must be sworn to secrecy.

VERY IMPORTANT PERSON: *(Impatiently.)* All right, all right, we swear, now what is it?

POPOV/CONSTABLE: *(In a stage whisper.)* He is Rasputin's brother!

SLINKOV: He's *who*?

POPOV/CONSTABLE: Yes, indeed, Rasputin's brother! None other than!

There are murmurings amongst those on stage. Krechinsky maintains his disguise; his true identity is still unknown to Nelkin, Muromsky, Lydia, and Atuyeva.

SLINKOV: Objection, Your Grace—this beggars disbelief!

VERY IMPORTANT PERSON: Beggar *you*! I'm fed up with this mayhem—

POPOV/CONSTABLE: So as you see, Your Grace, Brother Bogdan is eminently qualified. After all, he's a mystic—like all good lawyers!

SLINKOV: Your Grace, allow me to research Brother Bogdan's credentials—

VERY IMPORTANT PERSON: *(Sharply.)* Never mind, State Councilor, I am satisfied. If Grigory Rasputin is good enough for the Imperial Tsar, then his brother, Bogdan, is good enough for me.

MUROMSKY: But, Your Grace, I don't know this man, or rather, this monk!

NELKIN: May I advise my friend, Your Grace?

VERY IMPORTANT PERSON: If you must—and who are you again?

NELKIN: Vladimir Dmitrevich Nelkin: a close family friend, and Lydia Petrovna's faithful servant, unto death.

VERY IMPORTANT PERSON: I'll allow it.

Troika

NELKIN: (*To Muromsky.*) Grigory Rasputin is Tsar's closest advisor. He's a mystic, a healer, and a holy man with great spiritual powers. The Tsarina has invited him to live in the Winter Palace, with hopes that he'll cure the young Tsarevich of hemophilia.

POPOV/CONSTABLE: (*Frightened.*) Omigod! Is that catching?

VERY IMPORTANT PERSON: That will be all, Constable!

NELKIN: Indeed, it's said that Rasputin is succeeding with the cure. So we must give Brother Bogdan a chance—it's our only hope!

ATUYEVA: Please, Your Grace …

VERY IMPORTANT PERSON: Well? What does the prisoner say?

MUROMSKY: I'll agree to anything to save our Lidochka!

VERY IMPORTANT PERSON: Proceed then, Brother Bogdan.

KRECHINSKY *(in disguise)*: Ahem. My brethren and sistren …

Popov/Constable applauds.

SLINKOV: Order in the Court!

KRECHINSKY *(in disguise)*: May it please Your Grace that I, a lowly monk, have ascended from the depths of the catacombs, where I have spent my humble life in service to the Lord and the law—

POPOV/CONSTABLE: "Lord and law"—that's catchy!

SLINKOV: Order!

VERY IMPORTANT PERSON: (*Glaring at Popov.*) Constable Klop?

POPOV/CONSTABLE: Apologies, Your Grace, just trying to improve my vocabulary. In service to the Tsar—

KRECHINSKY *(in disguise)*: (*Surreptitiously smacks Popov.*) As I was saying, Your Grace, I live a life of piety and seclusion, but when I heard of the sufferings of Pyotr Andreyevich, a landowner of the noblest reputation, a valiant soldier in the Tsar's army who suffered a head wound at Borodino—

POPOV/CONSTABLE: (*Helpfully.*) I thought it was a stomach wound.

KRECHINSKY *(in disguise)*: (*Surreptitiously smacks Popov.*)—when I heard of the sufferings of Pyotr Andreyevich, I thought: "This is my calling, to help those in distress." As you may have heard, I am known to have mystical powers, like my brother. Let's say it runs in the family.

POPOV/CONSTABLE: Amen.

Krechinsky surreptitiously kicks Popov.

KRECHINSKY *(in disguise)*: As such, I feel the deepest of Russian Orthodox empathy for Pyotr Andreyevich. And for the sufferings of his daughter, a damsel of the purest purity whom I feel, somehow, that I know intimately—

VERY IMPORTANT PERSON: "Intimately"? But surely, Brother Bogdan, you are a chaste servant of God—

KRECHINSKY: Oops—I meant "spiritually," of course, Your Grace. Like Constable Klop here *(he surreptitiously pinches Popov),* I have lapses in my vocabulary, owing to a childhood ailment that left me speechless for a brief period of time. Recovery is going well, though.

VERY IMPORTANT PERSON: Carry on, then.

KRECHINSKY *(in disguise)*: So when Constable Klop, knowing of my true identity, reached out to me, how could I refuse? It's God's will!

POPOV/CONSTABLE: Amen! *(Stops, cringes, anticipating another blow.)*

KRECHINSKY *(in disguise)*: And so, Your Grace, I am here to review the case and represent this noble nobleman.

VERY IMPORTANT PERSON: Proceed—*briefly*, Brother Bogdan, if you will …

Slinkov reluctantly hands Krechinsky the papers.

KRECHINSKY *(in disguise)*: Ahem. As I understand it, the case against Pyotr Andreyevich involves—

MUROMSKY: —the theft of my daughter's diamond brooch by that criminal Krechinsky.

KRECHINSKY *(in disguise)*: Ah, yes, so I'm told, but *was* Krechinsky a criminal, really and truly?

MUROMSKY: *(In tears.)* He promised to marry my daughter, to give me a grandson, to sit by my side through my waning years—

KRECHINSKY *(in disguise)*: What happened?

NELKIN: I'll tell you what happened, Brother. He robbed Lydia of her diamond brooch and her honor—

SLINKOV: (*Groaning.*) Not that story again!

NELKIN: —and now the villain has escaped and gone into hiding. He's allowing his fiancé's father to take the rap. The coward!

KRECHINSKY *(in disguise)*: *(Paces, attorney fashion.)* Villainous acts indeed, if, as you say, they were committed. On the other hand, could this not have been a terrible misunderstanding?

NELKIN: (*Scornfully.*) How so?

KRECHINSKY *(in disguise)*: Could this be a mix-up contrived by the so-called Ivan Ivanich Popov, the dim-witted aide of Krechinsky?

POPOV/CONSTABLE: (*Aside, to Krechinsky.*) Boss! What's going on?

VERY IMPORTANT PERSON: Can we find this so-called Popov and have him cross-examined?

POPOV/CONSTABLE: (*Hastily.*) Er, as a matter of fact, Your Eminence, I hear he's fled Moscow and is lost in Siberia at the moment. I hear he might have frozen, actually, you know how cold it is there—sometimes it's fifty degrees below, sixty below even, and once it went down as low as one hundred below—and of course there are the bears—

KRECHINSKY: (*With a black look to Popov.*) As I was saying, could it be possible that Krechinsky has changed his ways, and, out of a sense of sincere contrition, wants to do right by this poor suffering family? Indeed, as a qualified mystic, I'm feeling those vibrations right now, the vibrations of repentance. Krechinsky is truly sorry if he inadvertently caused Pyotr Andreyevich any harm, and he's making it right at this very moment!

VERY IMPORTANT PERSON: Vibrations are not allowed in this court, Brother. Let's stick to the facts—that is, if you can sort them out—

KRECHINSKY *(in disguise)*: Very well, Your Grace, and now we come to the allegation of bribery.

VERY IMPORTANT PERSON: A most grave one—

KRECHINSKY: You say that Pyotr Andreyevich has presented a bribe to this court?

VERY IMPORTANT PERSON: (*Hastily.*) Yes, Brother Bogdan. I'm about to order my clerks to inventory it carefully and keep it locked away in the safe—

KRECHINSKY (*in disguise*): May I inspect this so-called bribe, Your Grace?

257

SLINKOV: (*Alarmed.*) No, wait—

VERY IMPORTANT PERSON: (*Ignoring Slinkov.*) I have it right here ...

MUROMSKY: As far as the bribe is concerned, Your Grace, my family was only acting on specific instructions of one of your own—

SLINKOV: (*Interrupting.*) Your Grace —

KRECHINSKY (*in disguise*): Allow me, Your Grace, to offer my humble services to remove this tainted parcel from your Court and keep it safe in the deepest depths of the Novodevichy Monastery, where it shall be counted by the most devout of monks under my strictest supervision, and locked away—

POPOV/CONSTABLE: Right next to the jelly!

VERY IMPORTANT PERSON: Good plan, Brother Bogdan.

SLINKOV: (*Warning.*) Don't do this, Your Grace—

VERY IMPORTANT PERSON: Enough! Brother Bogdan, I entrust you with the safekeeping of this parcel— (*hands it to Krechinsky.*)

KRECHINSKY (*in disguise*): (*Bowing low.*) Your Grace.

POPOV/CONSTABLE: (*Aside.*) Heh-heh.

KRECHINSKY *(in disguise)*: And now for my summary, Your Grace: humbly, yet passionately, I beseech you to look into your Russian Orthodox heart, as well as into your learned books of the law, and pardon us, sinners that we are—Krechinsky, Muromsky, all of us!

SLINKOV: Your Grace, this is an outrage to the law. (*In a lower voice.*) And don't forget our quota of convictions!

KRECHINSKY *(in disguise)*: Moreover, your Grace, I ask you to clear the venerable name of Muromsky of any further blemish, and wash away the stain on his innocent daughter's name, a delicate, unplucked flower (*aside*) ... unfortunately—

VERY IMPORTANT PERSON: Brother Bogdan, you are the essence of piety, humanity, and wisdom. *(Lifts a giant gavel.)* Case dismissed!

Overjoyed, tearful, Lydia and Atuyeva embrace Muromsky.

LYDIA: Papa!

MUROMSKY: My angel!

ATUYEVA: But what about Lydia's jewels, the ones we gave to the court—

NELKIN: *(Kneeling before Lydia.) You* are my jewel, Lydia. My life, my faith, my salvation! Will you be my bride?

LYDIA: Dearest Vladimir Dmitrevich, of course!

VERY IMPORTANT PERSON: Brother Bogdan will keep the parcel safe in his catacombs until further notice.

KRECHINSKY *(in disguise)*: Thank you, Your Grace. Meanwhile, as a qualified man of the cloth, permit me to perform the sacred rite of marriage, right here, on the spot! *(To audience.)* Then I'm out of here!

VERY IMPORTANT PERSON: Permission granted!

POPOV/CONSTABLE: Goody! I love weddings.

LYDIA: My dearest!

NELKIN: My darling!

ATUYEVA: My niece!

MUROMSKY: My treasure!

POPOV/CONSTABLE: *(Producing a flask.)* My vodka!

ARTEMISA: *(Rushing in.)* My goodness!

All freeze.

POPOV/CONSTABLE: *(Seeing Artemisa, horrified.)* Ahhhh!

ARTEMISA: *(Seeing Popov.)* There you are, Ivan Ivanich, you wily fellow, I've found you at last!

Krechinsky hides behind Popov.

VERY IMPORTANT PERSON: Now what?

ARTEMISA: Where is it? (*To Popov.*) I know you have it, you little devil!

SLINKOV: Who is this person?!

POPOV/CONSTABLE: Never saw her before in my life!

ARTEMISA: *(To Slinkov.)* Ooooh ... what a nice robe...!

SLINKOV: This is a court of law, Madame. I must ask you to state your business or leave at once!

ARTEMISA: *(To Popov.)* I've been looking for you everywhere, golubchik!

POPOV/CONSTABLE: *(Feigning ignorance.)* Who, me?

ARTEMISA: Yes, of course, you! So? Where is it?

POPOV/CONSTABLE: Where is *what*?

ARTEMISA: You're cute, you really are ... my diamond brooch, silly! Your master never gave it back to me!

KRECHINSKY (*in disguise*): (*To audience.*) Uh-oh.

POPOV/CONSTABLE: I don't know what you're talking about! Who *is* this woman!

Enter Constable Klop in disarray, dressed as Popov.

CONSTABLE: There he is! (*Points at Popov.*) Arrest that man!

POPOV/CONSTABLE: (*In a high, squeaky voice.*) Help!

VERY IMPORTANT PERSON: Who are *you*?

CONSTABLE: Your Grace, allow me to explain! (*Pointing at Popov.*) That constable is not a constable!

Popov faints.

VERY IMPORTANT PERSON: Will someone please tell me what's going on!

ARTEMISA: *(Sidling up to the Very Important Person.)* Haven't I seen you somewhere before?

Very Important Person starts coughing loudly.

ARTEMISA: Ooooh, now I remember. That was quite a night we had together at Maksim's, wasn't it, golubchik?

VERY IMPORTANT PERSON: Water! (*Choking.*) Someone *do* something!

KRECHINSKY: Good idea, Your Grace! "Dearly beloved, we are gathered here—"

CONSTABLE KLOP: What's going on here?

KRECHINSKY: Let us put our own selfish cares aside, and unite this loving couple in holy matrimony. You ordained it yourself, Your Grace. Why should they wait any longer? They have suffered enough!

POPOV: (*Revived.*) Amen.

ATUYEVA: Are you qualified to perform a wedding ceremony, Brother Bogdan?

KRECHINSKY: Oh yes, it's one of the skills we learned in the Novodevichy secret law school. We're highly experienced. All those monks, you know —

LYDIA: Oh yes, please do! Now that Papa is free, Vladimir Dmitrevich and I have peace of mind ... *(She blushes, looking at Nelkin lovingly.)*

NELKIN: *(Relieved.)* Proceed, Brother Bogdan—

KRECHINSKY *(in disguise)*: Amen. Dearly beloved, we are gathered together to unite this woman and this man in holy matrimony, blah, blah, blah ... you may present the rings!

LYDIA: But we gave them away to the court—

NELKIN: Never mind, my darling, your eyes are our diamonds—

KRECHINSKY: Blah, blah, blah, I now pronounce you "man and wife"! (*All applaud.*) You may kiss the bride, Vladimir Dmitrevich, but first, if you don't mind—

Krechinsky grabs Lydia and locks her in a passionate, prolonged kiss. All gasp.

NELKIN: Wait a minute, Your Grace!(*Approaches Krechinsky.*) I think I know what's going on here! (*Tears off Krechinsky's hood, revealing his face.*)

MUROMSKY: Omigod!

NELKIN: I knew it!

LYDIA: Mikhail Vasilyevich!

ATUYEVA: Krechinsky!

ARTEMISA: (*Overjoyed.*) Golubchik!

CONSTABLE: The prisoner!

VERY IMPORTANT PERSON: Who?

Popov faints again. Everyone freezes.

KRECHINSKY: *(As himself, to the audience.)* Time to wrap up, don't you think? (*Shouts out.*) Never fear, Ivan Ivanich. I am Rasputin's Brother ... I have the gift of prophesy; I see into the future!

NELKIN: What future? You won't have a future, you scoundrel!

KRECHINSKY: Good point. In that case ... to the happy couple! Congratulations!

(Krechinsky rips open the parcel and showers Lydia and Nelkin with jewels and rubles. Stuffs his own pockets too. Pandemonium ensues.)

KRECHINSKY: (*To audience.*) It would be rude not to give a wedding present!

POPOV: (*Revived again.*) But what about my share, boss?

SLINKOV: And mine!

CONSTABLE: And mine!

KRECHINSKY: *(To the audience.)* Share and share alike, my fellow Russians. That's the future, in case you didn't know! (*Waving to the audience.*) *Do svidanya!*[11] (*He runs offstage.*)

Mayhem. Merry wedding music plays. Lydia and Nelkin embrace. Muromsky embraces them. Popov and Slinkov try to stuff bills into their pockets. Atuyeva retrieves the brooch from the melee, crying: "Your brooch, Lydia! Here it is!" The constable tries to take his uniform jacket off of Popov. The Very Important Person surreptitiously swigs vodka, while Artemisa tries to sit on his lap. General pandemonium.

End of Play

Cast Breakdown

Here is a cast breakdown for a company of 10 (7 men, 3 women), doubling in the following roles:

Act One/Act Two

Actor #1 Krechinsky

Actor #2 Muromsky

Actor #3 Popov

Actor #4 Nelkin

Actor #5 Tishka, Blekh, Constable Klop, Petitioner

Actor #6 Shebnev, Policeman, Slinkov

Actor #7 Fyodor, The Very Important Person

Actress #1 Lydia, Petitioner

Actress #2 Atuyeva, Petitioner

Actress #3 Artemisa, Petitioner

Author's note: This play was inspired by the long-lost trilogy of Aleksandr Sukhovo-Kobylin, written in the mid-nineteenth century (see introduction for brief literary history). I've taken a historical liberty in setting the play in the 1850s and referring to Rasputin as a contemporary of Krechinsky, although Rasputin actually came on the scene fifty years later. Rasputin's residency with Tsar Nicholas II began in 1907, and it is not known if he had a brother.

Pronunciations:

(Note: Accented syllable is highlighted in boldface **CAPS**)

Lydia Petrovna/Lidochka
    (**LI**-di-ya Pye-**TROV**-na) (**LEE**-doch-ka)
Pyotr Andreyevich Muromsky
    (**PYO**-tr An-**DRE**-ye-vich Moo-**ROM**-skee)
Anna Andreyevna Atuyeva
    (**A**-na An-**DRE**-yev-na A-**TOO**-yev-a)
Tishka
    (**TEESH**-ka)
Mikhail Vasilyevich Krechinsky
    (Mi-khay-**EEL** Va-**SEE**-lye-vich Kre-**CHIN**-sky)
Fyodor
    (**FYO**-dor)
Vladimir Dmitrevich Nelkin
    (**VLA**-di-mir **DMEE**-tre-vich **NYEL**-kin)
Ivan Ivanich Popov
    (Ee-**VAN** Ee-**VA**-nich **PO**-pov)
Timofey Timofeyevich Shebnev
    (Ti-mo-**FEY** Ti-mo-**FE**-ye-vich **SHEB**-nev)
Blekh
    (pronounced as spelled)
Kandid Kastorovich Slinkov
    (Kan-**DEED** Kas-**TO**-ro-vich **SLINK**-ov)
Klop
    (pronounced as spelled)

Other Names/Words:

madame (ma-**DAM**) (French)
golubchik (ga-**LOOB**-chik)
Michel (Mee-**SHEL**) (French for Mikhail)
Novodevichy (No-vo-**DYE**-vi-chi)
Papa (Russian) (**PA**-pa)
Slavyansky Bazaar (Sla-**VYAN**-skee Ba-**ZAR**)
do svidanya (Do svee-**DAH**-nya)
za vashe zdorovya (za **VA**-she zda-**RO**-vya)

Notes:

(1) Atuyeva is trying to teach Tishka to address her as "*Madame.*" In Russia, the educated upper classes spoke French at home. It was a sign of social status.

(2) *"comme il faut"* (French): "as it should be"

(3) *"sacre bleu!"* (French): an antiquated expression of surprise or dismay (e. g., "goodness gracious!")

(4) *"Parlez à ma tante et Papa"* (French): "Speak to my aunt and father"

(5) *"golubchik"* (Russian): "sweetheart," "sweetie"

(6) *"confiture"* (French): preserves, jam

(7) *"Cherie, alongez vous"* (French): "My dear, make yourself comfortable"

(8) *"tout de suite"* (French): "right away"

(9) *"Attention, s'il vous plaît"* (French): "Attention, please"

(10) "*za vashe zdorovye*" (Russian toast): "to your good health"

(11) "*do svidanya*" (Russian): "good-bye"

SUMMERFOLK

A REIMAGINING OF MAKSIM GORKY'S PLAY

Troika

Cast of Characters

Sergey Vasilyevich Kirov, an attorney
Larissa Mikhailovna (Lara), his wife
Katerina Vasilyevna, his sister, a poet
Vladimir Mikhailovich, Larissa's brother
Kirill Akimovich Dudakov, a doctor
Olga Aleksandrovna Dudakov, his wife
Yuri Andreyevich Belkin, Kirill's uncle, a wealthy industrialist
Pavel Nikolayevich Rudin, a young writer and pianist
Maksim Alekseyevich Peshkov, a.k.a. Maksim Gorky, a playwright
Vera Fyodorovna Kommisarzhevskaya, an actress
Pusto, a watchman
Stepka, a young workman
Sasha, a young servant
A little peasant girl
Beggars

Time: 1904
Place: A dacha in the Russian countryside, late June.

ACT ONE

Scene One

Setting: A summer community outside Moscow, somewhere in the Russian countryside. It's July 1904. The action takes place in front of the dacha of Sergey Vasilyevich Kirov and his wife, Lara. There is a broad veranda (with wicker chairs and a small table); on it, stage left, is a window, through which is Sergey's study. On the veranda, stage right, there are more windows, through which a combined living room/dining room area is visible, with a grand piano to one side. There are steps from the veranda leading downstage to a terrace, and stage right, a lawn. Offstage down left, there are woods. Offstage down right, there is a path to the river. During preset, on the terrace, there is a pile of trunks, suitcases, and assorted luggage. While the house lights are up and the audience is settling in, Pusto and Sasha are unlocking the front door and unshuttering windows, setting up furniture, sweeping the veranda, opening the house for summer residents, carrying in the luggage. Someone is practicing Chopin inside the house.

When the preset is completed, house lights are lowered and stage lights begin to rise as Sergey takes a seat at his desk in his study. Lara enters through the house onto the veranda. She takes a seat in one of the wicker chairs and reads a manuscript. It's late afternoon; long rays coming from downstage cast a glow on the scene.

SERGEY: *(Looking out of window from inside the study.)* Who's there?

LARA: (*Sitting in a rocking chair, looking downstage.*) No one ...

SERGEY: Is that you, Lara?

LARA: Only me ...

SERGEY: Oh ... What are you doing?

LARA: Nothing much ...

SERGEY: I thought you were reading ...

LARA: Trying to ...

SERGEY: What?

LARA: Pavel's new essay ... I keep nodding off, though.

SERGEY: No wonder! What's it about, this time?

LARA: "Historicism."

SERGEY: What?

LARA: "Historicism" ...

SERGEY: Never heard of it.

LARA: What does it mean?

SERGEY: Beats me.

LARA: Oh well, I'll sort it out.

SERGEY: Good God ... how can you read that stuff? It's too hot.

LARA: We have to keep up, don't we?

SERGEY: Everyone around here is writing something. If we did nothing but read each other's work, we'd never have time to do our own. Still there?

LARA: Mmmmm ...

SERGEY: Stuffy in here, can't seem to open the window. It's stuck.

LARA: Ring for Sasha; she'll help you.

SERGEY: (*Rings.*) These new dachas—they've got the latest in electric bells, but the sashes stick and the floorboards creak. (*He rings again.*)

Sasha appears on the porch.

SASHA: You rang, mistress?

LARA: Sergey Vasilyevich needs some help with that window. (*Kindly.*) And Sasha, please don't call me mistress, remember? I'm Larissa Mikhailovna.

SASHA: Yes, mistress. (*Sasha curtsies, enters the study and opens the window. Sergey comes out onto the veranda.*)

SERGEY: (*Mimicking Sasha..*) Yes, mistress. (*He goes to kiss Lara. She withdraws.*)

LARA: Sergey ... (*Indicating "not in front of the servants."*)

What time is it?

SERGEY: After six. Where's Vlad?

LARA: Not here yet.

SERGEY: He's been slacking off, your brother. Gotten lazy.

LARA: Tea?

SERGEY: No, I'm going over to the Suslovs to play chess.

LARA: Sasha, run over to the doctor's, please, and ask Olga Aleksandrovna if she'll come for tea.

SASHA: (*Curtseying, as Sergey mouths her response along with her*): Yes, mistress. (*Runs off.*)

LARA: (*Smiling in spite of herself.*) It's 1904, Sergey, no more "masters"; no more serfs, remember?

SERGEY: Seriously, darling, you'll have a word with your brother, won't you? Tactfully, of course ... and please get the message across.

LARA: About?

SERGEY: You know, tell him he should take his responsibilities more seriously.

LARA: (*Sighing.*) I know, Sergey, I know, you gave my brother a job, and we're grateful—

SERGEY: That's not the point. Never mind—let's not have any tension between us, darling, all right?

Lara avoids his embrace again. Goes back to reading.

SERGEY: You seem so distant these days, Lara—why? Have I done something?

LARA: Aren't you supposed to be going to the Suslovs?

SERGEY: You don't mind, do you? I haven't played chess in a while. And I haven't kissed you in a while, either—

LARA: Why don't we postpone this cross-examination, Sergey. It's too hot. Anyway, it doesn't matter.

SERGEY: Forgive me, Lara. You're beautiful, you're kind, you're ... perfect! If something were wrong where I'm concerned, you'd tell me, wouldn't you? Of course you would.

LARA: I'm fine.

SERGEY: You know ... you need to find something to do, my darling Lara. All you do is read, read, read. You're overdoing it! Too much of a good thing, you know.

LARA: Remember that when you're drinking wine tonight at the Suslovs.

SERGEY: (*Laughs.*) Fair enough! Still, a dose of Pavel's drivel can be more dangerous than Merlot, my dear! Never mind; a real writer is descending on us any day now, isn't that right?

LARA: (*Feigning disinterest.*) If you say so.

SERGEY: Wonder how he's changed since last summer

... all that notoriety, you know. The great Maksim Gorky, arrested for subversion, expelled from the Academy.... They even say he's a personal friend of Lenin. In Moscow and St. Petersburg, they talk of nothing else—it's probably gone to his head. And a successful opening at the Moscow Art Theatre? He's a real celebrity now!

VLAD: (*Coming out of the house.*) My cue! (*Bows.*) Please, hold your applause—

SERGEY: There you are, Vlad, I've been waiting hours for you. Where have you been?

VLAD: Have you missed me, boss? How gratifying. Don't worry, I'll make it up to you! (*To Lara.*) Hello, sister dear. (*Kisses her.*)

LARA: Hello, Vlad.

SERGEY: I was on my way to the Suslovs, but I've got something for you to take care of. Wait here a moment—

Sergey enters the house into his study, and rummages at his desk.

VLAD: Any chance of getting a spot of tea?

Sasha enters from the house..

SASHA: The doctor's wife is coming, mistress. Do you want the samovar now?

LARA: Yes, thank you.

VLAD: *Tout de suite!* (*To Sasha*) Have pity on a poor pauper, fair maiden. Some tea, and something to eat—

SASHA: We've got some cutlets—

VLAD: Yum. And what about those cherry tarts? Bring anything you've got in the kitchen—I'm famished! I haven't eaten all day!

Sasha exits. Sergey enters from study and hands Vlad a pile of papers.

SERGEY: I'm counting on you, Vlad. A completed copy by nine tomorrow morning, yes?

VLAD: *Absolument, mon patron*! And may I wish *you* a sleepless night too!

SERGEY: Oh, and tomorrow, if you have the time, go down to the village and file a request with the district council. The roof on the local school is about to collapse— the head mistress asked me to requisition some funds on their behalf to repair it. It's pro bono work, I know, but we have to show some community support here for the locals, we summerfolk—

VLAD: I'll try, but with all you've given me, I'm drowning in paperwork —

SERGEY: Do your best, Vlad, there's a good fellow. Well then, I'm off to the Suslovs. (*Kisses Lara.*) Good-bye, my darling. (*Sergey exits.*)

VLAD: Where's Sasha with the tea?

LARA: Be patient—she's young.

VLAD: I'm starving!

LARA: Where have you been all day?

VLAD: Preparing papers for your dear husband from nine to three, and then running errands for him from three to seven—

LARA: (*Sighing.*) A lawyer's clerk ...Vlad ... it's so beneath you!

VLAD: I thought I was supposed to be grateful.

LARA: You should be!

VLAD: (*Teasing.*) I know, we must aspire to the highest of heights. But you know the old saying about the chimney sweep: He may have climbed higher than the rest of us, but do you really want to spend your life on a roof?

LARA: Why don't you look for more meaningful work, Vlad? You had such promise when we were young.

VLAD: Objection, exalted sibling! I serve a noble cause—the protection of private property from the teeming masses. And don't tell lies, sister dear, I never had any promise and we both know it. Ask your father—and mine too, by coincidence.

LARA: Be serious, just once.

Sasha enters again from the house, carrying a tray.

VLAD: Ah, nourishment for the laborers! (*Picks up a cutlet, puts it on a plate, starts to eat ravenously.*) Merci, kind damsel!

Sasha curtseys, confused, and rushes out. Lara paces up and down the room.

VLAD: All right, so tell me—what's wrong?

LARA: I don't know. I feel trapped. Everything around me seems so meaningless, so foolish … like you, for instance!

VLAD: "There once was a young man from Tiflis/Who contracted a slight case of syphilis—"

LARA: (*Laughing.*) Give it up, Vlad, you're no poet.

VLAD: Ah, but I have the soul of one, unlike our Katerina. She may write brilliant verse, but it's all Russian doom and gloom and I can't bear to listen to it! That's why *I'm* trying my hand at it, to lighten things up around here—

Pusto passes by with a lantern, whistling.

LARA: There goes Pusto.

VLAD: How very nineteenth century … what do we need a watchman for? This isn't an estate of the landed gentry, just a tract of summer dachas for the bourgeoisie—like thee and me. See? There's a decent rhyme.

LARA: Some of the homeless pass through every once in a

while, on the way to town. The association pays for Pusto's wages—

VLAD: "The association"? Sounds very communal. Any Marxist cells around?

LARA: Enough, Vlad!

VLAD: "Very well," he said, "and sadly fell silent." Have it your way—but you're not being a compassionate sister, are you? After all, I have to keep my mouth shut, all day every day, making copies of this grievance and that libel. No wonder my tongue runs wild in the evening.

LARA: I want to go away somewhere, live among simple people who do useful work, instead of all this talking and writing …

VLAD: Ah, "simple people," you sound Tolstoyan, like your Pavel—

LARA: Come on, Vlad—

VLAD: Anyway, you won't go, will you? You'll just sit on the veranda and read, and your life won't amount to anything, either—

LARA: Vlad, please—

VLAD: We're a pair, aren't we?

Sasha enters with the samovar.

LARA: Put it over here on the table, please, Sasha.

Sasha curtsies, sets up the samovar, and exits.

VLAD: I hear Peshkov is arriving tomorrow ... or Gorky—whatever he's calling himself this week.

LARA: Yes.

VLAD: Maksim Gorky—the great man of letters. Where's he staying?

LARA: With Uncle Yuri again.

VLAD: Didn't like his last novel. Too long, too dark. And heavy, like that latest hit play of his.

LARA: I remember the day I first saw him. I was a student, and he came to our school to give a speech. It was after his first arrest—he'd just been released, and already he was so famous! Imagine our excitement! He strode out onto the stage, his head held high, and when he turned to look out at us, I could feel his eyes burn right through me. What a thrill! He spoke with such passion—of Russia, of the misery of the workers—and all the while, he kept brushing that thick mane of hair out of those fiery eyes. I stood there, awestruck, thinking that someone like that could exist on earth, someone with such intensity and clarity. Eight years ago, that was ... then when he showed up at Uncle Yuri's dacha last summer, I couldn't believe it! I was terrified.

VLAD: Are we talking romantic fantasy here? Beware, sister. All writers are masters of seduction, or so I'm told—

LARA: Don't be vulgar, Vlad.

VLAD: Lighten up, Lara!

LARA: I've been counting the days till he arrives, and dreading it too. In case you haven't noticed, Vlad, I'm not very happy.

VLAD: *Quelle coincidence*! I'm not happy either. I don't belong anywhere, and I don't know what lies ahead.

LARA: So why then why are you always—

VLAD: Playing the fool? I don't want anyone to see how unhappy I am.

Katerina appears.

KATERINA: What a lovely evening!

VLAD: Enter Cassandra!

LARA: Don't start, Vlad. Hello, Katerina. Have you been walking in the woods?

VLAD: Where else? She's a birdwatcher, as well as a poet and clairvoyant. Did you spot any?

KATERINA: Birds? Oh yes, two whippoorwills and a spotted owl. They're rare at this time of year, you know—

VLAD: Do tell.

KATERINA: At sunset, the rays filter through the firs, and catch the wings of the birds in flight. A flash of silver and gold, here and there … magical …

VLAD: See? I told you. She opens her mouth, and presto—poetry. Why can't you write about nature, Cassandra, instead of dreary Mother Russia?

KATERINA: Poetry can't match nature's eloquence.

VLAD: So tell me, Cassandra, can you do a birdcall? I'll bet you can.

LARA: Vlad—

VLAD: What's the matter? Just being chatty. Come on, Cassandra, just one—

LARA: I apologize for my brother—

VLAD: Why? I'm trying to be helpful here. What do we need a night watchman for? Cassandra here can organize the owls and lead them in song—or do they hoot?

LARA: Come have some tea with us—Vlad won't say another word, I promise—

VLAD: Word of honor, Cassandra. Just give me one birdcall, and I'll shut up—

KATERINA: Tea would be nice. At this time of evening, your veranda is the loveliest spot to be—

VLAD: "—or not to be"—

LARA: Vlad!

KATERINA: Never mind, Lara, I'm used to it. It's his way of getting attention. Believe it or not, I think your brother likes me.

VLAD: Like you? I worship you—*and* your prodigious talent! If only your poetry were—how shall I put it—better?

KATERINA: Why don't *you* try writing poetry, Vlad?

LARA: You wouldn't want to hear it. *(They laugh.)*

Pusto passes and knocks on his lantern with his nightstick.

KATERINA: There goes Pusto ...

VLAD: There goes Pusto ...

KATERINA: I ran into Pavel in the woods—

VLAD: Lurking around, hoping to catch a glimpse of my sister ...

LARA: I know, it's sad.

VLAD: If only I were taller, and you were shorter, Cassandra, I'd lurk around you too!

LARA: Vlad—

KATERINA: Let him lurk all he likes, Lara, don't worry—

LARA: Anyway, he has no time to lurk. *(To Vlad.)* What did you promise Sergey? Tomorrow morning, nine sharp, remember?

VLAD: "Rebuked, he beat a swift retreat/With only one small bite to eat." (*Grabs another cutlet, exits into Sergey's study, sits at desk.*)

LARA: Don't start in with me about Pavel, Katerina.

KATERINA: I wasn't going to—

LARA: I never encouraged him, I promise you—

KATERINA: I know …

LARA: I did spend time with him, it's true—but only to help him overcome his depression. When I saw where it was leading, I tried to discourage him.

KATERINA: Did you talk to him about it?

LARA: What's there to say? Anyway, depression in Russia is as common as the head cold—

Sasha enters with more refreshments, places them on the table, and exits.

KATERINA: (*Smiling.*) He's like a lost lamb, don't you think?

LARA: *(Earnestly.)* Who, Pavel? But he's a Tolstoyan.

VLAD: (*Through the study window.*) For whatever that's worth …

KATERINA: He knows how to talk, but he doesn't know how to love, poor soul.

VLAD: (*Through the study window.*) Ironic, isn't it? Given all that Tolstoyan talk about love—

LARA: (*Calling out*) You'll never get your work done, Vlad, if you keep it up—

KATERINA: Now your brother, in contrast to Pavel, may have a case of too much passion—

VLAD: (*Entering onto the veranda again, feigning formality.*) Having examined all the evidence related to this case, it is my regret to inform you, Your Honor, that this humble servant finds himself unable to complete the onerous assignment of copying the depositions by nine tomorrow morning.

LARA: I'll help you later. Drink your tea.

VLAD: Sister mine! I love you dearly. And meanwhile, Cassandra (*with a full mouth*), love thy neighbor as thyself, and have a cherry tart!

LARA: Speaking of neighbors, where's Olga?

VLAD: Don't worry, the "Duds" are arriving soon ... or one of them, at least.

LARA: Don't call them that, Vlad, it's vulgar, their name is Dudakov—

VLAD: But "dud" suits them, don't you think? Anyway, it's short, and it saves time saying it—

KATERINA: What's that on your back, Vlad?

VLAD: (*Startled, mouth full.*) Huh?

KATERINA: That hump?

VLAD: What hump?

KATERINA: *Your* hump—you know, the deformity that all twisted people have.

VLAD: (*Catching on.*) Oops—does it show? I'll wear a jacket next time.

KATERINA: Vulgarity is like a hump. Whereas stupidity is more like a limp. Do you limp too, Vlad?

VLAD: Your poetry limps.

KATERINA: And yours —

LARA: All right, enough, you two—

VLAD: I'm deeply offended. Just for that, I'll have another cherry tart. You know, to feed my hump. (*Bursts out laughing. Katerina joins him.*)

Olga rushes in, breathless.

OLGA: Here I am, at last! (*Kisses Lara, then Katerina.*) Good evening, Vlad. What's so funny? Are you laughing at me? Is it something I'm wearing? (*Vlad and Katerina continue to laugh.*)

VLAD: Greetings, mother hen. How's the brood?

LARA: Sit down, Olga. Tea?

OLGA: Yes, please.

LARA: What kept you so long?

OLGA: Don't ask, I'm a wreck. *(Listens.)* Wait—did you hear?

They are silent. The sounds of owls, and the watchman's whistle.

OLGA: *(Anxiously.)* Who's out there?

KATERINA: It's only a night owl. From the sound of it, a horned one. They're lovely—have you ever seen one?

VLAD: Katerina will do you a bird call, if you ask her nicely. She specializes in the nocturnal hawk—

LARA: Don't listen to him, Olga.

OLGA: The woods are creepy. I always feel there's something lurking there.

VLAD: The only thing lurking would be Pavel.

OLGA: Still, Lara?

LARA: I can't help it.

VLAD: Don't like the country much, do you, Olga?

OLGA: I can't get used to it. But the children love it. Anyway, I would have come earlier, but you know how it is.

Nadya wouldn't go to bed—she's coming down with whatever Volka has. Did I tell you? He spiked another fever. And after supper, while I was bathing Sonya, Misha ran off into the woods and came back all dirty and hungry, so I had to feed and bathe him all over again. Meanwhile, Kirill came home in a foul mood, and he didn't even say hello. I don't know what to do. The new nanny is driving me mad. She boiled the baby bottles and they all broke!

LARA: (*Smiling.*) Poor thing! You must be done in.

VLAD: (*To Katerina.*) The trials and tribs of the Duds!

KATERINA: Nice try, but no rhyme.

OLGA: (*Hurt.*) I know, you find it all very funny, and boring too, and who can blame you? But you don't understand. "Children ..." It's like an alarm that goes off in my brain: "Chil-dren, Chil-dren!" Of course you wouldn't know, Lara.

LARA: Forgive me, dear—it's just that, well, we all know you exaggerate a bit.

OLGA: (*Agitated.*) How can you say that? And who are you to judge me? You have no idea what a burden it is to raise children, what a huge responsibility it is. And then, when they grow up, they'll turn around and ask you: "What do I do with my life *now*?"

VLAD: Why worry about it? They'll figure it out for themselves.

OLGA: No they won't. They'll ask terrifying questions for

which no one has any answers, let alone a mother. And they'll blame you for everything. How hard it is to be a woman!

VLAD: Try being a human, then—

LARA: (*To Vlad.*) Out!

VLAD: I'm being banished. Workers of the world, retreat!

Vlad grabs another cherry tart and takes it into Sergey's study. He sits at the desk.
Entering from the back of the house, unseen, Pavel appears in the living room and starts to play Chopin, softly.

KATERINA: (*Looking up at the sky.*) The Milky Way … path to the unknown …

VLAD: (*Through the window.*) Cassandra, brightest star in the summer firmament—

KATERINA: That's Cassiopeia, actually. (*To Lara.*) Your admirer is playing Chopin in the drawing room. He wants your attention, Lara.

OLGA: How did he get in?

LARA: The back way, probably. Sasha has a soft heart.

Lara paces restlessly.

OLGA: I've made everyone depressed, haven't I? Just like that old night owl. Enough then. Why are you pacing, Lara? Fed up with me again?

LARA: Not at all, Olga. I feel bad for you, that's all.

OLGA: Frankly, I can't stand myself, either. I'm pathetic. My soul is shriveling up, I look like one of those little old pug dogs, you know, the nasty ones with the sagging faces that no one likes and that try to bite you when you're not looking.

VLAD: *(Through the window.)* Ask Cassandra to read one of her dreary poems about Mother Russia. That'll cheer you up.

OLGA: Is anything the matter, Lara? Sergey mentioned to Kirill that you've not been yourself. Is that true? You seem distracted. What's wrong?

LARA: Nothing, I—

OLGA: Kirill says that Gorky, the writer, is arriving tomorrow.

LARA: I know. What of it?

OLGA: *(In a low voice.)* You remember ... that business last summer?

LARA: Please let's not speak of it. I'm sorry I even mentioned it to you, Olga—I should remember that you can't keep a confidence. More tea?

OLGA: Yes, please.

LARA: It's gone cold. Vlad—please ring the bell for Sasha. We need to reheat the samovar. Poor Pavel, he's inside playing, waiting to be invited out here.

VLAD: (*Teasing.*) Not in my job description ... but just this once. (*Rings for Sasha, calls out to Pavel.*) It's all right, Pavel, you can come out now; you've earned your tea.

Pavel appears at the door.

PAVEL: May I, Larissa Mikhailovna? I can come back another time, or not—whatever you say.

LARA: Come, sit, Pavel.

Sasha appears.

LARA: Please reheat the tea for Pavel Nikolayevich.

PAVEL: Your husband is at Suslov's now, they're drinking cognac, and I have the impression they've lost count. Uncle Yuri is on his way over—

VLAD: All that lurking in the woods —it pays off, doesn't it, old man? You see everyone's comings and going.

PAVEL: Only trying to be helpful, Vladimir Mikhailovich. I'm grateful to be among you, I'm grateful to be alive. Life is an art, you know—the art of finding beauty in everyone and everything around you, from the quotidian to the sublime.

VLAD: Cassandra finds beauty in everything. After all, she's a poet, isn't that right, Cassandra?

KATERINA: It's the beauty of silence I love most of all.

OLGA: Lots of luck with this group! Anyway, I'm glad Uncle Yuri is coming over. He lifts my spirits.

VLAD: Why does everyone call him Uncle Yuri? Whose uncle is he, anyway? I've forgotten.

OLGA: Kirill's, silly. He's very rich, and the one who developed the land we're on and built all these dachas, so in a sense he's our landlord—

VLAD: The Lord is my landlord—

LARA: Enough, Vlad—

OLGA: He's always happy, the life of the party, they call him. He says he's leaving all his money to us—well, to Kirill, that is—but Kirill says he'll give it away to build a new clinic here in the village. Won't someone try to discourage him, please? After all, we need it!

PAVEL: What a noble gesture! I admire your husband.

OLGA: Sorry I brought it up.

PAVEL: I apologize, Larissa Mikhailovna. Perhaps we're overwhelming you, descending on you so late in the evening.

VLAD: Nonsense. The party's just getting started.

LARA: It's fine; we're in the country. Anyone's welcome anytime. Where is Kirill, Olga?

OLGA: Still at the clinic. He never stops working. All week at the clinic in town, and all weekend at the clinic here.

And I never stop taking care of the children.

PAVEL: That's noble, too. The purity of the child's mind is sacred, to be protected at all cost. How else can they learn to love?

LARA: We were just talking about that with Olga.

VLAD: I told her not to worry. They'll find out how hard life is all by themselves.

PAVEL: Olga's right. Keep them innocent and pure as long as you can. Show a child the face of truth too early and you'll destroy him.

VLAD: So it's better to destroy a child bit by bit, to avoid your own responsibility?

PAVEL: Don't twist my words, Vladimir Mikhailovich, please. I'm only saying that it's cruel to strip life of the poetry that adorns it. You're a poet, Katerina Vasilyevna, wouldn't you say so?

KATERINA: The answer is all around us, in the summer evening.

VLAD: Well, that helps!

PAVEL: We must keep dressing life in beautiful garments, not stripping it bare.

VLAD: Somebody tell me: What are we talking about?

PAVEL: About innocence, about the right to deceive oneself. Life is raw and ugly. The longer we live, the more we see the banality, vulgarity and injustice that surrounds us, and the more we long for beauty, purity and clarity. Allow us, I beg of you, to avert our eyes from that which would destroy us. All we want is to live in the moment, in peace and love and tolerance—

VLAD: I'm lost.

PAVEL: (*To Lara.*) Forgive me—I see that I've offended you. Was it something I said?

LARA: It's not that—

PAVEL: What then? Tell me, I beg you—

LARA: (*Trying to be serious.*) It's just that ... last summer you were saying something quite different, as well as the summer before ... (*She starts to laugh; Vlad joins in.*)

PAVEL: (*Defensively.*) A man can change. And so can his ideas.

KATERINA: Devilish little things, these Russian ideas of ours, flitting around our heads like bats.

LARA: (*With compassion.*) You're frightened, Pavel; you want to hide from life—

OLGA: Good lord! When I hear a passionate philosophical discussion like this one, it makes me anxious. I start to itch ... brrrr ... I'd better go home now. I do love coming here, Lara, I always learn something. If only we could be kinder to one another.

LARA: Stay, Olga! Don't worry, if they need you, they'll come get you.

OLGA: All right, I'll stay just a little longer.

Pavel retreats to the drawing room and plays more Chopin.

LARA: How strange our lives are ... we talk, and talk, and talk! We grasp at new theories, one after the other, and no sooner do we embrace them than we discard them, like old, unwanted clothes that have gone out of fashion. As for a clear vision, or a single-minded purpose—we don't seem to have that, either.

VLAD: What about me? I have a purpose. I want to be a poet.

LARA: I'm talking about all of us. Our lives are empty and boring.

OLGA: Not yours, Katerina. Kirill tells me you've written some new poems for the children in the local school—about the future of Russia. I want to hear them. Everyone, please, persuade her to read!

PAVEL: (*From inside.*) Oh yes, please, I love her poems—

VLAD: You'd be the only one.

KATERINA: They're nothing, really.

LARA: I apologize for my brother, yet again—

OLGA: Never mind. Clearly, he's been deeply wounded in his past—

LARA: He has been, actually. He had to live with our father, who was always drunk, and who beat him—

OLGA: (*Embarrassed.*) My sincere apologies, Lara—I had no idea. Had I known, I certainly wouldn't have said—

VLAD: The well of human kindness has run dry around here, it seems—

OLGA: Come on, let's get the others. Lara, ask Sasha to go fetch Sergey from the Suslovs. Tell him that Katerina is reading her new poems. And stop by my dacha and see if Kirill is back yet. What could be keeping him?

Enter Uncle Yuri as Sasha exits.

YURI: May I intrude on this happy little tea party? Good evening, lovely Larissa Mikhailovna! (*He kisses her hand.*)

LARA: You're most welcome, Yuri Andreyevich.

OLGA: (*Clapping her hands.*) Hello, Uncle, perfect timing!

YURI: Always, my dear— timing is everything in life! Good evening, Katerina Vasilyevna—(*kisses her hand*)

LARA: Do sit down, Yuri Andreyevich.

YURI: Please! "Uncle Yuri" to all. Vladimir Mikhailovich— you've lost weight!

VLAD: Lack of food, I imagine?

YURI: And Pavel Nikolayevich—you're looking saintly, as always. What new idea do you have for us this summer?

PAVEL: Oh. I—

OLGA: We have a surprise for you, Uncle—Katerina is going to read her poetry. I don't want Kirill to miss it.

YURI: He won't. I just saw him coming through the woods. He's right behind me—

OLGA: I think he was working late at the clinic again.

Enter Kirill.

YURI: Ah, here's the good doctor himself! He'll tell you.

KIRILL: Greetings, all, pardon me for barging in like this—

LARA: Delighted, Kirill Akimovich. Won't you have some tea?

KIRILL: No thanks, I'm too tired.

OLGA: Where have you been, Kirill? I've left the children with the new nanny, I wouldn't have come, but Lara sent for me, and, anyway, I'd had it up to here with Volka running off in the woods looking for you—

KIRILL: Slow down, Olga, we'll go home now, if you like.

LARA: Stay a moment, Kirill, you look tired—

KIRILL: Well, I *am* tired. They're complaining over at the hospital that we're feeding the patients too much. The fools! What are supposed to do, starve them?

OLGA: Must you get so worked up over trivialities, Kirill? You should be used to it by now.

KIRILL: My entire life is composed of trivialities. Does that mean I should like it? Economize, they tell me at the clinic in town. How can you economize in the practice of medicine? Not feed the patients? Hold back on their prescriptions? All right, I'll economize. As a result, the sick will get sicker while the hospital balances its budget. I shouldn't even be working in the summertime, but I do, because—

OLGA: Because what? Because you have a large family? Isn't that what you want to say? I've heard it all before, of course, but do you have to say it here in front of all these people, and humiliate me? You rude and tactless man! *(She throws on her shawl and exits.)*

VLAD: Here we go again.

LARA: Olga! Please!

YURI: Pavel? A little Chopin, perhaps?

Pavel enters the living room and starts playing.

KIRILL: Of course, I didn't mean it. Forgive me, Lara—I didn't know what I was saying. It's been a long day. I'll run after her and bring her back. *(He exits.)*

VLAD: Exit the Duds.

LARA: I'm worried about Kirill. He doesn't look healthy—

VLAD: —that's not a good sign, especially if you're a doctor. And he's so absent-minded, too. He puts his spoon in his glasses case and stirs his tea with the little hammer he carries around in his medical bag. Who knows what you'll end up with if he prescribes you something?

Enter Sergey.

SERGEY: Look who I met coming down the path from our dacha. They were on their way home, but I insisted—

Olga (composed) and Kirill (embarrassed) return.

LARA: Of course, and thank you.

YURI: Ah, Sergey Vasilyevich, we're all here now—

OLGA: (*Attempting to save face.*) I came back to hear Katerina recite her poetry.

YURI: A poetry reading? Now?

VLAD: Apparently it's unavoidable—

LARA: Sit, Vlad, you promised—

VLAD: "And the crowd fell silent. The poetess walked among them, her diaphanous robes shimmering in the evening light—"

YURI: I'm afraid that we'll have to postpone our reading, ladies and gentlemen—

LARA: Why, Yuri Andreyevich?

YURI: Because ... I have a little surprise for you! (*Claps his hands.*) Sasha?

LARA: Why are you calling for Sasha?

YURI: It appears that our distinguished guest has unexpectedly arrived a day early—

KIRILL: What guest?

YURI: He's coming up behind me, on the path.

SERGEY: You don't mean—

Enter Maksim. He wears a peasant shirt, in contrast to the others, who are in Western clothes.

YURI: Ladies and gentlemen, I give you the voice of the Russian people, the great Maksim Gorky!—

MAKSIM: Greetings, everyone.

Surprise, delight, everyone applauds and exclaims greetings. Only Lara is silent, stunned.

YURI: —and his leading lady, Vera Fyodorovna, all the way from the Marinsky Theatre in St. Petersburg!

Enter Vera, wearing a stylish dress and a summer hat. Lara, shaken, moves aside.

SERGEY: What a surprise, indeed. Greetings, Maksim Alekseyevich, and you are most welcome too, Vera Fyodorovna.

MAKSIM: So kind of you to invite us.

VERA: What a warm welcome! Thank you! Greetings, all.

YURI: And here's another surprise: they're going to put on a play! Imagine: Maksim Gorky's newest play, just for us! They've already contacted the local company to work with them, so it's all arranged.

General ooohs and aahs. Lara remains frozen, speechless.

YURI: Listen, everyone: I've sneaked some champagne through the back door, they're setting it up, as we speak.

SASHA: (*At the door.*) All ready in the dining room, mistress!

VERA: Please, don't make a fuss on our account—

YURI: Why not! *(General laughter.)*

SERGEY: (*Quickly stepping in, clapping his hands..*) Inside, everyone! Let's give our eminent writer a proper greeting.

All walk up the veranda steps, laughing, talking excitedly, and exit into the house. They gather inside, and can be seen through the window, standing around the dining room table, to the sound of champagne corks popping. Lara remains outside, alone. Sergey appears at the door.

SERGEY: Can you believe it, darling? The one and only Vera Fyodorovna, all the way from St. Petersburg! Aren't you coming inside? Lara?

LARA: In a minute …

SERGEY: A new play by Maksim Gorky—imagine! Come on, darling!

Sergey exits into the house. The sound of a rousing toast— "Za vashe zdorovye!"— clinking of glasses, cheers and applause from inside. Lara stands there, motionless, moonlight on her face.

Lights. Piano music.

Scene Two

The following week. A bright afternoon. Upstage off right of the dacha a platform is being built for the performance of the play. Part of it can be visible onstage. Pusto is repairing a cane chair and assembling benches for the performance. A whistle is heard offstage. Pusto whistles back. Enter Stepka downstage left from the woods, a rake and bag slung over his shoulder.

PUSTO: Everything all right?

STEPKA: So far.

PUSTO: Where have you been?

STEPKA: Cleaning up the litter in the woods.

PUSTO: What a mess.

STEPKA: You said it, Uncle. Everywhere. Paper, cigar butts, you name it.

PUSTO: That's summerfolk.

STEPKA: They live like pigs. Leave their droppings all over the place.

PUSTO: Come on, help me—

STEPKA: They said I'm needed at the dacha next door, to repair the fence.

PUSTO: Says who?

STEPKA: The people renting it this summer. I forget their name. As if I care.

PUSTO: Suslov, the engineer.

STEPKA: New people, eh?

PUSTO: New ... old ... they're all the same.

STEPKA: You said it.

PUSTO: Anyway, that'll have to wait. We've got a platform to build—

STEPKA: Who for?

PUSTO: For the fancy folk from Petersburg, that's who. Master's orders.

Pusto stops to light his pipe. Stepka lights a cigarette.

STEPKA: *(With disdain.)* City folk.

PUSTO: Summerfolk is more like it. Now they're here, now they're gone ... like a rash on your face.

Offstage, guitar music is heard.

STEPKA: And now it's music.... What do they need *that* for?

PUSTO: For the play, I guess.

STEPKA: Why are they putting on a play?

PUSTO: That's what these people do. They put on plays.

STEPKA: They do whatever they damn please.

PUSTO: Why shouldn't they? They got all the time and money in the world.

STEPKA: Never seen a play, Pusto. Have you?

PUSTO: Seen one, you seen 'em all.

STEPKA: So ... what do they do, then?

PUSTO: Who?

STEPKA: You know, the people who are putting on the play.

PUSTO: I dunno. First, they get all dressed up in clothes that aren't theirs. Then they stand on a platform and say whatever they like. They run around, wave their arms, bother one another, make things up ... sometimes they shout. There's good types, there's bad types ... oh, yeah, and they bow at the end. Don't ask me why.

STEPKA: That's it?

PUSTO: That's it.

STEPKA: So where does the music come in?

PUSTO: To make it less boring. When they've run out of things to say, they sing.

STEPKA: Who's the new one walking around, so full of himself?

PUSTO: That's the fellow who wrote the play. He bosses everyone around—they call it "directing."

STEPKA: Why is he wearing a peasant shirt?

PUSTO: Beats me. Enough questions, Stepka—get to work.

STEPKA: *(Bitterly.)* Who do they think they are, anyway?

PUSTO: They're our employers, that's who. (*Voices are heard in the distance.*) I think the master is coming.

STEPKA: Don't call him that.

PUSTO: Well, he *is* the master, fool. He owns the place!

STEPKA: So? A man is a man.

PUSTO: Stop talking nonsense, Stepka. Come on, help me set these benches up. Make like you're working hard.

STEPKA: I am.

PUSTO: Not hard enough. You'll never come to anything in this life unless you work.

STEPKA: You mean that I should work like a dog all my life so I can end up like you?

PUSTO: What's wrong with that? Anyway, who else do you think will give you work? You have no schooling, your father was driven out of the village for stealing … you have to accept your lot.

STEPKA: No, I don't. Why should I?

PUSTO: Because you'll come to no good like your father—

STEPKA: *(Heatedly.)* And what chance did *he* ever have? He was a woodcutter who hurt his leg and couldn't support his family. No wonder he stole! He never had a fancy job like you, Uncle, working for the summerfolk.

PUSTO: Maybe one day, if you work hard, you'll get your chance, like your sister—

STEPKA: What do you mean?

PUSTO: She works in the village school, doesn't she?

STEPKA: *(Bitterly.)* That's right, as a cleaner. She scrubs the floors after the children go home. Is that what you call "a chance"? Getting down on your hands and knees?

PUSTO: Maybe some of that learning will rub off on her, being at the school.

STEPKA: Anyway, it's too late for me.

PUSTO: You have to *want* a better life, Stepka—

STEPKA: Better life? Hah. Like you said, no one will hire me, because of my father. I'm marked—

PUSTO: Look sharp—here they come!

Pusto returns to repairing the cane chair. Stepka starts moving benches. Enter Kirill and Yuri.

YURI: Carry on, Pusto—don't let us distract you. Important work …

PUSTO: Yes, Your Honor.

YURI: And don't call me "Your Honor," Pusto—my name is Yuri Andreyevich.

PUSTO: I'll try to remember, sir.

KIRILL: Sit for a moment, Uncle. On this bench here. *(They sit, while Pusto and Stepka continue to work upstage, setting up the theatre platform and chairs.)*

YURI: I'm fine—but what about you? You look all worn out. Be like me, Kirill, and don't take life so seriously!

KIRILL: That's hard, if you're a doctor.

YURI: All right, good point, but still, you work too hard. As I was saying, I keep trying to retire, but I can't help it. The money keeps flowing in. Last year, some Germans showed up in town with a ton of capital. Built a factory, started putting out stuff, trebled my output and undercut my prices. So I say to myself: if you can't fight 'em, join 'em.

KIRILL: You sold your factory?

YURI: For a pretty pile of rubles, too. I kept the house in town, of course, and I rattle around in it all by myself. Got nothing to do but count my money. Ha-ha! To tell you the truth, I'm bored. And lonely. Once I sold everything, I felt like an orphan. And I haven't a clue what to do with myself. Look at these two hands—useless now. They just hang off my arms like lumps of clay.

Lara appears on the terrace, pacing, lost in thought.

YURI: There's Sergey's wife. Beautiful woman ... if only I were twenty years younger ...

KIRILL: Why don't you marry again?

YURI: Once was enough—although to tell you the truth, it was more than once, as you may or may not know. Before your aunt Avdotya died, may her soul rest in peace, there were a number of them.

KIRILL: Wives? Really? I didn't know that.

YURI: The one before her died, and the one before that ran away. I had two little girls—did you know that? They died in infancy ... and there was a little boy who drowned—

KIRILL: We don't have to talk about it—

YURI: It's all right. Anyway, your uncle has had quite a success with women. It's easy to steal a wife in this country. Do you know why?

KIRILL: Why?

YURI: Because Russians make lousy husbands! (*Laughs.*) There was a time when I would roll into town, brush the country dirt off my trousers, spot a beauty passing by, and swoop her up just like that! Ah well.

KIRILL: What about the future?

YURI: Who knows? I like building things, developing things. Like this place. I built these dachas, and now I come down here, live among the *literati,* learn a new idea or two, or twenty-two.... (*Laughs.*) Anyway, I've got the biggest dacha in the area—

KIRILL: And rightly so—

YURI: —so I can invite the latest genius of Russian art, or music, or theatre to spend the summer here— like your Gorky, for example—

Vlad sticks his head out of Sergey's study.

VLAD: Lara, where are you?

LARA: Out here.

VLAD: Want company?

LARA: No thanks, Vlad, I'm fine. *(Exits into the house.)*

YURI: There's her brother.

KIRILL: The class clown.

VLAD: (*Appearing on the veranda.*) And you're the class capitalist, Yuri Andreyevich.

YURI: They say you're quite bright, but not very serious about your work. In fact, do you work at all?

VLAD: Not as hard as you do, Yuri Andreyevich. It takes a lot of effort to squeeze the blood out of your fellow man.

YURI: (*Laughs..*) It's tough when you're young, I know. Your heart hasn't hardened yet. But give it a few years, and you'll find out that the sooner you get a tight grip around your neighbor's neck, the better.

VLAD: I'll remember that. Meanwhile, I bow to the voice of experience. (*Bows and exits.*)

YURI: (*Laughs.*) Glad he enjoyed our little repartee. Let him feel he got the better of me.

KIRILL: Believe me, he needs it.

YURI: Ah, here come the lawyer and the writer. Had a nice stroll, gentlemen?
Enter Sergey and Maksim.

SERGEY: Just came back from a swim! Maksim's been hard at work on the rewrites—

MAKSIM: So Sergey lured me away.

SERGEY: God, the water's cold!

MAKSIM: No, it's just right! Bracing, refreshing! I've been toiling at rehearsals, or hunched over my writing desk all week.

YURI: Come on, Kirill—let's you and I go for a boat ride. Maybe I'll drown and you'll get your inheritance before you're even dry.

KIRILL: Only for a quick one, Uncle, I've got to stop by at the clinic—

YURI: Your patients can wait!

SERGEY: And tonight is the performance, don't forget!

YURI: How could we? They've been talking of nothing else, every dacha is buzzing in anticipation

Pusto and Stepka pass by, carrying some benches.

SERGEY: Hey, Pusto, Yuri Andreyevich wants to go boating. Can you get the boats and the oars, in case they want them too?

PUSTO: Yes, sir, only I'm afraid I won't finish these benches for the performance tonight.

SERGEY: Don't worry, Pusto; you'll have time! Who's this here?

PUSTO: Oh, that's my sister's boy, Stepka, from the village. He needed some work, so I let him help out. The master said I could—

YURI: —and he's doing a fine job. Aren't you, Stepka?

PUSTO: (*To Stepka, under his breath.*) Say thank you, fool!

STEPKA: Thank you ... *(Pusto nudges him.)* ... er ... master—

YURI: Carry on, then—don't let us keep you.

SERGEY: And don't forget those oars!

STEPKA: *(Under his breath.)* I hope they all drown.

SERGEY: Oh, I almost forgot. Pusto, when you're through with the boats, be sure to set up that croquet game on the lawn here, you know, in case Vera Fyodorovna wants to play.

MAKSIM: How thoughtful. She'd enjoy that, Yuri Andreyevich.

STEPKA: *(Under his breath.)* What'll they want next?

PUSTO: Stepka—go down to the river and prepare those boats. I'll set up the croquet, and meet you there. *(In a low voice.)* And keep your mouth shut! *(To Sergey.)* Right away, master.

YURI: Yuri Andreyevich, my good man, don't forget!

MAKSIM: *(To Yuri and Kirill.)* Enjoy the river—it's lovely.

Yuri and Kirill exit downstage right, followed by Stepka. Pusto exits upstage right. Katerina appears on the verandah.

SERGEY: Oh, Katerina, have you seen Lara?

KATERINA: No, I haven't—not all day.

SERGEY: Can you ask Sasha to bring some beer for our playwright?

Katerina goes in the house.

SERGEY: So glad you've taken the time off this morning, Maksim. How are rehearsals?

MAKSIM: As well as can be expected, Sergey. We're using a local company—Vera knows some of their actors, but not all. I was worried at first—after all, it's her theatre in St. Petersburg that's producing the play, and it's for her sake that I'm staging this reading, to give her an opportunity to hear it in front of an audience.

SERGEY: Have you rewritten much since you've been down here?

MAKSIM: Some ... craft the character to the actor, and the actor to the character, as they say in the theatre.

SERGEY: But your plays are always about the lower classes. Not many of them around here, I'm afraid.

MAKSIM: Enough.... Anyway, this new play is quite a departure from the previous ones.

SERGEY: In what way?

MAKSIM: (*With a cryptic smile.*) You'll see ...

Two beggars enter from the woods (downstage left), chanting: "Alms, alms for the poor. For the love of our Lord Jesus Christ, for the memory of your beloveds, alms, alms ...," etc.

SERGEY: Pusto! Where are you? Pusto!

Pusto appears from upstage right.

PUSTO: Yes, sir?

SERGEY: Get these people out of here!

MAKSIM: It's all right, Sergey—

SERGEY: No, it's not—Pusto, take care of this, would you, please!

PUSTO: (*To the beggars.*) Move on, move on ... Go! Get out of here! (*He shoos them off downstage left.*) *(To*

Sergey.) Sorry, Your Honor. *(Exits upstage right.)*

SERGEY: My apologies, Maksim.

MAKSIM: For what? This is Russia ... and this is what we're trying to change!

SERGEY: My wife has read all your stories, you know—

MAKSIM: I remember, from last summer.

SERGEY: She says *Chelkash* is her favorite.

MAKSIM: My novella? Yes, we talked about it, I recall.

SERGEY: We saw *The Lower Depths* at the Art Theatre—devastating! "The most wrenching depiction of poverty and suffering ever seen on the Russian stage"—that's what the critics wrote.

MAKSIM: Thank you. But you can't repeat yourself in the theatre, Sergey Vasilyevich. Art must lead the way—it must lead the artist himself, to take risks, to be bold. I was possessed when writing *The Lower Depths*. In retrospect, I think my focus was too narrow. But now, with this new play, I think I've discovered a new way for Russians to see how they truly live.

SERGEY: Sounds intriguing!

Vlad is listening through the window. Lara appears far downstage right, and is listening through the trees. Both are unseen to Sergey and Maksim.

MAKSIM: You'll see. A writer cannot keep silent. Believe me, I've tried to. I came down here last summer at Yuri Andreyevich's invitation, to rest. I needed to gather my thoughts. After all that business two years ago—

SERGEY: I know, your opposition to the regime, and the arrests. You were heroic—

MAKSIM: It's not a question of heroism, Sergey Vasilyevich. It's a question of necessity! An unseen but mighty hand is whipping me on with a scorching lash. Russia needs me—and I must speak out. We live in a country where the writer—and only the writer—can be the spokesman for truth. That is our obligation. Then, and only then, will there be change. Russia is a sleeping mammoth. I want to give her a good shove—to awaken her from her torpor, her complacency ...

SERGEY: After that crisis, you know, when you exposed government censorship and the Tsar expelled you from the Academy, what could you do? You needed to regroup. Chekhov was supportive, he resigned in protest, he championed you—

MAKSIM: Yes, he did. I'm fond of Anton Pavlovich, he's been good to me. And I admire his plays. But he didn't go far enough. Today, I walk down the streets, here, or in the capital, I see the people's faces, they're apathetic, indifferent, uncaring. They need someone to shake them. This Russia of ours is such an absurd, clumsy country, and the mantle falls on the shoulders of the writer to make them see it, if they're averting their eyes—

SERGEY: Do it, then!

MAKSIM: But I get frustrated. At the Art Theatre, they said: "Why don't you write something beautiful? Why must it always be raw and ugly?" So I showed them my new work this spring—

SERGEY: And?

MAKSIM: (*Agitated.*) The notes that Nemirovich sent me were insulting. I can't be inhibited by artistic control. I must be free. So I took my new play to Vera in Petersburg, and now she'll put in on in the fall at her new theatre; that is, if she's pleased with it tonight.

SERGEY: Of course she'll be pleased.

MAKSIM: Her reputation is on the line too.

(Lara disappears; Vlad continues with his work in the study.)

SERGEY: You know you'll have a supportive audience here, Maksim. Speaking of which, spend a little time with Lara, would you—

MAKSIM: Your wife? She's been avoiding me since I arrived. I've hardly said a word to her.

SERGEY: She's so self-effacing, my Lara. She knows you're busy, and doesn't want to get in your way.

MAKSIM: Do I detect a note of sadness?

SERGEY: No, it's just … show her some attention, talk to her, cheer her up.

MAKSIM: *(Perceptively.)* Does she need cheering up?

SERGEY: I ... don't know, really. I only know that when you walk into a room, she comes alive. She admires you.

MAKSIM: Happy to oblige, Sergey Vasilyevich—but not today. I shouldn't have even taken time for our swim. I've got to finish some touches on Act Three, rewrite a speech, and then talk to the actors.

Enter Sasha, with beer. Katerina follows behind.

SERGEY: Please give the beer to our guest, Sasha. There's a good girl.

MAKSIM: (*Looks at Sasha with appreciation.*) Thank you, dear.

Sasha curtseys and exits. Katerina takes her place at the table and starts playing solitaire.

MAKSIM: Oh, by the way, Vera's told me that one of the actors isn't feeling well. Is that funny brother-in-law of yours around?

SERGEY: Who, Vlad? He's certainly a clown off-stage—

MAKSIM: I remember him well from last year, he'd be perfect as a stand-in.

SERGEY: Vlad? Are you in there?

Vlad comes out of study.

VLAD: Yes, boss? What can I do for you? Good day, Maksim

Alekseyevich …

SERGEY: Would you be able to help our distinguished artist-in-residence?

VLAD: In any way I can.

MAKSIM: We may be losing an actor, could you stand in for him tonight? You'd be on book, of course—

VLAD: *On* book? You mean I have to perform *on* a book…?

SERGEY: I told you, Maksim—he's a funny fellow—

MAKSIM: He's ideal—

VLAD: At your artistic service, sir! When can I see the script?

MAKSIM: I'm just putting on the finishing touches, and we'll have a run-through in an hour or two. If Oleg—that's the actor—isn't feeling up to it, the part is yours!

VLAD: *(Elated.)* My calling! I've found my calling!

SERGEY: Another hour of work, Vlad, and then you're free—

A poor young village girl in shabby dress enters from downstage left.

GIRL: Please, sir, have seen Volodya?

SERGEY: Who?

GIRL: A little boy—this high, with fair hair. Has he passed this way?

SERGEY: (*Impatiently.*) No, he hasn't.

GIRL: (*Distressed.*) Oh no! He's my brother. I'm supposed to be watching him.

VLAD: Sorry, dearie.

WOMAN: Oh no, oh no ... (*Calls out, while exiting downstage left.*) Volodya! Where are you? Volodya!

SERGEY: *(Irritated.)* Where is Pusto? I told him to keep these people away of here. They should not be wandering the woods.

MAKSIM: I'd best be going. Thank you, er—

VLAD: Vladimir Mikhailovich, at your service! (*Elated.*) My new career! (*Exits into the study.*)

MAKSIM: Good-bye for now, Sergey, and thank you.

SERGEY: The show must go on, after all.

MAKSIM: Let's hope so. *(Exits.)*

SERGEY: Katerina—I didn't even know you were there!

KATERINA: Yes, brother dear, here I am.

SERGEY: I'll finish up with Vlad. Maybe he'll get some work done, after all.

Sergey goes into the study. Through the window, Pavel can be seen sneaking through the living room/dining room. He sits at the piano and plays Chopin.

KATERINA: Ah, right on cue. That must mean Lara's nearby. *(Still playing solitaire, without turning around.)* You can come out, Lara, wherever you are, the coast is clear.

Lara enters slowly from down right, embarrassed. She sits on the steps of the veranda.

LARA: It's hotter than yesterday.

KATERINA: Where have you been?

LARA: Out walking. There are so many people around. I keep seeing the actors from the company. Do they have to walk down by the river? There's no place to find any peace.

KATERINA: You've been avoiding them all week, Lara.

LARA: Who? The actors?

KATERINA: Maksim Gorky and Vera, our guests, our distinguished artists in residence ... they'll think you don't want them here.

LARA: I don't want to disturb them. They're so involved in rehearsals.

KATERINA: Is it that? Or is it because he's changed so much.

LARA: Who?

KATERINA: Your writer.

LARA: He's not "my" writer, Katerina. He's Russia's writer now.

KATERINA: Yes, fame has certainly gone to his head, hasn't it?

Enter Olga from upstage right. Sits on bench.

OLGA: It's too, too hot. I'm done in. (*To Katerina and Lara.*) What are you looking at me like that for?

LARA: Is something the matter, Olga? You look upset.

OLGA: How could I not be? Kirill got home from the clinic, took one look at the children and me, and left again.

LARA: Shall I ring Sasha for some tea?

OLGA: He's running away from us, that's what he's doing. I know, he's overworked, he needs some peace and quiet. But what about me? I'm exhausted, too. And there's nothing I can do. It enrages me! I've sacrificed everything for him—my looks, my strength, everything.

LARA: You do like complaining, don't you, Olga? Just a little—

OLGA: And what if I do? I should tell him that I'm leaving, and taking the children with me—

LARA: All you need is a little time apart. Go take a trip, I'll find you the money.

OLGA: I owe you so much already!

LARA: Never mind, Olga—

OLGA: I hate myself because I can't survive without you! Do you think it's easy for me to keep taking your husband's money? I take it because I know that one day Uncle will die and Kirill will inherit and I can pay you back—

LARA: You mustn't say such things—

OLGA: But then Kirill will give all the money to the clinic, and I'll be more in your debt! (*Sobs.*) I hate you!

LARA: Olga!

OLGA: That's right, I hate you! You're so calm and composed, you have no passion! Anyway, let's be honest. In their heart of hearts, benefactors despise their charity cases, don't they? So much for your magnanimity, Lara. You're a hypocrite—and so is Pavel, that driveling Tolstoyan, or whatever he is, who preaches love for "the noble Russian peasants." I hate the Russian peasants! They're dirty and narrow-minded—

KATERINA: Olga!

OLGA: I hate you, Lara, and I hate your husband. He's weak, and he's afraid of you—

LARA: I think that you should stop, Olga—

OLGA: He's got a lot of money, your Sergey, but he's not completely honest in all his business dealings—

LARA: What are you implying?

OLGA: I'm not implying, I'm only saying what I've heard from others. No wonder you worked it out not to have children—

LARA: Stop! Don't say any more—

OLGA: Kirill's a doctor, he knows what you're doing, he says—

LARA: (*Holding her hands over her ears.*) I don't want to hear it!

OLGA: Anyway, we all saw how you gazed at that playwright all last summer. Everyone saw—Kirill, me, Katerina—

KATERINA: Olga, enough!

LARA: You've been like a sister, Olga. I know how difficult things have been for you. And I've confided in you about myself too. Now I regret it, deeply—

OLGA: *(Dismayed.)* Forgive me, I don't know what I'm saying—

LARA: I've always been here for you, to listen to you, comfort you, give you tea. Together we dreamed of what life could be like—a new shining life—

OLGA: I'm ashamed.

LARA: *(Simply.)* You've hurt me, Olga. Go away.

OLGA: You mean ... forever?

LARA: Just go away.

Enter Yuri.

YURI: Ah, the lovely ladies—all ready for the performance?

An awkward silence.

YURI: What's happened? Olga? Larissa Mikhailovna? Somebody say something—

OLGA: Should I go now, Lara?

LARA: Yes. *(Olga exits quickly.)*

YURI: Forgive me. Clearly, I've come at an inopportune moment—

LARA: *(Regaining her composure.)* Will you be joining us this evening at the performance, Yuri Andreyevich?

YURI: I thought I might invite you for a stroll before, while everyone's preparing. It's clear to me that you don't belong here. Well? Am I right? *(Laughs.)*

LARA: *(In disbelief.)* Forgive me, but that's a rather bold statement, isn't it!

329

YURI: (*Laughs.*) Come on! I'm old! I've seen it all!

LARA: That doesn't give you the right to interfere in my private affairs—

YURI: (*Good-humoredly.*) I didn't mean to interfere, my dear—I just thought that since you don't belong here, and neither do I, that I could—how do you say it—cut to the chase and offer my supports. I don't have the facility with words that all these writers around here have—

LARA: (*Sighing.*) Now it's my turn to apologize for being rude. I'm just not used to anyone speaking his mind. Ironic, isn't it?—since that's all anyone does around here. What I meant was ... I'm not used to hearing people speak the truth. There's a difference.

Enter Kirill, breathless.

KIRILL: Where's Olga? I've been looking for her everywhere.

KATERINA: She was just here ... I think she went for a stroll.

KIRILL: But who's home minding the children? My God! (*Rushes off.*)

KATERINA: (*Shrugs.*) Summertime ...

Enter Pavel.

LARA: Not now, Pavel—

PAVEL: Permit me, dear Larissa Mikhailovna, I couldn't

help overhearing what Olga Aleksandrovna said to you—

LARA: There are no secrets here, are there?

PAVEL: —and I am offended for you, dear lady. We must show kindness and mercy to one another, we must show love—

LARA: How can we, if we don't love ourselves? We complain, we whine, we fill the air with our cries, and meanwhile, what do we contribute to the world?

PAVEL: I play piano ... for you.

KATERINA: And so you do, Pavel. The world is sad. We need music.

LARA: But you also talk and write, talk and write, every summer a new idea that's out of date by the time the next summer comes along.

PAVEL: (*Blurts out.*) Then why do you admire that playwright?

LARA: What are you saying?

PAVEL: I saw your face, the night he arrived. So full of joy, and fear, and excitement. I wanted to—

LARA: That's enough, Pavel.

YURI: Maksim Gorky is a famous Russian writer. He's fashionable. So what? Nothing wrong with that.

PAVEL: Did you read Tolstoy's review of Gorky's play, *The Lower Depths*? He called it manipulative and untruthful.

LARA: Your Tolstoy is just jealous. Gorky is a brave and honest writer!

PAVEL: You think his ideas are new and true and strong and enduring, don't you? Only time and history will tell. Meanwhile, what has history ever taught us, anyway? Nothing. The only enduring truth is love—

KATERINA: —and music.

YURI: (*To Pavel.*) Maybe you and I should take that walk together, young man.

PAVEL: (*Imploring.*) Do you want me to take a walk too, Larissa Mikhailovna? I know I've offended you.

LARA: Do whatever you like.

PAVEL: (*Dejected.*) I've made a fool of myself. (*Rushes off the veranda into the woods, downstage left. Yuri tips his hat to the ladies and follows.*)

Enter Sergey from downstage right, carrying a fishing pole and some fish.

SERGEY: Our Tolstoyan's in a hurry, isn't he? Hello, darling! Just back from fishing. Look what I've caught—

LARA: I'm tired, Sergey. I think I'll go lie down before the performance.

SERGEY: Good idea, my dear. I'll hand the fish over to Sasha, then I'll finish up some work. (*He goes to kiss her. She is unresponsive.*) Go then, darling. Rest ... where's Vlad? He should be inside, working.

KATERINA: Don't worry, Lara, I'll supervise Sasha ...

Lara enters the house, followed by Katerina; Sergey enters the study. Vera and Vlad enter from the woods, downstage left, breathless, laughing.

VLAD: (*Excitedly.*) Surprise! You see? The path through the woods leads right to our dacha.

VERA: It's lovely. Absolutely lovely. I'd adore to go mushrooming one day—

VLAD: But not in that ravishing dress—omigod, what have I said? You know what I mean—(*Laughs in embarrassment.*)

VERA: (*Laughs along with him.*) Of course! You meant—

VLAD: —that the material is so exquisite, so delicate, that you'd want to wear something simpler. I'd be devastated if that precious fabric tore on my account. I'd never forgive myself—

VERA: Don't worry, I'll find something suitable. I love mushrooming—

VLAD: Then allow me to take you, Vera Fyodorovna, please! It would be an honor. I know where all those little devils are hiding.

VERA: I like pearl mushrooms, don't you? Delicious …

VLAD: I always marinate them in oil, put plenty of salt on them, steam them with a large dollop of sour cream, and then—

VERA: Sounds utterly delectable.

VLAD: I'm quite a cook— did you know that?

VERA: How impressive!

VLAD: Oh—and sometimes I find "hens of the woods"—

VERA: *(Puzzled.)* Hens? You mean there are chickens wandering around in there?

VLAD: *(Bursts into laughter.)* No, no, no, no, no—I'm talking about "hens-of-the-woods"—you know, they're a kind of wild mushroom, quite rare and delicate, but plentiful in these parts!

VERA: Oh, of course. Silly me. We theatre types don't get to the country enough, do we? *(Laughs; Vlad joins in.)*

They sit on a bench.

VLAD: Yes I'm a talented cook. And now, as fate will have it, I'm about to become an actor.

VERA: So kind of you to offer to stand in for Oleg—

VLAD: Though I'm a bit worried. I'll be reading the script for the very first time, you know. And I wouldn't want to compromise the words of Russia's greatest writer—

VERA: Not to worry. Maksim seems to think you're a natural. (*Looks around.*) Let's enjoy these lovely surroundings, shall we, before rehearsal? Thank you for showing me the river, too. It sparkles ...

VLAD: My pleasure, Vera Fyodorovna, my pleasure. I sense this will be life-changing opportunity for me.

VERA: Why? Does your life need changing, Vladimir Mikhailovich?

VLAD: If only you knew. I've had a hopeless life—at least so far. My mother toiled as a laundress, my father toiled as a drunk—and a cook too, when he was sober. He forced me to work in his kitchens. Then when he left to work on the railroads, he put me into trade school. Well, that didn't stick, so the next year it was agricultural school, then art school, then business school. By the time I turned seventeen, I had such an anathema for schooling that I found it impossible to learn anything, not even how to play cards or smoke a pipe.

VERA: How sad.

VLAD: Although I did teach myself French, so I guess that qualifies me as an autodidact. Anyway, I do have the culinary skills my father gave me. How I long to make you my pearl mushrooms! They're tiny gems—oh, did I mention that, as a final touch, you sprinkle a bit of basil on them? That gives them a delicate flavor, but it must be fresh basil, not dried, and then if you happen to find any lemon thyme hiding under an unsuspecting tree, pluck it fresh and—

VERA: I'd like that, Vladimir Mikhailovich.

VLAD: People say I'm a natural comic—but to tell you the truth, I'm sick of playing the fool. I don't like these people. They're tiny and pathetic and annoying, like gnats. When I'm around them, I can't help myself, I grow more and more foolish and say outrageous things. I'm becoming one of them, banal and insignificant—

VERA: There, there—

VLAD: (*Earnestly.*) Take me away from them, Vera Fyorodorovna, open your arms and enfold me in the bosom of the theatre. It will be my salvation.

VERA: You do have a flair for the dramatic—

Vlad suddenly grabs Vera and tries to kiss her. She gently resists.

VERA: Please …

VLAD: (*Taken aback.*) What have I done? My God—

VERA: (*Gently.*) Don't worry—

VLAD: I'm so ashamed …

VERA: It will be our little secret …

VLAD: (*In a choked voice.*) I spoil everything, don't I?

VERA: Not at all—

VLAD: You have no idea how unhappy I am, Vera Fyodorovna—

VERA: Poor fellow—

VLAD: And now I've made a fool of myself ... such a fool ...

Vera puts her arms around him.

VERA: There, there ... (*She strokes his hair.*)

Enter Maksim. Vlad breaks from the embrace, abruptly.

MAKSIM: Ah, there you are, Vera darling. Not too hot, I hope—

VERA: Maksim, dearest, we just went for a short walk. The woods are magical! I've been waiting for you to finish—

MAKSIM: And I have. It's fixed, that problem in Act Three. I have the new pages—

VERA: Good, I'll go tell the actors, and we'll do a final bit of rehearsing—

Enter Pusto and Stepka, carrying the curtain and heading to upstage right.

MAKSIM: Hey, good man—

PUSTO: Yes, sir.

MAKSIM: Take care when you hang that curtain, will you?

PUSTO: Yes, sir.

MAKSIM: (*Sharply, to Stepka.*) Look out, it's dragging on the grass, it will get torn—

STEPKA: (*Sullenly.*) Sorry, master—

PUSTO: (*To Stepka, under his breath.*) Idiot—can't you do anything right?

STEPKA: (*Under his breath, angrily.*) I said I was sorry—

MAKSIM: We'll be along shortly, at five o'clock.

Sergey appears at the door.

SERGEY: Hello, Maksim—can I help?

MAKSIM: Your men are preparing to hang the curtain, but I'm concerned. It has to be done properly, and that fellow *(points at Stepka)* was dragging it on the grass—

PUSTO: It won't happen again, I'll make sure of it.

SERGEY: Don't worry, Maksim, I'll supervise it myself. Let's walk over to the theatre, we'll help them put it up. You too, Vlad—

VLAD: All right …

Pusto puts the scenery down.

PUSTO: Begging your pardon, sir—may I have a word?

SERGEY: Yes?

PUSTO: My apologies, sir. I've been waiting to find the right time to speak to you all day, but I didn't want to disturb you—

SERGEY: Speak up, then, what is it?

PUSTO: It's just that—

SERGEY: (*Impatiently.*) We haven't got all day, man, we've got a show to put on!

PUSTO: Sorry for taking your time, sir, I wanted to remind you, that, well, Stepka here, his sister cleans the school down in the village, and she keeps telling us that the roof is about to cave in—

SERGEY: (*Impatiently.*) Yes, yes, I know, I told Vladimir Mikhailovich to take care of that last week—

VLAD: But you haven't given me a moment, Sergey! I asked your friend Suslov if he'd look into it—he's an engineer, you know—but he says he's on holiday and he'll get to it if he can. Meanwhile, he's the only qualified one around to assess the problem—

SERGEY: Never mind; we'll take care of it tomorrow. And anyway, isn't school out for the summer?

PUSTO: It still has a few more days to go, sir. (*Summoning up the courage.*) So here's what I'm thinking. If you'd just allow Stepka and me to go over to the school after we hang the curtain, sir, we can see if we can start fixing the roof—

SERGEY: I'm afraid we'll need you both here tonight for the performance. You know, to get more chairs and benches if needed, to open and close the curtain—

VLAD: It will be exciting, you'll see—

STEPKA: *(In a low voice, to Pusto.)* Go on, tell them what my sister said.

PUSTO: *(Pleading.)* Sir, so sorry, but Stepka's sister says that the crack in the ceiling is so wide that rain has been dripping through it, and pieces of plaster are falling. It's a dangerous situation—

STEPKA: *(In a low voice, urgently, to Pusto.)* Tell him about the children—

PUSTO: Oh yes, sir, and there are children coming and going—well, of course, it's a school, and—

SERGEY: I'm sorry, fellows, it's just too late to pay attention to it today. I'll send Suslov over to the school first thing tomorrow, he'll supervise—

STEPKA: *(In a low voice.)* If he's sober—

SERGEY: What's that?

STEPKA: *(Blurts out.)* For God's sake, there are twenty children in that school! You've got to do something!

PUSTO: *(Sharply.)* Stepka! *(To Sergey.)* Forgive my nephew, master. He's just a little worked up, that's all. Apologize to the master, Stepka.

SERGEY: No need. As I said, we'll take care of it tomorrow, after the performance.

VERA: *(Trying to smooth things over.)* Never mind, everyone—come, Sergey Vasilyevich, let's walk over to the theatre together.

VLAD: Me too!

MAKSIM: Oh, Vladimir Mikhailovch, I forgot to tell you, Oleg's feeling better, and he'll go on tonight as planned, so we won't need you to step in for him after all.

VLAD: *(Stunned.)* What?

MAKSIM: I know that's a disappointment—

VLAD: *(Deflated.)* I ... I don't know what to say ...

MAKSIM: But if you don't mind standing in the wings, in case he should take another turn for the worse, then do come along.

VLAD: I ... I don't mind at all, Maksim Alekseyevich. (*Crestfallen.*) At your service.

VERA: (*Hastily.*) We thank you, Vladimir Mikhailovich, for your willingness—don't we, Maksim?

MAKSIM: Yes, yes, of course. And watch Oleg closely, Vladimir Mikhailovich—I think you'll find his character very interesting.

VLAD: (*Mumbling.*) Hired and fired in the same day—that's me ...

VERA: That's the *theatre*, Vladimir Mikhailovich! But you never know, keep an eye on Oleg from the wings, you may still get your chance. Meanwhile, come along, I'll find something for you to do backstage.

VLAD: (*With emotion.*) You are too kind.

SERGEY: Let's go, everyone! Pusto, pick up the scenery and follow us—quickly! You, Stepka, take care with that curtain!

VLAD: I'll help!

Sergey and Vera exit upstage right; Vlad follows. Pusto and Stepka pick up the scenery and follow. Lara appears on the veranda.

MAKSIM: (*Seeing Lara, calling out to Sergey and Vera.*) You go ahead ... I'll catch up in just a moment. Good afternoon, Larissa Mikhailovna, or should I say 'good evening'?

LARA: It will be an hour before the sun sets—

MAKSIM: And then you'll hear my play. Are you looking forward to it?

LARA: What do you think? (*Turns to go.*) Excuse me—

MAKSIM: Larissa Mikhailovna, I don't know why you've been avoiding me. We were such good friends last summer. But since I arrived last week, every time I walk into a room, you leave it—

LARA: You're busy with your work. I don't want to be in the way.

MAKSIM: *(Softly.)* You could never be in my way. How are you? Sergey says you've been reading all summer—

LARA: *(With emotion.)* Your new story, "Song of a Falcon"— it's so strong, so brave—

MAKSIM: What does it matter? It hasn't changed a thing, Lara. The months go by, the years go by, and where is the change? It's time for change. Prose can't make it happen. Theatre can!

LARA: Can it really? How? If *we* are the only ones who go to the theatre—

MAKSIM: You'll see. Tonight …

LARA: *(Abruptly.)* She's beautiful—

MAKSIM: Who?

LARA: Vera Fyodorovna, your leading lady—

MAKSIM: Ah …

LARA: *(Blurting out.)* Does your wife like her?

MAKSIM: *(Laughing.)* Why yes, actually, very much. She admires Vera's talent. We're all very good friends.

343

LARA: I didn't mean ... how rude of me ... I'm ashamed ...

MAKSIM: Friendship in the theatre can be a fleeting thing, you know. I thought Stanislavky and Nemirovich were my friends, my comrades in art. But they've turned their backs on me.

LARA: How could they?

MAKSIM: They criticized my new play.

LARA: But surely criticism can be constructive—

MAKSIM: They compromised my artistic integrity. So now I've cultivated a new friend.

LARA: (*In a low voice.*) Yes, one who has her own new theatre, how convenient.

MAKSIM: (*Not having heard.*) Pardon?

LARA: Nothing. Oh Maksim, you who are the bravest of us all, don't lose your principles, your daring, your idealism—

MAKSIM: (*Laughing.*) Now you're getting carried away. Save it for tonight. And afterwards, I'll want your comments, as you gave them before. You really have promise, you know, to become a writer—

LARA: Of what?

MAKSIM: Of the truth. What else is there to write about? Doesn't Sergey encourage you?

LARA: My husband? The only one who has ever encouraged me was my poor mother, bless her soul. She made sure I was well schooled, although I don't know how—there are so many bans on education of the working class, let alone young women. But you've heard the story of our tragic childhood before, my brother Vlad tells it at every opportunity—

MAKSIM: And what have you done with your education?

LARA: I read. I read everything. I can't stop reading. But none of it makes sense.

MAKSIM: Not yet.

LARA: There are so many of us reading, writing, but no one has any idea of how to make things better, not really. I think my mother's life made more sense than mine. She toiled for forty years in the laundry, and when she died, she said: "Don't cry for my sake. You live, you work, you die, that's it." As for those of us who read and write, they say we're the intelligentsia, but that can't be right. We're so unintelligent! We read, we talk, we read, we talk, our lives glide slowly by like ices floes on the river—they're shiny, they're solid (at least they appear to be), but under the cracks you see the dark waters of complacency and greed. And then every once in a while a new and honest work comes along—a story, or a novel, or a play, like yours, Maksim Alekseyevich—and it's like a sunbeam that melts through that ice, and all the dark waters wash away and new, purer ones surge forth—

MAKSIM: How poetic! Yes, you'll be a writer some day.

From the theatre, Vera calls: "Maksim! A-oooooo."
Stepka appears.

STEPKA: (*Gruffly.*) They're wanting you at the theatre, Your Honor ...

MAKSIM: Thank you, good man.

Stepka stands there waiting.

MAKSIM: Off you go, then.

STEPKA: *(Gruffly.)* Sir, I mean master, I—

MAKSIM: Can it wait, good fellow? I'll be along in a moment.

Stepka pauses, and then exits.

MAKSIM: So I'm off, Larissa Mikhailovna. Would you like to wish me good luck?

LARA: Of course ... forgive my manners ...

MAKSIM: Is that the best you can do?

LARA: What do you mean?

Maksim approaches, stands very close to Lara. Touches her shoulder.

MAKSIM: (*In a low voice.*) Don't you remember, last summer, that moment we had by the river? We sat on the bank—

LARA: I remember.

MAKSIM: You'd just read my memoir, the one about my childhood. I don't remember what you said, but I do recall how you looked. Your eyes were shining with tears—

LARA: They were real.

MAKSIM: I knew then that I had the power to move people, to shake them to the core. As I hope to do tonight. (*He draws closer to her.*) You've given me a gift, Lara.

LARA: Me?

From offstage, Vera calls: "Maksim! A-oooooo."

MAKSIM: You've shown me the power that I have as a writer. Let me thank you for that—

LARA: I—

MAKSIM: Shh ... not a word ...

He draws even closer to her and pulls her into an embrace. He is about to kiss her when, from offstage, Vera calls out again, impatiently: "Maksim, where are you?"

MAKSIM: (*Pulls back.*) I'll see you at the theatre—

LARA: Wait—

Maksim exits.

Lara stands frozen for a moment and then goes back in the house. Stepka emerges; he lights a cigarette. Shadows fall across the veranda and the lawn. Offstage up left, in the area of the theatre, we hear instruments tuning, and the sounds of animated voices laughing and talking. Katerina comes out onto the porch, with a shawl. Pavel appears at the drawing room window.

KATERINA: Don't bother, Pavel. She's dressing to go to the play.

PAVEL: The play, the play ... what difference will the play make? Will we love each other more? Care for each other better? Change each other's lives?

Vlad's voice, from afar, offstage up left: "Ladies and gentleman, your attention please! Half hour ... half hour!" The sound of offstage voices continues.

From the corners of the stage, shapeless shadows of men and women silently appear, standing on the periphery, waiting, watching, listening.

Lights.

ACT TWO

Scene One

Early the following morning. The sounds of birds singing. Sasha sleepily carries out the samovar and sets it up on the table on the veranda. Pusto sweeps the terrace. There are paper lanterns lying on the grass.

PUSTO: What a mess! Lanterns everywhere, sparklers ... I spent an hour picking up broken champagne bottles on the lawn.

SASHA: Where?

PUSTO: Behind the stage ... up all night carousing, those theatre people. A wild bunch, if you ask me. Why do they complain about the peasants? Theatre people drink more than peasants do. Is the tea on, Sasha?

SASHA: It'll be ready soon, Papa.

PUSTO: Not for me, silly, for the master and mistress.

SASHA: They keep telling me not to call them that, Papa—

PUSTO: Old ways, girl, keep to the old ways, if you want to hold onto your job.

SASHA: But they're not fancy people, like the ones Babushka used to serve. They're working class, like you, Papa. They've worked hard to get where they are.

PUSTO: Don't you believe it, girl; don't you believe it for a moment.

SASHA: But the master's a lawyer, his neighbor's a doctor—

PUSTO: They may have been born into the working class, but they're richer now than any of those landowners down in the Crimea with the big estates. They got more money than they know what to do with—and don't you forget it!

SASHA: I'll try.... What happened last night, Papa? Mistress came home and locked herself in her room. Master had to sleep in his study—

PUSTO: Such goings on at the doctor's dacha too. I heard 'em when we were cleaning up—

SASHA: Who, you and Stepka?

PUSTO: Stepka disappeared after the show. I had to take down the curtain, carry the benches, everything ...

SASHA: Where did he go?

PUSTO: Home, I think. His sister sent a message to come down to the village immediately, so he disappeared. I warned him he might lose his job, it's hard to have a watchman's post these days.

SASHA: I know, Papa, you keep telling me—

PUSTO: And then, when I walked by the doctor's house, I heard this crying and wailing—

SASHA: Must've been the children—

PUSTO: Not that kind of wailing. Then I heard the doors slam and I don't know what happened next. Or let's say I don't want to know. The lights went on in the engineer's dacha and there was a lot of loud talking there. Such goings on ...

SASHA: How was the play?

PUSTO: You're asking me? I dunno. All I know is, the actors talked a lot of rot on the platform, or the stage, whatever they call it, and that new actress—Vera what's-her-name—you know, the fancy one staying with Yuri Andreyevich—she kept changing her clothes and bowing at the end, like they do, and then the actors got all wound up and partied all night long. Lord, the bottles and the streamers and the mess ... I had to clean it up all by myself.

SASHA: I wonder why Stepka isn't back yet.

PUSTO: No idea.

SASHA: Maybe he got drunk?

PUSTO: Don't you worry about Stepka, child, just do your work—

SASHA: Yes, Papa.

Katerina enters. She sits on the veranda.

KATERINA: Good morning, Sasha.

SASHA: *(Curtsies.)* Good morning, miss.

KATERINA: *(Sighing.)* Any chance for some tea?

SASHA: Just preparing it now, miss. *(Curtsies and exits.)*

KATERINA: Good. It's going to be a beautiful day ...

PUSTO: *(In a low voice.)* Don't be so sure of that ...

Enter Kirill, hurried, disheveled.

KATERINA: You're up early, Doctor. House call?

KIRILL: *(Agitated.)* Good morning, Katerina Vasilyevich— so sorry to come by so early. You haven't seen Olga Aleksandrovna, have you?

KATERINA: Your wife? But I would think *you'd* be the first to see her this morning, no?

KIRILL: (*Shaken.*) As a matter of fact, yes, I mean, no—sorry, I'm so confused—I haven't seen her at all. She seems to have ... disappeared ...

KATERINA: (*Interested.*) Really?

KIRILL: The house is in chaos. Sonya is screaming, Volka ran away again, the nanny is searching the woods for him, Nadya is crying, Misha is hungry, I'm beside myself—

KATERINA: Didn't she say where she was going ... or ... ah ... leave a note?

KIRILL: Note? What would a mother write to her children: "Went for a swim"?

KATERINA: Don't get alarmed; she must have gone out for a walk. How was she last night?

KIRILL: You mean after the performance? Don't ask.

KATERINA: I'm afraid I just did.

KIRILL: She came home in a state, hysterical, woke up the children, we had words, and then ... and then ... (*his voice choking*) she left.

KATERINA: In the middle of the night? Interesting.

KIRILL: (*Miserable.*) This has never happened before. I don't know where she is ... (*Starts to tremble, his shoulders shaking in silent sobs.*)

KATERINA: There, there, Doctor; she'll turn up.

PUSTO: (*Stops sweeping. Takes off his hat.*) Excuse me, Doctor—

KIRILL: Who's this? The watchman?

PUSTO: Yes, sir—

KIRILL: Sorry I didn't recognize you, Pusto, we've all had quite a night—

PUSTO: I may be of assistance, sir.

KIRILL: What do you mean?

PUSTO: Er … I think I saw your wife last night … walking to the engineer's house.

KIRILL: Suslov's house? That drunk? She hates him! And Mrs. Engineer, she's a witch.

PUSTO: I'm only saying, sir, that the engineer's dacha is next to yours, and I may have seen your wife go in … and not come out.

KIRILL: *(Sinks onto a bench.)* I'm lost.

Sergey comes out onto the veranda.

SERGEY: I see everyone's up early. Good morning.

KIRILL: Good morning, Sergey Vasilyevich.

SERGEY: Rough night.

KIRILL: You could say so.

SERGEY: Where's Olga?

KIRILL: That's what I'd like to know.

SERGEY: What do you mean?

KATERINA: *(Quickly.)* Don't ask so many questions, Sergey, it's too early in the morning.

Enter Sasha.

SERGEY: Is my wife up yet?

SASHA: I haven't seen the mistress this morning, sir.

SERGEY: And her brother?

Sasha shrugs.

SERGEY: So ... now what do we do? *(Sits on bench, stage right, next to Kirill.)*

KIRILL: Wait, I suppose.

SERGEY: Any tea yet, Sasha?

SASHA: Almost ready, sir.

SERGEY: You shouldn't be doing that all by yourself, Pusto. Where's Stepka?

PUSTO: Well, that's just the point, sir. I don't know where he is, either.

KATERINA: Everyone seems to have disappeared this morning.

SERGEY: *(In a low voice.)* Small wonder.

Enter Olga slowly, followed by Pavel. Sergey and Kirill rise quickly.

SERGEY: Olga!

KIRILL: Darling!

Olga walks pasts them, head high, stone-faced, without acknowledgment.

PAVEL: Excuse me, Doctor. I met your wife on the path. She seemed not to know where to go, so I offered to escort her here.

OLGA: *(With cold formality.)* Is your mistress up yet, Sasha?

SASHA: *(Warily.)* Not yet, I don't think, Madam.

OLGA: Will you let her know I'm here, please? Tell her I'm here ... to apologize.

SASHA: Very well, Madam. *(Curtsies and exits into the house.)*

KATERINA: Won't you sit down, Olga, dear. You are always welcome here.

OLGA: I didn't know where else to go.

KIRILL: Where on earth have you been all night?

Olga is silent.

KIRILL: Olga, darling, it's me, Kirill, your husband—

OLGA: I'm aware of who you are, Kirill. I'm also aware of my status in this community, which, after last night, has been put into peril of such a magnitude that I cannot possibly ... well, let's just say that it has been the worst night of my life—

KIRILL: But Olga, where were you? You didn't come home!

OLGA: If you think I wanted to sleep at the Suslovs—that souse, and his wife, what a harpy—but I didn't know where else to go. I couldn't face anyone who went to that performance!

KIRILL: It was a play, Olga—only a play. You are a wife, and a mother—that's what comes first, that's what counts—

SERGEY: Let's face it, Kirill, it was rough for all of us who sat through it.

KIRILL: What difference does it make? I spent a night without my wife, afraid, with our children crying for their mother—

PAVEL: We must all stay calm.

KATERINA: Yes. Too much drama so early in the morning.

Enter Maksim. Everyone freezes.

MAKSIM: (*Cordially.*) Good morning, Sergey Vasilyevich. Am I ...disturbing you? It's early, I know ...

KATERINA: We're up. As you see.

MAKSIM: I came to bid you good morning and thank you all for coming last night. You were a good audience, and I—

The rest are silent.

MAKSIM: —I'm only sorry that you all left so quickly. What a pity! Yuri Andreyevich brought champagne, there was caviar and salmon, and I wanted to toast you and thank you for your presence. It really helped to see the play in front of an audience for the first time, and though the acting may not be up to St. Petersburg standards, for which I do apologize ... still, Vera Fyodorovna was not displeased, and that's what counts.

Silence.

So I thank you for your service to the cause of art. And to the enlightenment of the Russian people—

Another silence.

MAKSIM: (*Puzzled.*) Sergey?

PAVEL: *(To Maksim.)* How dare you ...

MAKSIM: Beg your pardon?

PAVEL: How dare you!

MAKSIM: How dare I ... what? What's going on here? Why are you all looking at me that way?

Vlad appears on the veranda.

MAKSIM: Vladimir Mikhailovoch, thank you for your help backstage last night, Vera Fyodorovna said you were of great assistance. So sorry you didn't have the chance to go on, but I do think—and Vera agrees with me—that you have the natural energy, and, er, comedic talent, to become an actor if you so choose, and since you have been searching for a new career, so Vera tells me, why then anything I can do for you in the future to further your purposes, if indeed the theatre is your passion, I'd be more than happy to—

PAVEL: What are you saying? Don't you know what you have done?

MAKSIM: Really, I'm at a loss. I wrote a play, that's what I've done.

PAVEL: Yes, you wrote a play. You wrote a play *about us* ...

MAKSIM: Hold on, man—

PAVEL: You came down here last summer, into our lives, as our guest, as the guest of this man's uncle (*indicating Kirill*) who admires and trusts you, and you—how should I put it?—you studied us. That would be putting it nicely—more accurately, you *spied* on us. You exploited us. You took from us, you stole from us. That's right! You're a thief. You took our lives, our ways of speech, our behaviors, and you made us into, into what?

SERGEY: Caricatures, Maksim. We were your friends. You used us. And more. You humiliated us.

MAKSIM: I honestly don't understand your reaction, my dear Sergey. I'm an artist. You know that. I write the truth. That's my responsibility. I write life as I see it. So that people can look and see and ask themselves: Is this who we are? Is this the way we want to live? That's what I write. I write living, breathing characters—not caricatures, as you put it. Leave that to Gogol and the old guard, who've accomplished nothing in this miserable land.

VLAD: You don't write caricatures? Then what do you call that jumped-up, hysterical clown, the brother of the lovely young woman who's married to the crooked lawyer—

SERGEY: Calm down, Vlad.

VLAD: —you know, the fool whose father beat him, who dropped out of every school he went to, a washed-out failure before his life even began, a laughingstock, a nothing, a nobody—

SERGEY: Vlad!

PAVEL: And what about the pathetic Tolstoyan who can make music but can't make love, who changes his ideas every year the way a dandy changes clothes—

VLAD: You used us! No, worse, you cannibalized us! For your own insatiable appetite for fame, notoriety, and

God only knows what other motivation. Good thing that Suslov didn't come last night—I wonder how he'd like the character of the bigoted engineer? Too bad—when he's drunk he's prone to violence, and if he'd seen himself up on that stage, who knows what he would have done!

KIRILL: Gentlemen, let's all calm down—

OLGA: We will not calm down! (*To Maksim.*) What about the doctor's wife, eh? Who was that big foolish woman up there on the stage, moaning and whining about "*Kinder, Küche, Kirche*"[1] while everyone snickers behind her back?

MAKSIM: An artist must write what he sees. That's his obligation!

OLGA: Who are you? God? You used us, our friendship, our confidences. And most shocking of all, Maksim Alekseyevich, you betrayed us. What did you call the doctor's wife? A little Jewess? At least you called her "little"—

MAKSIM: You confided in me one afternoon last summer, remember, by the river?

KIRILL: By the river, Olga? You walked alone with a writer by the river? Where was I?

OLGA: Oh be quiet, Kirill—at work, where you always are, or lying in the hammock, exhausted.

SERGEY: But—is it true?

OLGA: What? Is what true?

SERGEY: (*Stunned.*) That you're ... a Jew ...

OLGA: (*Raising her voice.*) Yes, it's true. All right? It's true. I told Maksim Alekseyevich our little secret, Kirill's and mine, in confidence. I'm a Jew—that's right. I gave up my faith to marry Kirill. His parents wouldn't have allowed him to marry me otherwise—

KIRILL: I would have defied them—

OLGA: I did it for *you*! I turned my back on my family. I converted so that my husband wouldn't be turned down for a job in a prestigious clinic—

SERGEY: (*Incredulous.*) You're ... a Jew?

OLGA: What's that to you, Sergey?

SERGEY: Nothing ... only ... I think we had the right to know.

Lara appears on the veranda. She's been listening all along.

LARA: The "right"? The "right"? What does that mean, Sergey?

SERGEY: Now Lara, hang on—I was only saying that ... that sort of information is something we should know about each other—

LARA: "We"? Who is "we"? We "Russians"? We pure, Orthodox Russians?

SERGEY: Please let's discuss this later—

LARA: I want to discuss it now. Look what you've done to us, Maksim Alekseyevich. All in the name of art. You've taken advantage of us—your adoring, admiring audience. You used us to write a play about the bourgeoisie, about their greed, their narrow-mindedness, their selfishness—

Enter Yuri.

YURI: Good morning, friends. I see we've gotten started early. Talking—the great Russian callisthenic!

KIRILL: Why weren't you at the play last night, Uncle?

YURI: (*Laughing.*) I was hoping you wouldn't notice. Actually, I went fishing with Sergey, and after he left, I dozed off in that lovely little boat Pusto set up for me, and when I awoke, well, as they say, the curtain was already up! By the time I got home and dressed and got to the theatre, the curtain was down!

VLAD: (*Bitterly.*) *Finita la commedia!*[2]

SERGEY: So you're saying you didn't see what your distinguished guest has done to us?

YURI: What have you done, Maksim? Can't be that bad.

PAVEL: He's put you in his play, that's what he's done. You and all of us "summerfolk." You're a rich, greedy selfish merchant, Yuri Andreyevich. What do you think about that?

YURI: (*Laughs good-naturedly.*) Actually, he got it right! I *am* rich. So what? I've worked hard. I've earned it. I'm entitled to enjoy it. Why should I be ashamed? And why should I give it away, like my nephew here wants me to do? Actually, I'll enjoy it even more, seeing it on the stage!

VLAD: He made you into a fool, Uncle! A big, blind, foolish fool!

PAVEL: Look how you've turned us one against the other. Is this what truth does? Is this how it helps?

MAKSIM: Hamlet said that the theatre should "hold a mirror up to nature"—and human nature too—to show us how we live, so we can see the truth and change our lives—

PAVEL: Ah, so now you're the Russian Shakespeare!

LARA: You come into our lives, and you talk of change. You write of the people's sufferings—of the injustice in Russia, of the cruelty of the Tsar, of the corruption of the government. You write of the Russian worker—the squalid, degrading, harsh, savage, beastly life that he leads, the pain he suffers, the morass that he calls his life. Maksim Gorky, the poet of the worker! We read your every word, we hang on your every phrase. You educate us, you enlighten us. And now … Now you turn on us. Instead of inspiring us, you put *us* on the stage—to mock us, to shame us, to make us look like fools—

VLAD: —and we're supposed to be grateful!

MAKSIM: (*To Lara.*) Isn't that what you were saying to me yesterday afternoon? Word for word?

LARA: What?

MAKSIM: That you—the new generation of privilege, the bourgeoisie, who came up from the working class, who now have money and status—that you're all superficial, selfish, greedy fools who do nothing but talk?

LARA: When?

MAKSIM: Yesterday afternoon, when we were alone—

SERGEY: *(Alarmed.)* Alone? (*To Lara.*) When were you alone with Maksim Alekseyevich?

LARA: Stop this! Stop! Listen to me. This is not about us. It's about Gorky. Maksim Alekseyevich Gorky—

VLAD: —who changed his name from "Peshkov," isn't that right?! Not good enough for you, eh? Now you're Maksim Gorky. Maksim the Bitter. Wow! That's rich! What do *you* have to be bitter about?

MAKSIM: Haven't you read my autobiography? If you had, you'd know. Don't show your ignorance, man!

VLAD: You're right, I'm ignorant. Why bother to go to the theatre at all!

LARA: You speak of progress, of change, that can be brought about by the theatre. How can that happen if you offend your audience, if you assault us, bludgeon us?

Troika

MAKSIM: Bludgeon you? I'm trying to get you to look at yourselves, to see what shallow, selfish lives you lead.

LARA: Oh, so now you're God, you're judging us.

PAVEL: No one has the right to judge his fellow man.

MAKSIM: I do! That's my right, as a writer. Indeed, it's my responsibility.

VLAD: And you think you're entitled!

MAKSIM: All right, do you want to know what kind of life *I've* led? For the first ten years, I wished I were dead. No childhood like your pampered brood, Olga. My father died young, and my mother abandoned me. So I lived with my grandparents. My grandfather—the bastard— beat my grandmother senseless. I pulled out the hairpins he drove into her scalp while my drunken uncles looked on. Then he'd beat me senseless too. No fancy education like yours, Sergey. I went to school hungry and sold rags on the street. At age twelve I ran away, and I've been on my own ever since. My first job was in the kitchen on a riverboat. By the time I was seventeen, I'd worked every job you can imagine—bird-catcher, dishwasher, icon maker, gardener, baker's assistant, and yes, even watchman, like your man Pusto here. I've hauled fish from the Black Sea, dug salt from the Siberian mines, harvested grapes in Bessarabia, built roads in the Crimea, dragged cargo on the Odessa docks. I even attempted suicide—did you know that? Life swallowed me whole and then turned around and spat me out. Yes, I've seen this country, I've seen it all: the sufferings, the miseries, the degradations—not of those "gentle peasants" whom your Tolstoy slobbers over, Pavel, those lazy, shiftless, creatures—but of the *worker*. The Russian worker, who pulls barges on the Volga like a human mule. That's my life's purpose—to sing his song of suffering, to shout his protest till it's heard from the Urals to the Pacific.

VLAD: That's a pretty impressive résumé of misery. What are we, in a competition? To see who had the roughest life? We're all from the working class, we all had a father who beat us, and we all have the scars to show for it. Shall we each count them up and compare them, blow by blow?

MAKSIM: You're right. You're the children of the working class, sons and daughters of cooks and laundresses and laborers. But now that you've succeeded, you have a responsibility to be different, not rich! To imbue in us all a desire to improve and illuminate the lives of the masses, the people you've left behind—people who toil, trapped in darkness. We must work! We must set an example. Not as an act of charity, but for our own souls, to nourish them, to broaden our horizons, to break out of the isolation we feel up here on our pedestals, gazing across the chasm of the poor huddled masses who have nothing—no bread, no sugar, no wood. This country of ours has an abundance of resources—enough to feed every last mouth—but where is it all? In the hands of the swindling bourgeoisie, who consume all, or worse, throw it away.

YURI: *(Eagerly.)* I have bread and sugar, I have wood—

MAKSIM: The bourgeoisie is consolidating—it's become

stronger and stronger, it's robbing this country, depleting its resources as they've never been depleted before, till soon there will be nothing left. Meanwhile, the intelligentsia is lazy, careless, and apathetic, drowning in a sea of its own self-serving rhetoric.

PAVEL: Tolstoy says that what matters is the child. With emotional nourishment, a child becomes an adult who can love his fellow man, who—

MAKSIM: Tolstoy? You mean *"Count"* Tolstoy? What does your *Count* Tolstoy know of life? He was born a child of privilege! *Emotional* nourishment, you say? I had nothing to eat till I was ten!

VLAD: Ah, but look at you now! You're a star, Maksim Gorky! Bitter? Your life is saturated in the sweetness of success. You're hypocrite! A sell-out!

SERGEY: Let's try to be reasonable. I agree with you, Maksim Alekseyevich—I've always said that what this country needs, more than anything, is men who want to do good. Men who know that it takes *time* to do good. Not through revolution, but through *evolution*—

PAVEL: That's not the way. It has to start in rural Russia, where the peasants—

LARA: (*Shouting.*) Stop it! Everyone! Here we go again, round and round and round. What's the point, Maksim Alekseyevich? Who is going to see your plays? Pusto? Stepka? Sasha? They're too busy carrying our boats, setting up our croquet games, cleaning up after us, trying to survive. It's *we* who see your plays. So tell us, what do you want us to do with what we've seen?

Enter Vera, carrying a basket.

VERA: Have I come at a bad moment?

MAKSIM: I've glad you're here, Vera—

VERA: Good morning, everyone. I came to thank all of Yuri Andreyevich's friends for coming to the performance last night. Since you weren't at the reception afterwards, I've brought you some special sweets—straight from St. Petersburg. And of course I'm interested to hear what you thought of the play.

VLAD: No you're not.

VERA: I beg your pardon?

YURI: Have we all lost our manners?

VERA: (*Sincerely.*) Vladimir Mikhailovich? Larissa Mikhailovna? Really and truly. I want to hear your response to what you saw last night on the stage.

LARA: (*To Vera.*) Do you intend to put on this play? This travesty of our lives?

VERA: Forgive me, but I'm not sure what you mean by "travesty." Actually, I thought it was a drama. A drama, with—frankly—some comedic moments, emanating from the truth of the characters.

VLAD: Really, is that what you thought?

VERA: I …think I've interrupted something here. Shall I go and come back later?

VLAD: No, no, no— we all want to hear what *you* really thought of the play. Right now.

VERA: To be honest—

LARA: Yes, please, after all this, let's be honest—

VERA: I quite like the play, and I think that my audiences would, too. It's a new direction for Maksim, and I think that it will surprise them. And it will certainly capture the attention of the critics. As for the characters, I think they'll be very interesting roles to play, and would suit a number of members of my company. In fact, I've already talked with Maksim about casting possibilities. As for my own part—

Enter Sasha, breathless.

SASHA: (*Hysterical, to Pusto.*) Papa, Papa!

PUSTO: You're forgetting yourself, Sasha!

SASHA: It's a message, from the village, from Stepka. Stepka says ... Stepka says—

PUSTO: Calm down, child; speak clearly—

SASHA: (*Crying out.*) The school roof collapsed. His sister's leg has been crushed. And two children ... two children ... (*Bursts into tears.*) Please, come quickly! (*She collapses, sobbing.*)

All are stunned. Pusto crosses himself. Katerina moves to Sasha and puts her arms around her.

SERGEY: My God!

PUSTO: *(To Sergey.)* Master, I beg you, I must go to the village, to help—

KIRILL: I'll come too—

PAVEL: I'll get Suslov, the engineer. *(Exits.)*

SERGEY: *(Shaking his head.)* Too late. Too late.

Pusto and Kirill rush off stage left.

MAKSIM: Vera, please, go back to the dacha.

VERA: I'm so terribly sorry to hear this news. If there's anything we can do—

MAKSIM: Just … go …

Vera exits.

SERGEY: I'll never forgive myself for this.

MAKSIM: Ladies and gentlemen, I'm very sorry—

YURI: Never mind, my boy, never mind—

LARA: Never mind? But we do mind, Uncle. We do.

YURI: Now Lara, show Maksim Alekseyevich some respect. He is our guest.

LARA: What respect did he show us, Uncle? Tell me. He disgraced us—

OLGA: I can't face you, any of you—

VLAD: You've taken away my hope, Maksim Alekseyevich.

MAKSIM: It was not my intention. But with all due respect—

LARA: Oh, so now you're giving us our due respect?

MAKSIM: Hear me out, Larissa Mikhailovna, though you haven't heard my play out. For there to be change, there must be sacrifice. If yours is a sense of discomfort—

OLGA: Discomfort? What about shame?

MAKSIM: —then that is your contribution to the cause.

LARA: What cause?

Pavel enters.

PAVEL: Suslov is on his way down to the village—

LARA: Wait a minute, Pavel. *(To Maksim.)* What cause, Maksim Alekseyevich? Your writing is facile, it's glib, you're a sensationalist, you're in love with your own miserable childhood—

MAKSIM: You were always my most exacting critic, Larissa Mikhailovna. Time will tell, time will tell.... Meanwhile, I'm willing to take my chance before the Petersburg audience—

LARA: The Petersburg audience is *us!*

SERGEY: So now you're talking about reviews.

VLAD: We have a clairvoyant here (*pointing to Katerina*). Cassandra will tell you what your reviews will be— that is, if this play ever sees the light of day again—

SERGEY: Leave Katerina out of this—

PAVEL: Let *me* be your first reviewer, then. After I saw your play last night, do you know what I think, Maksim Gorky? You're confused.

MAKSIM: Now, wait a minute—

PAVEL: You don't know which way to turn. Your work is noisy, it's showy, but it lacks real content—as well as a plot, I might add. Nothing happens. They just sit around and talk and talk and talk—

KATERINA: Just as we are doing right now, while down in the village—

PAVEL: —let me finish, please. Do you know what your friend Chekhov wrote about your last play? I do. Tolstoy told me, in confidence. And I'm breaking that confidence, right now, for the sake of truth. Chekhov wrote: "A time will come when Gorky's works will be forgotten. But not Gorky."

MAKSIM: *(After a beat.)* Since it's coming from my mentor, I'll take it as a compliment.

VLAD: Don't. Can't you hear what he's saying? You're a celebrity, that's what you are! A cult of personality!

MAKSIM: Balzac taught me—

PAVEL: Balzac? What does he have to do with this?

KATERINA: Everyone, please, we should be going to help—

LARA: No, I want to hear this through—

MAKSIM: Balzac said that sordidness is a crucial theme in art. You saw my play last night, and now you know. It's not only the masses—it's *your* lives that are sordid, too. Every time I pick up my pen, I ask myself: "Is this worth writing about?" And the answer, in this case, is yes. The sordid truth must be revealed down to its very roots—how else can we change this shameful life of ours?

PAVEL: Oh, so now you're calling our lives "sordid" and "shameful"?

VLAD: I didn't think you could offend us more than you did last night, Maksim Alekseyevich, but you're outdoing yourself this morning!

An offstage cry is heard. Vera rushes in.

VERA: They've broken into our dacha! They've smashed the windows, they've ransacked my trunk ... my costumes are everywhere! My pearls are gone! *(Collapses in tears.)*

YURI: What? Who would do such a thing?

LARA: Who do you think? Maybe Maksim found his audience last night after all ...

Lights.

Scene Two

Late that afternoon. Sasha sits alone, huddled on the stairs leading up to the veranda. She wears a shawl, which she has wrapped tightly around her. Katerina enters from the woods.

KATERINA: Sasha?

SASHA: (*Jumping up.*) At last, miss, I've been waiting and waiting ...

Katerina collapses in her chair on the terrace.

KATERINA: I'm all done in.

SASHA: (*Agitated.*) What's happening? How is Papa?

KATERINA: Don't worry, dear. He's working with some of the others to repair the roof. Vladimir Mikhailovich and Pavel Nikolayevich are helping them too.

SASHA: (*Trembling.*) And Stepka's sister?

KATERINA: They wouldn't let me in the clinic, but Dr. Dudakov is doing his best. Don't worry, she's in good hands.

SASHA: What about the children? Omigod, don't tell me—

KATERINA: They say that two children were there when the roof fell—they were the last to leave the school yesterday afternoon. But they'll survive, and the doctor is looking after them, too—

Sasha breaks down and weeps.

SASHA: I'm so frightened, I didn't know what to think, with everyone shouting, and then with you gone, and the master and the mistress gone, too—

KATERINA: Have you seen Stepka, Sasha? He was nowhere around the village.

SASHA: He didn't come by here, no—

KATERINA: He still hasn't shown up. Pusto is worried sick. And now with the break-in, well, the longer he remains missing, the more incriminating it is for him—

SASHA: Incriminating? What does that mean?

KATERINA: It means … that his absence indicates guilt—

SASHA: Guilt? For what?

KATERINA: For breaking into Vera Fyodorovna's rooms.

SASHA: But that's terrible! Stepka would never do such a thing!

Enter Yuri.

YURI: What's so terrible, young lady?

SASHA: (*Throws herself on her knees.*) Oh, Your Honor, forgive him, please, he didn't mean any harm—

YURI: Who?

SASHA: Stepka ... the break-in at your house, and Vera Fyodorovna's lovely costumes all in disarray—

YURI: Don't you fret, now. A broken window, that's all—

KATERINA: And the pearls?

YURI: We found them on the grass behind the dacha. Whoever broke in must have taken them, and then dropped them as he was fleeing. "All's well that ends well ..."

KATERINA: Or at least "ends"—

SASHA: Are you going to press charges, sir? Against Stepka? He's my cousin, sir, he's not a bad boy, spare him, please—

YURI: Charges? Why would I press charges? These things happen, you know. At my factory—well, I won't bore you with stories—let's just say I've seen it before.

SASHA: But he's fled, sir.

YURI: Are you sure it was Stepka who broke in?

SASHA: No, sir, but they all think he did it. The business about the schoolhouse roof, and all, and his sister—

YURI: Ah, the roof, yes. Well. Unfortunate, but they're attending to it now. Sergey is over at the town council, applying for funds to cover costs for the repairs. I offered to pay for it myself—don't tell Kirill—but Sergey said that for him it's a matter of principle. Vera Fyodorovna is relieved to have her pearls back, so she won't press charges, although she'll be leaving today with Maksim Alekseyevich. Something about getting back to rehearsals in St. Petersburg. Pity, with most of the summer still ahead. It's lovely here, and I was so looking forward to having them as my guests for a while. As for Stepka, let's not come to any conclusions, shall we?

SASHA: So ... Stepka can come back?

YURI: (*Laughs.*) Maybe not as night watchman, but we'll find him something to do.

Sasha grabs Yuri's hand, kisses it, and runs off.

KATERINA: I admire you, Yuri Andreyevich.

YURI: Oh, don't do that. Save your admiration for the writers and artists. I'm just a capitalist. If it works, do it, and make it bigger and better. If it breaks, fix it. Or sell it. Keep moving. Survival is all.

Enter Olga.

OLGA: You're back, Katerina Vasilyevna, I've been worried sick—

KATERINA: You have your own worries, Olga—

OLGA: (*Anxiously.*) The children at the school—are they all right?

KATERINA: Your husband is taking care of them, and Stepka's sister, too. He's a good doctor ...

OLGA: (*Bursts into tears.*) I'm such a fool.

KATERINA: According to your playwright last night, I'm afraid you are—

OLGA: Don't be cruel, Katerina. Anyway, he's not my playwright.

KATERINA: Well, he's not mine, either.

OLGA: Strange, you were the only one of us he didn't put in that play, Katerina. I wonder why? Are you insulted?

YURI: From the sound of it, Katerina should be relieved.

KATERINA: Never mind; we're past that now.

OLGA: Where's Lara?

KATERINA: She was with me at the school. I think she went to see if they'd let her help at the clinic—

OLGA: So what do we do now, wait? I'm exhausted.

Enter Pavel.

PAVEL: Have you seen him?

KATERINA: Who?

PAVEL: Forgive my manners, please. Larissa Mikhailovna told me to look for Stepka. I've been searching everywhere for him. The doctor says he should be at his sister's bedside at the clinic, in case—

KATERINA: In case what?

PAVEL: No, I can't say it—

OLGA: Omigod!

YURI: Please let's not jump to conclusions. Let's wait until the doctor comes home.

PAVEL: I can't imagine that Stepka would do such a thing. I have faith in the integrity of the Russian peasant—

OLGA: Is he a peasant or a worker? I'm so confused, I can't tell the difference!

KATERINA: Does it matter? No more theory, please, for God's sake! Haven't we talked enough?! Lara doesn't understand Pavel, Pavel doesn't understand Sergey, Sergey doesn't understand Yuri—

YURI: Me? I'm easy to figure out. I'm a capitalist.

KATERINA: Never mind. We drift along like boats on the Baltic, crashing into each other, until we all sink.

YURI: What's hard to understand here? Some innocent people have been hurt, people who are our neighbors.

PAVEL: I can't let her down!

OLGA: Who?

PAVEL: Lara ... I mean Larissa Mikhailovna.

OLGA: Grow up, Pavel!

PAVEL: What did you say?

OLGA: I said "grow up" and "give up." Can't you face the truth? All that education, all that reading and writing, and you can't see what's right in front of you.

PAVEL: What truth? I've loved her all my life ... before I even met her. She is the woman of my dreams. You can search and search your whole life through and never find her. But I have found her.

OLGA: My God, Pavel, where did you find that line? In *War and Peace*?

PAVEL: There. I've said it. Aloud. And now you know.

OLGA: As if we didn't know already ...

PAVEL: The truth is, I wanted her to feel sorry for me. Life frightens me.... You're a poet, Katerina, you understand.

KATERINA: As a matter of fact, I do.

PAVEL: What have I learned at university? Endless rhetoric, random speculation, useless theory, mere guesses at the meaning of life—

YURI: That's more than I learned. I never went to university—and look at me, I own more than I want to own. Who's better off—you or me?

PAVEL: Anyway, tell Larissa Mikhailovna or don't tell her. I don't care. I feel better now. Thank you for hearing my confession.

KATERINA: What will you do now?

PAVEL: Look for Stepka ...

OLGA: And if you find him, then what will you do? Come back here and play that mopey Chopin?

PAVEL: Music, and only music can express the grandeur of love.

KATERINA: You know what, Pavel? Go. Leave here. Forget Tolstoy. He didn't teach you anything. Study piano again—this time, exclusively. I hear Rachmaninoff is taking pupils in Moscow. Immerse yourself in music, there's where you'll find truth—

Enter Kirill.

OLGA: There you are. My poor, poor Kirill.

KIRILL: (*Collapses exhausted on a bench.*) Yes, poor Kirill ... I'm exhausted.

OLGA: How are the children? Tell us! We've been frantic with worry.

KIRILL: The boy has a broken arm and some crushed ribs. I sewed up the gashes on the little girl's head, and got most of the plaster out of her eyes—at least I hope so. I saved the right eye ... not sure about the left one, though. Probably not. (*Sighs.*) Still, they'll be all right.

KATERINA: And Stepka's sister?

KIRILL: Ah ... that's another matter. I've done all I can for now. We'll see over the next forty-eight hours.

OLGA: Oh, God.

PAVEL: Excuse me, Kirill Akimovich, I'm off to find Stepka. At times like these, we must show forgiveness. It's the only way. *(Exits.)*

OLGA: Kirill, I—

KIRILL: Please, Olga, not now, I can't ... I need to rest. If it bothers you that I'm here, I'll leave.

OLGA: I want to apologize.

KIRILL: *(In a choked voice.)* For what? I could strangle Maksim for humiliating you—

OLGA: Perhaps it's not a humiliation after all. It's who I am. I only thought ... that it would make your life, our life, easier, if no one knew. That's all.

KIRILL: I see that now.

OLGA: Come, Kirill, let's go home. The children haven't seen you in two days.

KIRILL: Olga, I try, I really do. I toil away at the hospital in town all week, just for—you know—for your sake, and the children, then I come out here—and I can't help myself—they need me at the local clinic, so what can I do? Turn my back on them?

OLGA: Of course you can't. Come ...

Kirill and Olga exit together. Yuri whistles softly. Enter Sergey.

SERGEY: Katerina, where's Sasha? Tell her that Lara will be home soon. She'll want Sasha to start preparing something. No one's eaten a thing all day. And Vlad's right behind me.

YURI: How did it go at the town council?

SERGEY: I have connections. They'll come up with the money ... meanwhile, Pusto has found a few men to get started on that roof. He'll be working double time, and he knows it. After the break-in, we can't be without a watchman, and now that Stepka has disappeared ...

KATERINA: Pavel's gone off to find him.

SERGEY: Good luck.

Enter Vlad, dusty, disheveled.

VLAD: Two new professions in the past twenty-four hours—actor and now plasterer. At least now I know how to repair a roof.

SERGEY: Where's Kirill? Did he come back from the clinic yet?

KATERINA: He's just been here.

SERGEY: And?

KATERINA: The children will survive, but Stepka's sister ... we won't know yet for a day or two whether or not—

SERGEY: (*Sinks onto a bench.*) I will never forgive myself for this.

VLAD: It's my fault! You asked me to go to the council. I got carried away with everything that was going on here—

SERGEY: No, the responsibility was and is mine. How can I make it up to them?

Yuri whistles softly.

SERGEY: And Lara ... she won't even look at me ...

YURI: *(To Vlad.)* Well, now that the writers aren't in residence anymore, I think I'll go pay a visit to my place in town. Want to come with me, Vlad? It's a big old house, plenty of space, we'll never get in each other's way. So many rooms that you can whistle in one and hear the echo for hours. I'll find something for you to do. Sergey says you've assisted him—don't worry, I won't ask him for a reference—but you're quick, and if you can plaster, you can do anything. Give you a fresh start. What do you say?

VLAD: There's nothing for me here, or anywhere else—so why not? I seem to specialize in being someone else's assistant.

YURI: I might even be persuaded to build a new school in the town. I told them they'd have to pay the laborers, of course, I'm not *that* philanthropic, but I may advance them some funds, make a deal with *their* town council ...

VLAD: Worth a try.

YURI: Good! I'd better get back to the dacha, to help sort out Maksim and Vera. They'll be leaving soon. Back later, my friends ...

Yuri exits.

SERGEY: What are you talking about, Vlad?

VLAD: Come on, Sergey, we both know I'm useless here. And after last night, I want to get away ... start a new life.

SERGEY: What will Lara say?

VLAD: What can she say? She's as unhappy as I am.

SERGEY: What do you mean?

VLAD: We have a lot to face—all of us, Sergey.

SERGEY: I don't know what you're saying.

VLAD: I'm going in now, to sort out your papers. Then I'll start packing.

Vlad exits into the house. Sergey and Katerina sit quietly. Enter Lara, exhausted.

KATERINA: You're back.

LARA: I'm going into the house now, to find Sasha. She's got to start preparing a meal. No one has eaten all day.

SERGEY: Lara—

LARA: Not now, Sergey—

SERGEY: Listen to me, Lara, I just came back from the town council meeting. They approved a budget to repair the new roof.

LARA: Of course they did. The prestigious city lawyer among the humble locals? They'll do anything to please you. After all, you have influence with some real estate investors who might—

SERGEY: What do you mean?

LARA: So now you can play the big man. You did some pro bono work, you swooped down from your Olympian heights and saved the community—

SERGEY: (*To Katerina.*) What is she saying?

LARA: Only it's too late, Sergey, too late! It's fake, Sergey— you're a fraud, I'm a fraud, we're all frauds!

KATERINA: (*Discreetly.*) I'll go into the house and tell Sasha to start preparing.

LARA: (*Sharply.*) No—you stay here, Katerina—

KATERINA: It's all right, Lara. (*Exits into the house.*)

SERGEY: Influence? What are you saying, Lara? What influence are you talking about?

LARA: I'm only saying what others have been implying for quite some time now, Sergey.

SERGEY: What are you accusing me of, Lara? I have a very high standing in this community.

LARA: Yes, Sergey, I know my role: the grateful wife of a great man. But I'm getting tired of playing the part, Sergey. The disguise is wearing thin.

SERGEY: We're the elite of this country, Lara. Remember that. Everyone here knows it—

LARA: No we're not! We're just the summerfolk. We don't belong here, we don't belong anywhere, for that matter! We just drift from one lovely spot on earth to the next, and when we find one that we like, we buy it or lease it, we litter it, we use it up, and then we move on to pollute another place. And wherever we go, we talk, and talk, and talk!

SERGEY: As you are doing right now—

LARA: Listen to us! What lies we tell—to ourselves and others! We spout pretentious ideas, flamboyant phrases we've stolen from one book or another—ideas that we flaunt to conceal our spiritual poverty. Who are we to talk about the poor people of Russia? We may have come from them, but now we've turned our backs on them. We can't live without our newfound comforts. We're frauds! And we're lost—we can't go back to the way we were, we can only continue to get richer and fatter and talk and talk and—

SERGEY: You know what your problem is, Lara? You've read too many books and you've seen too many plays! Like the one we saw last night ... don't take it to heart. In fact, don't take it at all. Put it out of your mind. We're above all that.

LARA: Oh, so now we're above art, as well as philosophy and literature. What else are we above? I'm so confused ... why can't we find the courage to be silent? We pollute the air around us with our talk talk talk, just as we pollute our cities with trash, and whatever else is left in our decaying souls. Our flawed ideas spread like viruses, infecting everyone they touch, leaving us weakened and depleted. Empty.

Vlad and Katerina come out of the house.

VLAD: (*Clapping.*) Brava, sister!

SERGEY: (*After a pause.*) I've failed you, Lara. I know. Can you find it in you to forgive me?

LARA: Just as Uncle Yuri wants to forgive Stepka for stealing Vera's pearls?

Enter Pavel, out of breath.

PAVEL: Larissa Mikhailovna, pardon me, I've looked everywhere, but I can't find him.

SERGEY: Who, Stepka? You're wasting your time.

PAVEL: Why?

SERGEY: Because when I was in town, I notified the police. They'll be looking for him—

LARA: You did what?

SERGEY: This is a gated community. I'm not going to put my wife and sister in jeopardy—

PAVEL: What are you saying, Sergey Vasilyevich? Haven't you heard?

SERGEY: What?

PAVEL: Uncle Yuri was here before. He told us that Vera found her pearls in the garden behind the dacha. The thief—whoever he is—must have dropped them.

LARA: So that means Stepka is hiding because he's afraid we think he stole the pearls. How could you, Sergey?

Enter Yuri and Vera. There is immediate tension in the air.

VERA: Larissa Mikhailovna, Sergey Vasilyevich, I've come to say good-bye. The train leaves in a half hour—we're packed—we have to get to the station.

YURI: Maksim Alekseyevich sends you his sincerest regards—he had to wait for the carriage to come, to load the luggage. Otherwise, he would be here in person to thank you—

VLAD: For what? For being fools? So he could become even more famous by exploiting us, like he got famous by exploiting the workers in his last play?

KATERINA: Vlad—

VERA: Maksim said—

VLAD: I've heard enough of what Maksim said.

KATERINA: Let her speak, Vlad—

VERA: He said ... he learned a lot from the audience response last night. He's going to do another revision based on your comments.

VLAD: Bully for him.

VERA: He wants you to know, of course, that he looks forward to welcoming you at the performances this fall in St. Petersburg. And I'll be happy to arrange house seats at our theatre.

VLAD: (*Laughs*) You're joking!

VERA: He's very excited about this play—and so am I. We think our audiences will find it very provocative. As for me, the role of ... (*she glances at Lara*) ... well, let's say it will be an honor, as well as a challenge.

VLAD: Tell him good luck with the reviews.

VERA: (*Crosses to Vlad, touches his arm.*) Vladimir Mikhailovich— I wanted to tell to you personally how much I enjoyed our walk together. I think you could become a very fine actor—that is, if you want to. I'm sorry that you didn't have your moment last night. But if you want to pursue the stage, come see me in St. Petersburg, and I'll see what I can do. And I do hope you'll make me those mushrooms one day. The pearls and the hens ...

SERGEY: Mushrooms? What mushrooms?

Pause, in which no one knows what to say.

VLAD: And ... curtain! (*Disappears into house.*)

YURI: Come, Vera, Maksim is waiting—

VERA: Good-bye, Larissa Mikhailovna. (*Lara stands, stony, as Vera kisses her and waves to the others.*) Good-bye, everyone. (*Turns to go. Stops.*) Oh, yes, our hearts go out to the victims of that unfortunate accident in the village. We hope that they will soon recover—

YURI: (*Gently.*) You'll miss the train, Vera Fyodorovna.

Vera and Yuri exit.

SERGEY: Lara ... (*She turns away from him.*) I'll go look in on Vlad ...

Sergey exits into the house.

PAVEL: I've disappointed you again, Larissa Mikhailovna. I'd have done anything to find Stepka, just to please you.

LARA: It doesn't matter.

PAVEL: I seem to be worthless around here. But Katerina Vasilyevna has been so kind. She's suggested I go to Moscow, to study piano with Rachmaninoff. I could learn composition too. I've always wanted to compose. And while I was walking around in the woods, around and around, I realized that ... it would be a fine idea to go at the end of the summer. But am I worthy? Do I dare? What do you think?

LARA: Honestly? I don't care.

(Pavel looks stunned, as if struck in the face.)

KATERINA: Lara! How could you?

Another pause.

LARA: (*Suddenly.*) Pavel?

Lara rushes at him, throws her arms around him, and kisses him fully on the mouth. He gasps.

LARA: You're a wonderful pianist. Thank you. Of course you should go. But before you do, please, play for me one more time.

Pavel, stunned, stumbles into the house.

KATERINA: (*Calmly.*) Why don't you go away for a while, Lara? After the summer ... go abroad. Study, work.... Who knows what you'll find?

LARA: Yes, who knows?

Sasha enters with a tray of delicacies.

SASHA: Where shall I put this tray, mistress?

LARA: I don't know. Anywhere. You decide, Sasha.

Sasha looks confused.

KATERINA: Put it here, Sasha. (*Indicates table. She clears her deck of cards.*)

LARA: Maybe you're right, Katerina. Maybe I should go abroad. Otherwise, we'll sit here on the veranda, and read and talk, until some dark force swoops down and wipes us off the face of the earth.

KATERINA: Why don't you go lie down for a bit?

LARA: I'm tired.

Lara exits into the house. Strains of Chopin are heard from the living room.

SASHA: What should I do now, miss? Now that the mistress has gone inside. I don't know what to do.

KATERINA: Stay here … sit for a minute.

Hesitantly, Sasha sits on the steps. Katerina crosses and sits alongside her. Together they listen to Pavel, who is playing Chopin softly.

SASHA: *(After a moment.)* What about the play, miss? Will they put it on again?

KATERINA: If only we could predict the future ...

SASHA: It made people angry. It made them cry.

KATERINA: Ah, well ... it happens ... you never know.

Silence.

KATERINA: Perhaps we've had enough theatre for now.

SASHA: If you say so, miss.

KATERINA: Would you like to hear a poem, Sasha?

SASHA: Who, me?

KATERINA: Have you ever heard poetry before?

SASHA: If you mean words that rhyme, then yes, I think so—when my mother sang to me.

KATERINA: Poetry is song without music.

SASHA: Oh.

KATERINA: Shall I read you my latest poem?

SASHA: As you wish, miss.

Katerina takes out a piece of paper.

KATERINA: Would you like something to eat, Sasha?

SASHA: Oh no, I don't dare.

KATERINA: Well then, take a plate over to the bench. I think we have a new arrival who might be hungry.

Pusto appears out of the shadows.

SASHA: (*Cries out.*) Papa!

KATERINA: Shhh ... Just take him a plate, would you, please, Sasha?

Sasha curtseys, makes up a plate, and tiptoes over to Pusto, who sits on the bench.

KATERINA: Ready? "The Storm Petrel." Do you know what a petrel is, Sasha?

SASHA: It's ... a bird, miss?

KATERINA: Very good. Very good, indeed. I study birds, did you know that?

SASHA: No, I didn't, miss. Well, maybe I heard about it.

KATERINA: Did you know that birds sense what's coming, what lies ahead?

SASHA: Really?

KATERINA: Really. That's why I study them. They know in which direction to fly. And when.

SASHA: Sounds scary.

KATERINA: No … what's scary is when they *don't* know … ready?

Sasha nods.

(*recites*) "The Storm Petrel."[3]

He circles the air, in a darkening night …
Behind him, the past
Before him, the future
Above him, the blackness,
Below him, the sufferers, tossing on a violent sea …
The air is thick with their cries …
His wings slacken …
Shall he turn back?
Or plunge into the dark vast ahead?
He searches for a sign,
But there is none …
Only a void …

(During the poem, Sasha listens, Pusto eats, music plays, fading, with the lights.)

End of Play.

Pronunciation Guide

Characters Names:

(Note: Accented syllable is highlighted in boldface **CAPS**)

Sergey Vasilyevich
    (Ser-**GEY** Va-**SEE**-lye-vich)
Larissa Mikhailovna
    (La-**REE**-sa Mee-**KHAY**-lov-na)
Katerina Vasilyevna
    (Ka-te-**REE**-na Va-**SEE**-lyev-na)
Vladimir Mikhailovich
    (Vla-**DEE**-mir Mi-**KHAY**-lo-vich)
Kirill Akimovich Dudakov
    (**KEE**-ril A-**KEE**-mo-vich **DUH**-da-kov)
Olga Aleksandrovna Dudakov
    (**OL**-ga Al-ek-**SAN**-drov-na **DUH**-da-ko-va)
Yuri Andreyevich Belkin
    (**YUH**-ri An-**DRE**-ye-vich)
Pavel Nikolayevich Rudin
    (**PA**-vel Nee-ko-**LA**-ye-vich)
Maksim Alekseyevich Gorky (Peshkov)
    (**MAK**-sim A-lek-**SE**-ye-vich **GOR**-kee) (Pyesh-**KOV**)
Vera Fyodorovna Kommisarzhevskaya
    (**VYE**-ra **FYO**-do-rov-na)
Pusto
    (**POOS**-to)
Stepka
    (**STYEP**-ka)
Sasha
    (**SA**-sha)

Other Words:

dacha (**DA**-cha) (summer house)
za vashe zdarovye (za **VA**-she zda-**RO**-vye) ("to your good health")
Babushka (**BA**-boosh-ka) (grandmother)

Notes:

1. "*Kinder, Küche, Kirche*"—(German) "childen, kitchen, church," an old German saying that stereotypes the traditional role of women.
2. "*Finita la commedia*"—(Italian) "the farce is over." an Italian saying. It is also a paraphrase of "*La commedia è finita*," a line in Leoncavallo's famous opera Pagliacci.
3. "The Storm Petrel" is the title of a poem by Gorky. Here I've taken the liberty of making it the title of Katerina's own poem (an original composition).

Author's Note:

This play is inspired by Gorky's 1904 play. Of the twenty-six characters in the original work, I retained only ten, and added three of my own, including Maksim Gorky himself and Vera Kommisarzhevskaya (also a figure in Russian theatre history). I kept the original setting and time period but completely rewrote the plot. So as you'll see, it's a "reimagining" of the original work. I've also taken one or two literary liberties—for example, "The Storm Petrel," the poem that Katerina recites at the end, is actually an original poem I wrote for this play. I've given it the title of one of Gorky's own poems (but not

Gorky's content.) *Mea culpa*, to Russian literary scholars and historians.

Production Notes:

1. Set: The play is performed on a unit set (see description at the top of *Act One, Scene One*)
2. Piano music: Pavel can play selected Chopin, according to the mood of the scene (or Schumann, Schubert, or Bach).
3. Role of "little peasant girl": That short scene in Act Two can be cut, if the theatre has casting limitations.
4. Two beggars: Other cast members can be "doubled" in the roles, wearing appropriate costumes.